# BEASTS OF BURDEN

# BEASTS OF BURDEN

## ANIMAL AND DISABILITY LIBERATION

Sunaura Taylor

THE NEW PRESS

25 YEARS

NEW YORK
LONDON

Requests for permission to reproduce selections from this book should be made through our website: https://thenewpress.com/contact.

Published in the United States by The New Press, New York, 2016
Distributed by Two Rivers Distribution

An earlier version of Chapter 3, "Animal Crips," was published as "Animal Crips," edited by Judy K.C. Bentley, Kim Socha, and JL Schatz in their special issue of *JCAS, Eco-Ability the Intersection of Earth Animal and Disability* in the *Journal for Critical Animal Studies*, Volume 12, issue 2, May 2014, 95–117.

Portions of Chapter 9, "Animal Insults," and Chapter 17, "Caring Across Species and Ability," were published as "Beasts of Burden: Disability Studies and Animal Rights" in *Qui Parle* 19.2 (Spring/Summer 2011), 191–222, edited by Katrina Dodson.

An earlier version of Chapter 17, "Caring Across Species and Ability," was published as "Domesticated, Dependent, and Dignified: A Case for a Cripped Ethics of Animal Care" in *Ecofeminism: Feminist Intersections with Other Animals and the Earth*, edited by Carol J. Adams and Lori Gruen (New York and London: Bloomsbury, 2014), 108–126.

An earlier version of Chapter 13, "Toward a New Table Fellowship" was published as "Vegans, Freaks, and Animals: Toward a New Table Fellowship" in Claire Jean Kim and Carla Freccero's special issue, *Species/Race/Sex*, of *American Quarterly*, Volume 65, Number 3, September 2013, 757–764.

LIBRARY OF CONGRESS CATALOGING-IN-PUBLICATION DATA

Names: Taylor, Sunaura, author.
Title: Beasts of burden : animal and disability liberation / Sunaura Taylor.
Description: New York : New Press, 2017. | Includes bibliographical
   references.
Identifiers: LCCN 2016035638 (print) | LCCN 2016044803 (ebook) | ISBN
   9781620971284 (hbk : alk. paper) | ISBN 9781620971291 (e-book)
Subjects: LCSH: Animal rights. | Animal welfare. | People with
   disabilities—Civil rights. | Social advocacy.
Classification: LCC HV4708 .T395 2017 (print) | LCC HV4708 (ebook) | DDC
   179/.3—dc23
LC record available at https://lccn.loc.gov/2016035638

The New Press publishes books that promote and enrich public discussion and understanding of the issues vital to our democracy and to a more equitable world. These books are made possible by the enthusiasm of our readers; the support of a committed group of donors, large and small; the collaboration of our many partners in the independent media and the not-for-profit sector; booksellers, who often hand-sell New Press books; librarians; and above all by our authors.

www.thenewpress.com

Book design and composition by Bookbright Media
This book was set in Bembo and Lydian Pro

Printed in the United States of America

To David, Leonora, and Bailey, three of my favorite animals.

And to Jeremy Ayers, a friend to all creatures.
In loving memory.

*They are all beasts of burden, in a sense, made to carry some portion of our thoughts.* —Henry David Thoreau

*Description of the cover art: The front cover depicts two white silhouettes on a mossy teal background. Emerging from the middle right is a human sitting in a wheelchair: head, chest, legs, and the wheelchair's casters and back wheels are visible. An unspecified shape is evident above the human's head. The human looks slightly downward across the page to the left where a cow stands with her neck hanging low and her head forward facing. The cow's arched back, chest, front legs, and head are visible, as is part of a large wheel near her hindquarters. As the image is cropped, the viewer cannot tell whether the wheel belongs to a cart the cow may be pulling or whether it is a wheelchair for the cow herself. As one looks at the image longer it becomes evident that the shape above the human's head is the tail and rear of a cow and that the emerging wheel could belong to the human's wheelchair, giving the image a wraparound effect. It is possible therefore to see the silhouettes as separate and distinct, or as a single united image of a human in a wheelchair sitting in front of the rear of a standing cow.*

*Cover art:* Beasts of Burden, *2015, by Sunaura Taylor*

# Contents

# Prologue: Chicken Truck

If there is one thing that has led me to my current thinking about animals and disability, it is a memory I have from growing up in Georgia in the early nineties. Summers in Georgia are sweltering, humid, sticky, and uncomfortable. I vividly remember driving along the highways in our family car—which always seemed to lack air-conditioning—being too hot to move, and drinking huge amounts of water and soda from Big Gulp cups. It was common to look out our car windows and see rows and rows of chickens on massive, fast-moving trucks. These chickens were alive, often packed so tightly beside one another that the truck itself seemed to have feathers. They were clearly dying, slowly being cooked as they zoomed down the road. They were scraggly, terrible-looking birds, sometimes literally falling through the wire cages that held them in.

My siblings and I thought these trucks were horrible. Vehicles of profound cruelty constantly whirred by, and no one seemed to notice. The four of us would hold our breath every time we saw one until it passed us. Originally this started because the smell was so horrendous—with our windows down we could smell the dying birds and chicken feces before we'd even see the truck—but eventually holding our breath became more symbolic. Not breathing was our way of recognizing that something deeply wrong was happening right next to us.

In 2006, long after I began noticing these trucks, I applied to UC Berkeley. I had been making art, mostly paintings, for many

years and wanted to go to graduate school for an MFA. Before I
left Georgia for California I got the strong desire to paint one of
those trucks that I had seen so often during my childhood.

I had learned a few months prior that I lived mere blocks away
from a chicken "processing" plant, which was the trucks' final
destination. As so often happens, this huge industry was invisible to most moderately well-off people in our city, tucked away
on strange, out-of-the-way roads where the pollution, the smell,
and the terribly paid, mostly immigrant workers would be out
of sight. I had the idea of photographing one of the trucks while
it was parked outside of the plant. I tried and failed to take the
photo—I went with my brother Alex and my partner David, but
we were quickly kicked off the premises—so I asked an acquain-
tance who did some work at the plant to take the photos for me. I
got the pictures, but the person who took them was fired the very
next day for taking them.

These photos eventually led to a series of paintings of animals
in factory farms, and in many ways they led to this book. I spent
a year painting a large canvas (about ten feet by eight feet) of the
chicken truck. At one point I counted the chickens whose portraits
I had been able to paint from the photo—there were more than
one hundred. I had wanted to paint a life-size image, but it would
have had to be three times as long. As I painted I slowly began to
appreciate the enormous scale at which animals are exploited and
killed in this country. My hundred-plus chickens were but a fraction of those on the truck that caged them. That truck was one
of countless trucks that were delivering birds to slaughterhouses
at that moment. United Poultry Concerns reports, "Worldwide
over 50 billion chickens are now being slaughtered every year."[1]

Through my research I found out that the chickens I was painting were egg-laying hens, which are actually a different breed
of chicken than the "broilers" used for meat. I learned about the
crammed spaces these birds live in, and I learned about the hundreds of millions of male chicks who are thrown away every year
in the United States because they are useless to the egg industry.
I also learned about the hens themselves, who after about a year
of egg-laying are killed and made into cheap ground chicken,

as their bruised and debilitated (in other words, disabled) bodies can't be sold at a higher price.[2]

Those hundred-plus chickens I spent a year looking at and thinking about inspired me to begin asking the questions that have propelled these pages—how does an animal become an object? How are we taught to view this objectification as normal? How can thinking about disability help us to see animals differently?

The feeling that first led me to hold my breath when seeing the hens caged on trucks eventually led me to understand animal issues as profoundly relevant and even essential to other social justice issues, including disability. But if anyone had told me when I was first trying to take photos of those hens at the processing plant that I would spend the next six years and counting examining animal oppression through the lens of disability studies and activism, I would have thought them absurd. However, the more I looked, the more I found that the disabled body is everywhere in animal industries. I also found that the animal body is integral to the ways disabled bodies and minds are oppressed in the United States today. A thought struck me. If animal and disability oppression are entangled, might not that mean their paths of liberation are entangled as well?

# BEASTS OF BURDEN

# Part One

Epiphanies

# 1

## Strange but True

I AM FIVE. It is the mid-1980s, my older sister's seventh birthday. Madonna's *True Blue* is blasting. Kids jump up and down, twirl in circles, bound across the room. I am filled with excitement. I want to dance. I have enough dancing energy inside my small body that the desire to boogie is enough to make me bounce chaotically around the room. But each time I pull myself up off the floor and begin to wiggle, I fall. I pull myself up onto the chair beside me, stand and take a step or two, start shaking in tune, and then . . . bump! I'm on the floor. The first couple of times it seems like an accident. Maybe I am just too excited. Maybe I am just losing my balance. By the third crash I realize something is wrong. I stop listening to the music and everything goes quiet. Flat on my butt, I stare at all the frantic dancers around me. "Oh," I think. "That's what handicapped means."

It's a year or two later and I am with my family on a vacation in Washington, D.C. While exploring the city my siblings and I come upon a table with information about animal rights. We rush to find our parents to inform them of the outrageous news we have just learned: meat is animals. We all have already agreed that if this impossible news is indeed true, we will never eat meat again. Our mother is pleased, having been a vegetarian on and off for most of her life. Our father not so much, but even he soon turns around.

The epiphany about meat remained with me longer than the epiphany about my own body. Being disabled since birth, I knew no other form of embodiment. I was so used to being me that the realization I had during that third crash to the floor quickly dissipated. Being physically different continued to be abstract—so abstract that on a conscious level it was of little consequence to me. I do remember getting my first wheelchair, briefly participating in physical therapy, convincing my parents that my hand braces were painful and unnecessary, but these were not visceral realizations of difference, whereas from the moment I learned meat was made from animals I was awakened to something hard to forget: cruelty.

Some may wonder whether the decades-long dedication to animal justice that followed is simply the consequence of being traumatized by the animal rights literature I was introduced to on that vacation. Perhaps this depends on your definition of trauma. I have no memory of violent images of animals being slaughtered. Instead I remember the power and the trauma of my suddenly altered understanding of the world. I had thought that I already knew about animals and food. Animals were our dogs Clyde and Mischief and our cat Sybil. They were the lizards and toads that were supposed to live outside but would sometimes come inside. They were Curious George and Winnie-the-Pooh. How could they possibly be in the same category as apples and sandwiches and birthday cake?

My siblings and I reinforced one another's dedication to not eating animals. None of us were ever the lone vegetarian in the family. Our convictions were strengthened by one another's commitment, especially in the beginning when our friends found us weird or our own dad tempted us with Burger King. In short, I had a community—even if a small one.

A community of disabled people was something I did not have as a kid. Disability community is something many disabled kids, and disabled adults, lack.

In her book *Contours of Ableism: The Production of Disability and Abledness*, disability studies scholar Fiona Campbell writes, "From the moment a child is born, he/she emerges into a world where he/she receives messages that to be disabled is to be *less than*, a world where disability may be *tolerated* but in the final instance, is *inherently negative.*"[1]

As a child I was instilled with a narrative of what disability scholars and activists critically call "overcoming." Clearly my disability was a drawback, a *negative*, but I could *overcome* it. I wouldn't let it define me. Even in a radical homeschooling household with socially conscious parents and virtually no TV, ableism crept its way into my family's home and my own self-perception because it was embedded in the environment around me: in the stairs, curbs, and narrow pathways that perpetually reminded me that my body wasn't right and wasn't welcome; in people's sidelong looks or attempts not to stare that rendered me both hypervisible and invisible simultaneously; in the absence of knowing anyone resembling me in a position of power or living a flourishing life; and in people's low expectations of me and other disabled people.

Ableism is prejudice against disabled people that can lead to countless forms of discrimination, from lack of access to jobs, education, and housing to oppressive stereotypes and systemic inequalities that leave disabled individuals marginalized. Ableism breeds discrimination and oppression, but it also informs how we define which embodiments are normal, which are valuable, and which are "inherently negative." Although the moments in which I recognized my physical limitations (like my Madonna moment) were poignant and challenging experiences, the suffering I experienced in these moments was minor compared to the ineffable suffering I began to experience due to ableism. I had no language with which to articulate these feelings and no context from which to interpret them. Instead I internalized the prejudice that I often felt and distanced myself from anything and anyone that had to do with disability.

The Americans with Disabilities Act (ADA) was passed in 1990, when I was eight years old. It was passed largely because of the disability community—disabled people coming together to protest, participate in direct action, and define for themselves and for policy makers what disability meant. I had no way of

knowing it then, but an entire other way of understanding disability existed—one that I wouldn't find for another thirteen
years.

I was six when I first learned that animals are often mistreated
and that there are people who protest this mistreatment because
they believe it is wrong. I was able to articulate the ways in which
animals are oppressed, and I wanted to help change the ways they
are viewed and treated. It wasn't until I was twenty-one that I
realized the same thing about disabled people.

# 2
## What Is Disability?

VARIOUS STATISTICS SHOW that disabled people make up anywhere from 15 to nearly 20 percent of the world's population.[1] Disabled people are the world's largest minority.[2] But how can this be true? Where are these 900 million or so people? Even in Berkeley, California, the supposed disability capital of the world, I didn't bump into *that* many disabled people—not enough to tell me that we are the world's largest minority, anyway. Where are these people?

Fiona Campbell writes, "Unlike other minority groups, disabled people have had fewer opportunities to develop a collective conscious, identity or culture."[3] Disabled people are everywhere, and yet we are often isolated from each other. This "dispersal," as Campbell calls it, leads to the isolating impression that disability is a rare experience, an individual's unique challenge to overcome. Even when disability impacts a community, as when a neighborhood has high rates of asthma or congenital disabilities due to pollution, it is still too often treated as an individual's isolated medical problem. The sociopolitical challenges that disabled people face can thus often become individualized narratives of misfortune and strife.

We actually interact daily with far more disabled people than we think we do; we just don't *consider* them disabled (and they may not consider themselves disabled either). Being disabled is often profoundly stigmatizing, so it is no wonder that many people choose to "pass" as nondisabled rather than identify themselves with a population that is largely considered to be unfortunate, broken, and burdensome. The general public usually associates disability only with those who have some clear marker of difference, such as using a wheelchair or crutches or being accompanied by a guide dog. But what about those who live with a chronic illness or have trouble walking long distances? What about people who are discriminated against and deemed unfit because of their weight?

Disability as a category of difference began to crystallize in the United States in the mid-nineteenth century. With the rise of populations that were pathologized and deemed unemployable came a variety of charities, institutions, eugenic practices, and welfare regulations designed to categorize and segregate individuals perceived as unfit and dependent.[4] The modern meanings of the term "normal" also came into use during this period, as increasing numbers of people were organized and defined into various bodies of difference.[5] Of course this is not to say that something akin to disability did not exist prior to the nineteenth century. Ideologies of able-bodiedness and able-mindedness, concepts of fitness and unfitness, and assumptions about the vulnerability and dependency of bodies defined as crippled, blind, deaf, dumb, mad, lame, and infirm can be found in various historical and cultural contexts.[6] Similarly to definitions of race, gender, and sexuality, definitions of disability—of what counts as disability and what disability means—are constantly changing depending on a myriad of factors such as religion, political and economic policies, kinship structures, and so forth. Definitions of disability have also intersected with the shifting meanings of race, gender, sexuality, and class in mutually reinforcing ways.

That the category of disability is a social construction is evident simply by trying to define disability in the United States today. What disability is and isn't is far from clear-cut. Definitions of disability change from regulation to regulation within various organizations and government agencies, and this says nothing of the many meanings disability has culturally, socially, or within disability movements themselves.[7] As cultural critic Michael Bérubé writes, "Any of us who identify as 'nondisabled' must know that our self-designation is inevitably temporary, and that a car crash, a virus, a degenerative genetic disease, or a precedent-setting legal decision could change our status in ways over which we have no control whatsoever."[8] Many invisible or less visible disabilities go unnoticed by people in their daily interactions because most people presume abledness in others. Disability studies scholar Alison Kafer writes, "If it is this difficult to ascertain who is 'disabled,' then it is likely equally difficult to determine who is 'non-disabled' or 'able-bodied.'"[9] The fact that disability is so hard to define is part of what has allowed it to play such a prominent role in shaping Western ideologies of difference and ability. In other words, disability is both a lived reality and an ideological framework that provides contours to fragile meanings of abledness.

Disabled people also don't seem to be out and about because many of us aren't. We are often segregated into separate classrooms, separate buses, separate waiting lines, and separate entrances. We may stay home either by choice (because it is easier than facing discrimination outside our homes) or against our will (because that is where our parents, spouses, caretakers, doctors, or benefit counselors want us to be, or because our homes are not accessible to leave). We may leave our homes only to be stopped by the end of a sidewalk with no curb cut. We may try our best to avoid inaccessible environments and to stay away from stores with physical barriers, such as stairs, or psychological barriers, such as gawking strangers. We may have such deeply internalized ableism that we don't leave our homes out of shame. Or we may be locked away in institutions.

In September 2003, having spent virtually no time with other disabled people up until that point, I participated in my first protest for disability rights. It was a decision made not out of a sense of political responsibility—I initially had only the vaguest idea of what the group was protesting—but out of desperation. I was a depressed twenty-one-year-old with two decades' worth of internalized oppression to unpack. Luckily I had a gut instinct that what I needed was other disabled people in my life—to learn from and to be in community with. A two-week disability protest march seemed like an appropriate way to make that happen.

There were at least two hundred protesters—more than I had ever imagined. And my God, were they disabled! Drooling, limping, wheeling, grunting—my initial desire was to flee and scream for rescue.

Thankfully, I didn't. I stayed the whole two weeks, and, as frustrating as it sometimes was, it also changed my life in amazing ways. The event, a 144-mile march from Philadelphia to Washington, D.C., was organized by one of the disability movement's most prominent groups, American Disabled for Attendant Programs Today (ADAPT).[10] At the time of the march, ADAPT had been at the forefront of disability rights in the United States for more than twenty years, organizing powerful and often dangerous direct actions. They had been doing this for almost my entire life.

The march was in protest of what ADAPT called the "stolen lives" of the more than 2 million people who are currently warehoused, many for profit, in nursing homes and Intermediate Care Facilities for Individuals with Intellectual Disabilities (ICF/IIDs) versus being given the opportunity to live in their own homes where they can have more control over their lives.[11] America has more than sixteen thousand nursing homes, two-thirds of which are for-profit ventures. Nursing homes have become a $116 billion industry.[12] The industry is a racket. The national average annual cost of a room in a nursing home is $87,000. Although it is difficult to estimate the cost of home care, as government policies and health-aide salaries differ widely state by state, and disabled people need varying levels of care, it is clear that it is nearly always far cheaper for disabled people to live in their own homes—so much so that home care workers could be paid a living wage and it would still be cheaper than institutionalization.[13] The standard of services in nursing homes is also often shockingly low.[14] There is a high incidence of physical and sexual violence as well as negligence of hygiene and psychological needs. Even at the best institutions, individuals are stripped of countless freedoms that people on the outside take for granted, such as choosing when and what to eat, when to sleep, and whether to engage in consensual sexual intimacy.[15]

Disabled people's right to live in their communities instead of in separate institutions is constantly being threatened. California, often referred to as the home of the disability rights movement, has some of the largest nursing homes in the United States, and year after year the state government tries to put essential services disabled people need to live in their own homes on the chopping block.[16]

Despite the fact that 2 million people are denied the privilege of determining where and how they live and who cares for them, the lack of press garnered by disability issues is not exactly a surprise. This is not to say that representations of disability are absent from the media—far from it. Disability as metaphor is deeply pervasive in the media, and as a human-interest story disability has almost mythic endurance. In these narratives disability is nearly always seen as a personal tragedy. Disabled people are supposed to find the courage to overcome their own personal limitations through strength of character rather than by overcoming discrimination and oppression. This has been dubbed the "super crip" narrative by many disabled activists and scholars. Anything a disabled person does, no matter how mundane or remarkable, is seen as amazing and inspirational, from getting married, to going to school, to simply leaving the house or not wanting to kill themselves (or even the fact that they *do* want to kill themselves). This narrative does not inspire other disabled people to participate in their communities and demand equal rights but instead motivates an able-bodied audience to work harder and be more grateful. Through this lens, disability becomes a hyper-sentimentalized version of the familiar capitalist narrative of the poor man lifting himself up by his bootstraps.

As I began my journey as a disability activist, I went from feeling like disability was my own isolated experience to seeing it everywhere. I realized that disability's presence in U.S. culture is inescapable even on a rhetorical level. We say that "the economy is crippled," or that someone who feels incapable or unable to do something is in a state of "paralysis." We talk of blindness as if it means ignorance or naïveté; we describe things that we think are ignorant or unfair as "retarded." "Disabled" is used ubiquitously to describe things as broken or not working.

Such examples are often brushed aside as innocent figures of speech. But words are political.

Whether in language or imagery, the most common disability metaphors are based on stereotypes and a lack of knowledge of disabled people's experiences. The figurative use of a word such as "crippled" reinforces the idea that crippled means broken, defective, and in need of fixing. Because the word is often used metaphorically, the actual lives of those who are crippled are simultaneously erased and stereotyped. "Crippled" is a particularly interesting example because of how the word "crip" (which comes from "cripple") has been adopted by disability activists and scholars in a way that is similar to how LGBT activists and scholars have reclaimed the word "queer." Many disabled people identify as crips, and to crip something does not mean to break it but to radically and creatively invest it with disability history, politics, and pride while simultaneously questioning paradigms of independence, normalcy, and medicalization.

During that first protest with ADAPT I was hesitant to identify so boldly as disabled. But as time went on, crip increasingly became a part of my identity. For disabled scholars, activists, and artists, crip has become an action, a way of radically altering meaning. We talk of crip time, crip space, crip culture, and crip theory.

Like antiracist and feminist scholars before them, disability scholars realize that words reinforce how we are treated socially and politically every day, and the same is true of other kinds of representations, images, and cultural narratives. There are countless ways that the lived experiences of disabled people are replaced with metaphors and stereotypes: from pity-mongering charity drives and sappy "super crip" characters in movies to representations of disabled people as scroungers, fakers, malingerers, or burdens in common political discourse. Disability is presented as pitiable, always in need of a cure, and a barrier to a full life, while disabled people are patronizingly referred to as "inspiring" and "special" and praised for "overcoming their disabilities." Other representations present disabled people as dangerous, violent, and ready to take revenge for their suffering (think of all the villains in movies who are disfigured or use a prosthetic). This is especially true for those with intellectual or psychological disabilities (consider the role mental illness plays in national conversations about mass shootings and other extreme violence). Such representations are not universal—they compound and shift across nationality, racial, gender, and class differences—but these particular stereotypes are some of the most prominent in mainstream U.S. culture.

Representations of disability are often born from medicalization —the idea that disability is an issue best suited for the fields of medicine and rehabilitation. During the nineteenth and early twentieth centuries disability went from being largely a moral, spiritual, or metaphysical issue to a medical one. Where disability had once been understood as an intervention by God or as the price paid for a karmic debt, it was now understood as medical deviance. What disability scholars and activists refer to as "the medical model of disability" positions the disabled body as working incorrectly, as being unhealthy and abnormal, as needing a cure.[17]

The medical model of disability locates a disabled person's struggles solely within their own body: something is wrong with the disabled person, which makes them unable to fully function in the world. This perspective is taken for granted now as common sense or as proof of our advancement as a civilization. Of course the need for a wheelchair is a medical issue. What else could it be?

Over the past few decades disability advocates have tried to tell a different story about disability. Many disabled people argue that disability is not simply a medical problem; it is a social justice one. This is not to say that disabled people don't sometimes need doctors or medical contributions. Rather, it is to say that medicine is not the only, or even the best, framework for understanding disability. Disability activists and scholars have countered medicalization with other models of disability, the most established being "the social model of disability," which argues that disability is not caused by impairment, but by the way society is organized.[18]

Consider the simple example of our daily movements through our cities and towns, entering and exiting buildings, stepping over curbs, getting on buses. If someone cannot step up onto a curbside, is that marginalizing fact the fault of the person's body? What about a bus that is equipped with stairs but not a ramp or lift? What about crossing lights that visually signal that it's safe to move across the street but don't beep or otherwise signal it through sound? Ableism encourages us to understand one technology as normal and another as specialized. We are so used to technologies and structures such as steps and staircases that they become almost natural to us. But curbs are no more natural than curb cuts, and blinking lights no more natural than beeping sounds.

Access is also a question of which cognitive characteristics are privileged and supported. Many simple things can give those with intellectual and psychological disabilities (as well as those with other kinds of disabilities, such as chronic illness) access to environments they would otherwise be left out of. In workplace and school environments such things as access to a paraprofessional, assistive technologies, extra breaks, more flexible means of communication (such as e-mail, telephone, online chat, or in-person meetings), changes in lighting, and scent-free and chemical-free policies can make the difference between a completely inaccessible environment and one open to more people.[19]

None of this is to say that access is simple or easy—access needs are vast and various—but it bears remembering that our environments have been built based on assumptions about whose bodies will be participating in them. Legacies of oppression shape the ways our social landscapes are structured. As disability justice activist Mia Mingus explains, the question of access is not unique to disability: "Accessibility is nothing new, and we can work to understand access in a broad way, encompassing class, language, childcare, gender-neutral bathrooms as a start."[20] Access is intersectional. It's important to consider who our societies have historically privileged and what kinds of bodies they have been built to accommodate. Our cities and cultures have not organically manifested themselves to reward certain embodiments over others. They are human made, with human biases and prejudices built into them, so we must ask why certain bodies have been presented as the standard against which others are compared.

Access isn't only about physical space, it's also about the economic and social systems that structure society. Disabled people are some of the most marginalized people on the planet. The connections between disability and poverty in particular are striking. Twenty percent of the world's poorest people are disabled, and 80 percent of the world's disabled population live in developing countries.[21] Across the world disabled people are likely to live in poverty and are often among the worst off in their communities.[22] This is true of the United States, where disabled people are more likely than their able-bodied counterparts to live below the poverty line.[23] As the World Bank reports, "Poverty causes disabilities and can furthermore lead to secondary disabilities for those individuals who are already disabled, as a result of the poor living conditions, health endangering employment, malnutrition, poor access to health care and education opportunities, etc."[24] This can be a vicious cycle for many people, as people who are disabled will often face additional barriers to accessing things that could help them get out of poverty, such as education and job opportunities. Additionally, while disabled activists often criticize the medicalization of disability, we are fully aware that access to health care is vital for people living with a disability—as it is, of course, for everyone.

The unemployment rate for disabled people around the world is also staggeringly high. According to a UN report, "In developing countries, 80 percent to 90 percent of persons with disabilities of working age are unemployed, whereas in industrialized countries the figure is between 50 percent and 70 percent."[25] Even with disabled people in the workforce rising in recent years, only 37 percent of working-age persons with disabilities in the United States are employed.[26] All of these numbers are worse for disabled women and disabled people of color. Senator Tom Harkin has written that things aren't looking up: "According to the Bureau of Labor Statistics, the disability workforce shrank by over 10 percent during the recession, five times faster than the non-disability workforce, which shrank by only about two percent."[27]

Our actual physical or mental disabilities are often the least of our worries. People with physical and mental differences have been oppressed by extreme and violent measures such as sterilization, infanticide, eugenics, and institutionalization, as well as through systematic inequalities such as impoverishment and denial of access to housing, work, and education. Disabled people not only face institutionalization in nursing homes and psychiatric hospitals but are also disproportionately represented in U.S. prisons and jails.[28] Disabled people are more likely to be victims of violence than able-bodied people, and hate crimes against disabled people are notoriously underreported and under-prosecuted.[29] For disabled individuals who are incarcerated, institutionalized, or unable to choose and hire their own attendants, violence and hate can be a daily occurrence.

Disabled people contend with stereotypes, stigmas, and civil rights infringements daily. We are some of the world's poorest people, some of the least educated, and some of the most likely to face violence. It is legal to keep us from participating in many social spaces through physical and attitudinal barriers and to segregate us into institutions and "special" programs. It is considered acceptable to talk for us instead of to us—or, in the case of those who are nonverbal and "severely" intellectually disabled, instead of to the people who know them and their interests best.

The profound systemic prejudice and discrimination faced by disabled people pervades nearly all aspects of society. Yet this prejudice changes with location, race, gender, class, and the nature of a person's specific disability. My own privilege as a white, middle-class, physically disabled American woman with no communication impairments and the means to live in my own home with assistants whom I choose and hire has often shielded me from the reality of many of these oppressions—realities that are inescapable for other people with disabilities.

Disability oppression and disability activism play out differently depending on place and experience. Individual populations face specific challenges particular to them. Further complicating matters is the fact that, as is becoming evident, the barrier between able-bodiedness and disability is far from clear-cut or permanent. Disability can be an identity one embraces, a condition one struggles with, a space one finds liberation in, or a concept that can be leveraged to marginalize and oppress. It can also be all of these things at once.

It becomes increasingly clear that disability is not only a lived experience that shapes individual human lives—it is also an ideology that plays a central role in forming our histories, politics, and cultures. Disability doesn't belong simply to the margins, or to medicine, or to a few specific historical events; instead, disability—like gender, class, and race—is a social force that affects the world in a pervasive manner.[30] As historian Douglas C. Baynton notes, "Disability is everywhere in history, once you begin looking for it, but conspicuously absent in the history we write."[31]

This becomes starkly evident when we consider that ideologies of disability have been central to the development of the modern world. For example, scholars have exposed the role of disability in the creation of capitalism and labor relations, particularly in contributing to definitions of a "work-based" system versus a "needs-based" system of distribution, as well as in definitions of concepts such as independence, efficiency, and productivity.[32] Others have shown how ideologies of disability have been key to formulating U.S. immigration policies, as justifications for the exclusion of various racialized and classed populations have often stereotyped certain populations as "likely to become a public charge" or pose a public health threat.[33] Such examples of the importance of disability in shaping our society abound. Perhaps most telling, though, is the role concepts of disability have historically played in reinforcing and defining categories of difference.[34] Ideologies of disability have contributed to the pathologization of various populations by infantilizing them, declaring them weak, vulnerable, unintelligent, prone to disease, less advanced, in need of care, and so forth. This pathologization is intricately tied up with ableism, which asserts that markers of disability, such as vulnerability, weakness, physical and mental abnormality, and dependency are undesirable. Consequently, any physical or mental attributes that can then be associated (falsely or accurately) with these conditions are seen as biological, natural deficiencies that need to be regulated and controlled. These ideologies of disability have helped define whole populations as disabled through claims of intellectual and physical inferiority, as can be seen in racist stereotypes that posit black people as physically robust but intellectually inferior to white people, indigenous communities as in need of management and prone to disease, and upper-class white women as too delicate for rigorous intellectual or physical work. The legacies of such histories are far from buried, as can be seen in the work of scholars such as Nirmala Erevelles, who has shown that in the United States children of color are disproportionately

categorized as having disabilities, giving the school system a supposedly biological justification for segregating them into special
(in other words separate) education classrooms.[35]

It's important to point out that when scholars argue that disability is central to structuring categories of difference, they are
not arguing that disability trumps such markers of difference as
race, gender, or class but rather that disability is mutually consti-
tutive of various forms of difference. In other words, ideologies
of race, class, sexuality, and gender form meanings of disability,
just as disability forms meanings about them. These categories
have developed alongside one another, shaping, impacting, and
sometimes merging with each other. Disability studies scholar
Ellen Samuels makes this point well in her book *Fantasies of Identification: Disability, Gender, Race*, particularly in her discussion of
nineteenth-century anthropologists. She writes, "Physicians and
anthropologists of the time did not in fact distinguish between
characteristics ascribed to race and those ascribed to physical and
mental ability as we do today." She explains that anthropologists
of the day were not analogizing differences so much as actually
"merging . . . [them] into a flexible category of mental immatu-
rity and incapacity."[36]

Samuels's statement is a powerful reminder that categories that
may seem distinct today have at times been inseparable from each
other. Though often overlooked, the category of animal is also
crucial to understanding this history and the frameworks that
define us. Who is human versus nonhuman may seem clear-cut
and uncomplicated today, but as we know all too well, at different points in time various human populations have been identified as bestial, more animal than human, or as missing links of
evolution—classifications that were inextricably entangled with
definitions of inferiority, savagery, sexuality, dependency, abil-
ity/disability, physical and mental difference, and so forth. Samuels's statement is actually in reference to the racist anthropology
that consigned Native Americans to the status of evolutionary
throwbacks, examples of a less advanced stage in human development. Such assessments operated in tandem with claims that intellectually disabled people were examples of a prior stage in human
evolution. Such dehumanization and animalization of race and

disability can be seen in the work of nineteenth-century geologist J.P. Lesley, who argued human evolution was demonstrated not only by the discovery of so-called primitive or apelike populations (in other words, non-Europeans) but by examining the "idiots" and "cretins" of all societies:

> Individuals scattered all over the world, through all the human races, with low foreheads, small brains, long arms, thin legs, projecting, tusk-like teeth, suppressed noses, and other marks of arrested development; to say nothing of millions of idiots and cretins produced by the same arrest in every generation of mankind, sustain the argument.[37]

The century prior, the 1700s, had seen the development of Linnaean taxonomy, the system of classification of different species that would lay the groundwork for the scientific classification system we still use today. This system helped position humans within nature, but it was also embedded in and representative of racialized and gendered debates over the categorization of humans, using assumptions about human difference to help name the boundaries between human and animal.[38] Systems of species classification have relied heavily on hierarchies that have placed humans above animals, and these hierarchies have always been entangled with constructions of human difference. My point here is not only to expose the importance of the figure of the animal to histories of categorization and dehumanization, it is also to make clear that the animal, and, consequently, the human, are complicated categories, socially determined rather than solely biologically.

Although such historical analysis is too complex to do justice to here, it's important to emphasize that histories of dehumanization invariably exposed Western understandings, assumptions, and bigotry; understandings that were bound up with racism, ableism, and prejudice toward animals (as can be seen in J.P. Lesley's work). In these constructs animals—a huge, unwieldy category that encompasses creatures as diverse as mosquitoes, jellyfish, dogs, and orcas—are understood to be unquestionably inferior creatures. In this anthropocentric view the world exists for "man" (that is, some men), with animals existing completely separate from and lesser than this pinnacle of creation.

With such histories of animalization and pathologization in mind, it's no surprise that many people would wish to distance themselves from both disability and animality. As much as I recognize the drive and sometimes even the need for such distancing, in this book I want to challenge such impulses. As disability studies scholar Michelle Jarman writes, "The very real need to challenge fallacious biological attributes linked to race, gender, sexuality and poverty—such as physical anomaly, psychological instability, or intellectual inferiority—has often left stigma around disability unchallenged."[39] In many ways a similar thing could be said of animality: that there has been an urgent need among dehumanized populations (including disabled people) to challenge animalization and claim humanity. As urgent and understandable as these challenges are, it is important to ask how we can reconcile the brutal reality of human animalization with the concurrent need to challenge the devaluing of animals and even acknowledge our own animality. This book suggests that inattention to disability and animality (and to how they intersect) is a mistake, because both concepts are so deeply implicated in other categories of difference and in the many social justice issues that oppressed populations face—from poverty, incarceration, and war to environmental injustice—that they cannot simply be relegated to the margins. Unless disability and animal justice are incorporated into our other movements for liberation, ableism and anthropocentrism will be left unchallenged, available for use by systems of domination and oppression.

However, as Jarman and many others have pointed out, disability scholars and activists have too often neglected an intersectional approach, ignoring issues of race, class, sexuality, and gender and leaving white and class privilege within disability movements and scholarship unchallenged. A similar critique of mainstream animal rights movements is in order; too often issues of race, gender, and class are neglected while white privilege and patriarchy are maintained, with animal rights advocates neglecting issues of intersectionality and centering a white and middle-class model of animal advocacy. The disability justice movement, which centralizes disabled people of color, poor people, and queer and gender-variant people, has emerged in response to the need for a disability movement that centralizes oppressions as inextricably connected.[40] In animal liberation movements, feminist and people of color framings of animal ethics have emerged to challenge traditional framings of animal rights by focusing on the interlocking oppression of humans and animals and by highlighting the concerns of communities that have largely been left out of animal rights discourse. This book is hugely indebted to such movements.

Many years after the ADAPT protest, and after I began identifying as crip, I realized in my art studio at UC Berkeley how important it is to think intersectionally about animals. As I painted the scores of chickens on the truck awaiting slaughter, I learned many things about animal industries and specifically about the hens in my painting—hens who I came to understand were virtually all disabled. I realized that ableism is a force that expands beyond disabled people. *All* bodies are subjected to the oppression of ableism. It helps form our cultural opinions and values as well as our notions of what it means to be independent, how to measure productivity and efficiency, what is normal, and even what is natural. In research for that painting, I learned that these values not only affect disabled individuals and the able-bodied population, but also the nonhuman animals with whom we share this planet.

# 3

## Animal Crips

A FEW YEARS AGO I found a story about a fox with arthrogryposis, which is the disability I was born with. According to the Canadian Cooperative Wildlife Health Centre, a wildlife conservation and management organization, the fox was shot by a resident of the area because "it had an abnormal gait and appeared sick." The animal, whose disabilities were quite significant, had normal muscle mass, and his stomach contained a large amount of digested food, which suggested to researchers that "the limb deformity did not preclude successful hunting and foraging."[1]

The resident seems to have shot the animal out of pity (a sort of mercy killing) and fear (perhaps assuming the fox was sick with a contagious disease). People shoot normal foxes too, of course, but for less purportedly altruistic reasons. However, this fox actually seemed to be doing very well. Did the resident assume the fox's quality of life was unacceptable? Did the person view the animal's disabilities as dangerous or as a fate worse than death? The concept of a mercy killing carries within it two of the most prominent responses to disability: destruction and pity. The fox was clearly affected by human ableism, shot dead by someone who equated disability only with suffering and fear of contagion.

The assumptions and prejudices we hold about disabled bodies run deep—so deep that we project this human ableism onto non-human animals. They are subjected to some of our most familiar ableist narratives. For instance, the "better off dead" narrative, which led to the shooting of the fox, is a common thread in discussions of pet euthanasia and animal farming. There is also the inspirational disabled animal who overcomes great odds, which is perhaps a more surprising narrative but one that seems to be gaining in popularity. Consider for example the 2011 movie *Dolphin Tale*, a true story of a dolphin who loses her tail and learns to swim with a prosthesis, or the animated fantasy film *How to Train Your Dragon*, which has a similar story line involving a dragon who gets a prosthetic tail. Then there are stories like that of Faith, a dog who was born with only her two hind legs and who has learned to walk bipedally. Faith has appeared on many television shows, including *Oprah*, and become an inspiration for viewers. "Cute" and "inspiring" disabled animal stories seem to be all the rage on social media these days, and various memes and websites tell the stories of disabled animals who "triumph" and "overcome" obstacles. Television shows are also beginning to catch on to this burgeoning market: a *Nature* episode titled "My Bionic Pet" aired on PBS in spring 2014, exploring animal prosthetics. Their promo declares, "Sometimes miracles do happen."[2]

Clearly we project ableism onto nonhuman animals; do we also project the notion of *disability* itself? If the category of disability is a social construction, then what does it mean to say an animal is disabled? We have no idea how other animals comprehend physical or cognitive difference. Does a dog perceive that something is different about another dog if she has three legs? Can a monkey tell that she is different if she limps? Can animals know to help other disabled animals? Can animals recognize disability across species? The animal world is filled with such an incredible and seemingly infinite variety of difference that trying to assess the difference disability makes almost seems futile. And yet a lot of fascinating evidence suggests that some animals can and do recognize something akin to disability.[3] Primatologist Frans de Waal tells the story of Yeroen, the oldest adult male chimpanzee in the Arnhem chimpanzee colony. Yeroen hurt his hand in a fight with a young rival. De Waal writes that Yeroen "limped for a week, even though his wound seemed superficial." The scientists soon discovered that Yeroen was only limping if he could be seen by his rival. Did Yeroen think that faking a limp would make his attacker more sympathetic to him? Or does that interpretation too quickly read Yeroen's actions through human assumptions about disability and the sort of response it should engender?

The meanings of the word "disability" are uniquely human, created and contextualized by human cultures over centuries. Despite this, I have chosen to use it here when discussing differences among nonhuman animals. I am drawn to the breadth of meaning the word has within disability movements, and I'm interested in what happens when we consider how disability as lived experience and as ideology impacts nonhuman animals. How do nonhuman animals relate to physical and cognitive difference themselves? How do human understandings of disability affect the ways we interpret what animals are experiencing?

That animal disability both inspires and horrifies people is clearly evident in discussions surrounding Internet sensation Chris P. Bacon. Chris is a pig who was born in January 2013 with very small hind legs that he cannot walk on. He "set the Internet on fire" when a video of him using a homemade wheelchair went viral. The tiny piglet, who was rescued by a veterinarian after a woman brought him in to be euthanized, has now gone through multiple wheelchairs and weighs more than seventy pounds.[4]

Many commenters on articles about Chris want him euthanized, saying it's cruel to "make him live like that." Others find him so heroic that he is invited to attend muscular dystrophy events for children. Chris is raising awareness—not about the plight of pigs, but about disability. After all, no matter how much Americans on the Internet love this pig, his name constantly reminds us what people think he really amounts to: bacon.

A telling example of the impulse to project human stereotypes of disability onto other animals can be found in the story of Mozu, a snow monkey (a Japanese macaque) who was born in Japan's central highlands. Mozu was born with abnormalities of her hands and feet thought to have resulted from pesticide pollution. Snow monkeys spend much of their time moving through trees, which allows them to avoid wading through the thick snow that covers the ground in the winter months. Mozu's disabilities meant she was mostly unable to move through the branches; instead she traveled the nearly two miles that her troop covered every day in search of food by alternately walking on her abnormal limbs and crawling and sliding on the forest floor. When Mozu was born, researchers who had been watching this troop feared she would not make it past infancy. To their surprise, Mozu lived for nearly three decades, rearing five children of her own and becoming a prominent troop member.

In an episode of the program *Nature* featuring Mozu's story, she is again and again referred to as "inspiring," "suffering," and a "very special monkey."[5] The dramatic music and voice-overs that describe Mozu's struggle in vivid detail make it nearly impossible to watch her move across the snowy forest floor, a baby clinging to her belly and other monkeys flying by above her, without thinking, "Poor Mozu!"

At the same time, I am aware that the piece was edited to elicit this reaction. There are few shots in which Mozu is not struggling, and I question the effect the videographers had on her and the troop. In one scene her desperation seems to stem from being chased by the cameraperson. The music and voice-overs of course also add a sense of struggle to Mozu's story.

Yet I have no doubt that life was hard for Mozu, and I find myself desperate to know what she thought of her situation. Was her instinct to reach for the trees unquenchable? Was she always in pain, exhausted, or fearful as she moved slowly across the forest floor? Did she wonder why she was different from her companions? I cannot help but wonder, although I realize how similar these thoughts are to the tiresome questions I have been asked again and again about my own life, my own disability. My desire for Mozu's life not to be seen as one of suffering and struggle is also a projection, one that wishes disability empowerment onto my fellow primate. Our human perspective shapes how we interpret Mozu's experience.

Many of our ideas about animals are formed by our assumption that only the "fittest" animals survive, which negates the value and even the naturalness of such experiences as vulnerability, weakness, and interdependence. When disabilities occur, we assume that "nature will run her course," that the natural process for a disabled animal is to die, rendering living disabled animals not only aberrant but unnatural.

How true is this? Mozu lived for twenty-eight years, raising children and grandchildren. Jeffrey Moussaieff Masson, author of the bestselling book *When Elephants Weep: The Emotional Lives of Animals*, writes that "it is something of a cliché among animal behaviorists that wild animals do not tolerate disabilities, and that animals who are unfortunate enough to be born with a deformity or fall ill rarely last very long. I am dubious."[6] Recent research offers numerous examples of disabled animals surviving and sometimes thriving, as well as evidence that animals can recognize when another animal is different and needs support. There are countless stories of primates, elephants, dogs, pigs, whales, ducks, geese, and chickens helping their disabled companions. It is known, for example, that male silverback gorillas will slow down their troop so that elderly, ill, and disabled members can keep up. Other species, such as elephants and wolves, have been shown to do the same. What do we make of animals such as Babyl, an elephant who lived in the Samburu Reserve in northern Kenya? Ethologist Marc Bekoff writes that Babyl was "crippled" and "couldn't travel as fast as the rest of the herd," and describes how the other elephants in Babyl's group would wait for her instead of leaving her behind. The elephant expert Iain Douglas-Hamilton told Bekoff that the elephants had been doing this for years; that they "always waited for Babyl. . . . They would walk for a while, then stop and look around to see where Babyl was. Depending on how she was doing, they'd either wait or proceed."[7] The matriarch would even feed Babyl on occasion. Bekoff asks why the other elephants in Babyl's herd would act this way since there was no practical reason to do so: "Babyl could do little for them." The only conclusion Bekoff and his companions could draw was that the other elephants cared about Babyl. As important (and radical) as it is to suggest that animals who are not directly related can care for each other in such a way, from a critical disability perspective it is also important to keep open the possibility that Babyl did offer something useful to the troop—something that may be hard for us to recognize if we understand disability only as a drawback or limitation.

Such examples of disability survival, adaptation, and care in the animal world are not limited to elephants and apes or even mammals. Consider Baks, a large boxer who was blinded in an accident. Unprompted by humans, a four-year-old goose named Buttons began leading the dog around. Buttons became a veritable guide-goose, hanging on to the dog with her neck or directing his movements by honking at him.[8] Examples such as this are indeed the kind of sweet stories of companionship popular on the Internet, but they also raise critical questions about empathy, vulnerability, interdependence, adaptation, and animal experience.

De Waal suggests that animals go through a process of what is called *learned adjustment*: "Healthy members do not necessarily know what is wrong, but gradually become familiar with the limitations of their less fortunate mates."[9] In other words, an animal may learn to recognize *over time* that the way another animal is moving or acting makes her more vulnerable to danger, supporting and protecting her, or treating her with less aggression because she is not seen as a threat. De Waal contrasts this to another response considered to be more complex, cognitive empathy, the ability "to picture oneself in the position of another individual." Cognitive empathy allows us humans to understand what sorts of limitations another being has simply by seeing them, as we are immediately able to imagine ourselves into their situation.[10] Research into animal empathy is still young, but it seems likely that humans are not the only species capable of cognitive empathy, as numerous animals, including wolves, apes, and elephants, have been shown to have the capacity for empathetic response.

A reaction to learned adjustment could go in multiple directions—if animals learn that another animal is vulnerable they might take advantage of her, abandon her, help her, or accept her and learn to accommodate her. The concept of learned adjustment, however, and the distinction between it and cognitive empathy leave important questions unanswered. De Waal writes, "Special treatment of the handicapped is probably best regarded as a combination of learned adjustment and strong attachment; it is the attachment that steers the adjustment in a positive, caring direction."[11] What is this attachment, then? Is it friendship or love? Is it empathy? De Waal acknowledges the concept's limitations—for example, it does little to explain the care and protection an animal can have for an injured or disabled animal they have had no time to adjust to, as when a troop member suddenly becomes injured.[12]

To unpack these terms further it might be helpful to look at an example de Waal gives. He asks us to picture a human being who has lost his arms in an accident: "Just from seeing his condition, or hearing about it, we will grasp the reduction in physical ability he has undergone. We can imagine what it is like to have no arms, and our capacity for empathy allows us to extrapolate this knowledge to the other's situation." He goes on to say, "Our friend's dog, by contrast, will need time to learn that there is no point in bringing her master a stick to fetch, or that the familiar pat on the back is being replaced by a foot rub."[13] Again, because it involves being able to imagine oneself into the life of the other, cognitive empathy is deemed more complex than learned adjustment.

A critical disability analysis, however, exposes something troubling about the distinction between learned adjustment and cognitive empathy. In the scenario de Waal offers, he describes cognitive empathy as "grasping" what a body with no arms won't be able to do; we human beings are immediately able to imagine what is lacking for a person with no arms. But this imagining may not be accurate, and more important, it is only possible with disabilities and injuries with which we ourselves are familiar— ones that are diagnosable and recognizable within our culture. If we encounter someone with a disability or illness we have never heard of and know nothing about, our interaction with them would arguably be one of learned adjustment. Thus de Waal's description of cognitive empathy naturalizes disability as a predictable diagnosable fact as opposed to something that is inextricably situated in our own cultures and histories. In contrast, he frames learned adjustment as a process of learning how another being moves and acts without prior assumptions or stereotypes. The limits of these definitions and distinctions are evident in de Waal's assumption that someone with no arms won't be able to play fetch with his dog. The dog may learn that fetch can still be played, as her human companion may use his mouth or feet to throw the stick. Which being—the dog or the presumptuous human observer—understands disability more accurately?

De Waal's framing shows how easy it is to assume an animal's behavior is less complex than a human's behavior. It also exposes how human assumptions about disability invariably shape the way animal behaviorists interpret it.

What stands out for me most, though, in the conversation about animal disability is how little it is discussed by those who study animal behavior. Perhaps this should come as no surprise, given that disability is often neglected as a legitimate area of study. What work does exist often focuses on the effect the disabled animals have on the able-bodied animal population of which they are a part rather than the insights into animal behavior offered by disabled animals themselves. We should be wary of this human tendency toward ableism, which assumes that it is the nondisabled population's response to disability that is most worthy of critical examination. Disabled animals are repeatedly presented as offering nothing back to their communities, but is this true, or are scientists neglecting to watch for more nuanced behavior because of their preconceived views on disability? We should also bear in mind that as tempting as it is to see disability engendering either compassion or neglect in other animals, these narratives also rehearse reactions common to disability in many human cultures. In these narratives disabled people are either perceived as inspiring compassion in able-bodied populations or as burdening communities and triggering animosity. This does not mean these narratives are always untrue, only that we should be careful not to simply read human stereotypes of disability onto other species. Disabled animals raise important questions about adaptation, creativity, and self-reflection. If scientists of animal behavior would look to disabled animals with an open mind—watching for more than what ableism teaches us to expect—than we quite possibly would find that disability plays a far more complex role in animal lives than has previously been thought.

Thus far we have thought mainly about wild animals, but what of those who are domesticated? What does disability mean to the domesticated animals we breed and profit from? As I learned from the chicken truck photographs I spent so many hours with, disability is ubiquitous among animals used in food production.

Industrially farmed animals live in such cramped, filthy, and unnatural conditions that disabilities become common, even inevitable.[14] They are often crammed into cages with cement, wire, or metal-grated floors, covered in their own feces and kept in virtually nonstop darkness. But the disabilities that arise from these toxic environments are often secondary to the ones they are made to have from birth. Farmed animals are bred to physical extremes: udders produce too much milk for a cow's body to hold, turkeys and chickens cannot bear the weight of their own giant breasts, and pigs' legs are too weak to support them. Chickens, turkeys, and ducks are also physically harmed by processes such as debeaking—done without anesthetic—which can leave them prone to serious infection and make it difficult for the birds to eat or preen themselves.[15] And then there are the bruises, abscesses, sores, broken bones, vaginal and reproductive disorders, chronic illnesses, and psychological issues that farmed animals are commonly reported to endure.

Masson reports that "nearly a quarter of all commercially reared birds are lame and experience excruciating chronic pain."[16] To satisfy the increasing demand for cheap meat and eggs, chickens have been bred to grow twice as fast as they usually would, leaving them with bones and joints that cannot bear the weight of their massive forms. A battery hen, whose sole role is to lay eggs, produces around 250 eggs a year, far more than the sixty or so her body is meant to handle.[17] The constant egg production combined with her complete inability to exercise make her prone to osteoporosis and broken bones. Scientists who expose such situations have been accused of being anthropomorphic.[18] The use of the word *anthropomorphic* is telling, as if acknowledging that humans aren't the only creatures who experience physical difference and illness brings animals too close for comfort. If humans can share this sort of vulnerability with nonhuman animals, what else might we share?

It is not only chickens who experience disabilities and illness on industrialized farms. At least 60 percent of dairy cows experience lameness, and 35 percent experience udder mastitis, a potentially

fatal inflammation of the udder tissue.[19] Cows used for milk production are kept either continuously pregnant or milking, their
calves taken away within hours or days of birth. They are bred
to produce far more milk than their calves would need. As the
Humane Society of the United States (HSUS) reports, "On average, a U.S. dairy cow produced 9,193 kg (20,267 lb) of milk in
2007, more than double the per-cow milk yield in 1967 and 47%
more than the per-cow milk yield in 1987. . . . Even though the
number of cows in the dairy industry declined from 1987 to 2007,
the total production of milk increased by 30%."[20] As with battery hens, this overproduction leaves cows susceptible to limping,
weak limbs, and broken bones, as they must walk with an unusual
gait to carry such large and heavy udders.[21]

Pigs are prone to disabling conditions as well. Most upset-
ting to the pork industry is porcine stress syndrome, which costs
the industry an estimated $90 million a year.[22] The condition is
genetic, resulting from half a century of selective breeding for
large and lean muscles. The condition makes pigs susceptible to
heart attacks if they are stressed, which is inevitable on industrialized pig farms. All of the pigs live in cramped and filthy conditions, but it is the female animals who are the worst off. They are
kept continually pregnant or nursing in cages so small that they
often cannot even sit up and are forced to lie on their side until
the next breeding cycle begins.

Pigs also experience disabling leg conditions because of a lack
of physical exercise and the unusual weight they are bred to carry. They are prone to a wide variety of disabilities and diseases, including severe arthritis that affects their ability to walk. A
slaughterhouse in Sioux City, Iowa, John Morrell & Company
(which closed in 2010) had the capacity to slaughter 75,000 hogs
a week, or one pig every four seconds. This is how one employee described it: "The preferred method of handling a cripple at
Morrell's is to beat him to death with a lead pipe before he gets
into the chute. It's called 'piping.'"[23] Another said, "If a hog can't
walk, they scoop the son of a bitch up on a dead run with a Bob-
cat [small tractor]. Whupp! Right up in the air. If he stays in the
bucket, he stays in. If he falls out, you run him over or pin him
against the wall, finish busting the rest of his legs so he can't run

any further."[24] Comparing this reality to the general enthusiasm over Internet sensation Chris P. Bacon, it becomes apparent just how conflicted human beings are about how we should treat and feel about animals.

One need not look past the daily newspapers to realize the impact of industrial farming on animal health. Outbreaks of bovine spongiform encephalopathy (mad cow disease), foot and mouth disease, swine flu, avian flu, and other diseases of industrially farmed animals have led to countless headlines over the past few years. In the spring of 2015 the worst outbreak of avian flu ever to hit the United States spread across a dozen states and, according to the U.S. Department of Agriculture, led to the death of more than 48 million birds. These birds did not die of the flu. If avian flu infects even one bird, the whole flock is killed. And these are not flocks of a few dozen animals. *The Guardian* reports that in Iowa, the worst hit state, an egg farm holds anywhere from seventy thousand to 5 million chickens. In such a scenario, "infection means slaughtering an unimaginable number of animals." If the affected birds are egg-laying hens, they are "euthanized" with carbon dioxide gas. Because carbon dioxide isn't effective in the enclosures that house broiler chickens and turkeys, they are suffocated to death with water-based foam, a process that can take three to seven minutes.[25]

In 2001 a highly publicized outbreak of foot and mouth disease—a virus that is not lethal to humans or animals—swept through the United Kingdom. Pyres of burning cattle carcasses could be seen across the English countryside and all over the international media. The fires were to dispose of the bodies of more than 10 million adult and baby cows, pigs, and sheep who were shot, burned, and then bulldozed into mass graves.[26] Reports described terrified animals running over each other in an attempt to escape their executioners. Millions of these animals did not have foot and mouth disease, which is preventable and can be easily treated with veterinary care. They were killed because trade policies required it.[27]

All of these animals—the 10 million cows, pigs, and sheep and the 48 million chickens and turkeys—were destined for early and traumatic deaths regardless of these culling campaigns. What was shocking about such mass killings was the way they openly and publicly displayed the complete lack of worth these animals are deemed to have. No longer having any market value, they were viewed not only as killable, but as discardable.

Industrial animal farms are widely acknowledged to be exceptional incubators for increasingly dangerous diseases like avian flu that can be infectious across species (including humans).[28] When thousands or even millions of immune-compromised animals are forced to live in tight and filthy quarters, viruses and bacteria spread like wildfire and have ample opportunity to adapt, especially with the widespread use of antibiotics in animal feed, which leads to increasingly resistant and virulent strains. Within these conditions any sort of contagious illness or sign of illness becomes a possible disaster with huge implications for profits.

As this discussion shows, any sympathy directed toward farmed animals is secondary to a concern for human needs—and these needs prove to be largely financial. The advice given to animal farmers to protect their animals from disease and disability is nearly always motivated by profit, and these profits and losses can be huge. In Iowa alone the avian flu cost $1.2 billion.[29] We can again find parallels to human situations, for example in public health framings of disability in which disabilities are spoken of in terms of their cost to industry or society. In one instructional video I found on what to do with animals born with disabilities such as congenital blindness, "hermaphroditism," or arthrogryposis (my own disability), there is no mincing of words: the advice is to "destroy" them before they contaminate your gene pool and damage your profits.

Profit has also been a leading reason given for why farmers shouldn't abuse their farmed animals. No one wants to eat damaged or bruised meat, as evidenced by the fact that egg-laying hens are used largely in dog food or canned products and dairy cows for cheap hamburger meat, where their unsightly flesh won't be visible. In a bizarre undated pamphlet by Swift & Co.,[30] this is made abundantly clear. The pamphlet, likely from the 1940s or 1950s, is really better described as a comic, and is filled with anthropomorphized, Warner Brothers–inspired drawings of smiling animals getting beaten by slaughterhouse employees—slapped, thrown,

Figure 1: The back cover of an undated pamphlet by Swift & Co., a meat processing plant, likely from the 1940s or 1950s. Its purpose was to warn employees to not use excessive force when handling the animals, because "crippling" and "bruising" cost the industry money. The pamphlet is filled with anthropomorphized, Warner Brothers–inspired drawings of animals getting beaten by slaughterhouse employees. Image Courtesy: Ethan Persoff, http://www.ep.tc.

prodded, and whipped. The first page reads, "Directly or indi-
rectly, every pound of meat lost because of bruises and crippling
costs you money."[31] The most fascinating page is the back cover
(figure 1). A cartoon pig stands on two legs with a pair of crutches
and his head wrapped up as if he has a head wound. Next to him
stands a cow with a sling around her front leg (which resembles an
arm, as she is also standing on two legs). With her uninjured hoof
the cow pushes an old-fashioned wheelchair in which sits a young
lamb. All three of them stare out at the viewer. No longer smiling, they look distraught and exhausted—but it's hard to imagine
it's over the loss of profits.

Nowhere is farmers' focus on profit more clear than in the extensive debate over what to do with "downed animals." Downed (or
"nonambulatory") animals are animals who are unable to walk,
occasionally due to a serious illness but more often as a result of
exhaustion, dehydration, weak and fragile bones, broken bones,
complications after giving birth, or simply falling. Because there
is a chance downed animals may be seriously ill, posing a risk to
humans who consume them, controversy has emerged in recent
years over the question of whether or not these animals can be
sent to slaughter.

It is in the immediate financial interest of the meat industry to
slaughter all animals they raise for food, so extreme and violent
measures are often taken to get downed animals to stand up. Horrific videos by various animal advocacy groups including HSUS[32]
and Mercy for Animals[33] have shown animals being dragged
by a single limb or kicked and beaten in an attempt to make
them stand and walk to slaughter. When an animal can't or won't
walk, abusive measures are taken to discard of them. For example, another video shows "crippled" pigs being hung to death by
chains. Other animals are picked up alive by human beings or by
equipment such as bulldozers and thrown in dumpsters, where
they are left to die in "dead piles." Often all these animals would
need to recover is patience and water. *Vegan Outreach* reports that
"the number of downer cattle on U.S. farms or feedlots or sent to
slaughter facilities is difficult to ascertain, but estimates approach
500,000 animals per year."[34] Most of these are dairy cows, many
of whom have just given birth.

Although the media does often mention the cruelty inflicted on these animals, it is the potential health risks posed to human beings that has driven interest in this issue. In 2009 President Barack Obama banned the slaughter of downed cattle in a large part because there is evidence that downed cows are more likely to carry mad cow disease.[35] Rather than be slaughtered, sick and disabled downed cattle are now supposed to be "humanely" euthanized, with euthanasia defined as a "single blow of a penetrating captive bolt or gunshot" or a "chemical means that immediately renders the animal unconscious with complete unconsciousness remaining until death."[36] But the Animal Welfare Institute reports that there are loopholes to these requirements: "Young calves 'unable to rise from a recumbent position and walk because they are tired or cold' may be held for slaughter. Because slaughter of these animals is permitted, slaughter plants have an incentive to attempt to get downed calves to rise, sometimes employing inhumane methods like kicking and the use of electrical prods." Currently there are no regulations for the treatment of nonambulatory pigs and sheep, or any animals during transport or at market. The institute notes that the federal ban on the slaughter of nonambulatory adult cattle "was enacted for reasons of food safety, not animal welfare."[37]

The public expresses some pity for these animals, but only at a distance and only if it is clear they will not mix with "normal" and "healthy" cows (who are actually neither healthy nor normal, thanks to the ways the animals are bred and the unhealthy environment wrought by factory farms). In the end they must be euthanized, a mercy killing that, like the shooting of the fox with arthrogryposis, allows human beings to continue to kill animals as we would anyway, upholding beliefs in human superiority over other species while also fulfilling two of the most prominent ableist responses to disability: pitying it and attempting to destroy it.

Disabled and ill animals bring up historical associations of disability with the fear of contamination. The downed, sick— or even potentially sick—animal becomes the symbol of what is unhealthy, dirty, and dangerous about industrialized animal farming. Ableism operates in such cases to create psychological and emotional distance from disability through inciting fear of contagion. Separating out downed animals, like the mass killings of animals exposed to a contagious illness, creates the idea that safety, health, and even compassion are a priority on factory farms, despite the obvious reality that the industry itself is clearly the creator and perpetuator of these problems. Disabled, ill, and otherwise nonambulatory animals are hardly the reason that industrial animal agriculture is dangerous and harmful. Countless investigative reports and studies have exposed just how cruel, toxic, and terrible these industries are, not just for animals, but for the environment, workers, and human health overall. This is not to say that the viruses born of factory farms are not a serious public health concern—they are—but rather that the slaughter of millions of animals is not the solution—the solution is to shut down these concentrated animal operations.

It seems impossible to consider the disability that farmed animals experience as separate from their environments. The mother pig is made utterly immobile not by physical difference or disease but by the metal bars of her gestation crate. The hen suffers from pain, but whether that pain is due to a broken leg, overcrowding, complete darkness, or the death of her cagemate is impossible to know. The dairy cow is euthanized not because she cannot walk but because she has become a symbol of contamination. Such animals' environments clearly disable them even more than their physical and psychological disabilities do—a fact that supports the social model of disability.

Trying to pinpoint disability and disease in these environments is no less challenging than trying to ascertain what does and does not qualify as disability among human beings. What does it mean to speak of a "healthy" or "normal" chicken, pig, or cow when they all live in environments that are profoundly disabling? Indeed, when they are all bred to be disabled? The Belgian Blue is a breed of beef cattle bred for "double muscling" for more and leaner meat. They are so huge that they have a hard time walking, and the females must have caesarians, as vaginal births are impossible.[38] Even so-called heritage breeds are often bred for characteristics that in human beings would no doubt be labeled disabilities or abnormalities; consider the Tennessee fainting goat, which "keels over when startled" and which Slow Food USA says "sounds more like a sideshow act than the centerpiece of a barbecue."[39] The issue of breeding itself raises all sorts of complex questions about normalcy, naturalness, and the boundaries between disability and enhancement. These animals are simultaneously disabled and hyperabled—made disabled by the very enhancements that make them especially profitable to industries and desirable to consumers.

Disabling animals is not incidental to animal industries. It is essential for the work they do and the profit they create. Of the tens of billions of animals that are killed every year for human use, many are manufactured to be disabled, bred to be machine-like producers of meat, milk, and eggs. And we haven't even looked at other animal industries. According to HSUS, the animals who are subjected to lives in fur farms (foxes, minks, chinchillas, and numerous other species) "are inbred for specific colors . . . causing severe abnormalities—deafness, crippling of limbs, deformed sex organs, screw necks, anemia, sterility, and nervous system disorders."[40] Animals in research labs, circuses, and zoos also experience a variety of conditions and problems that are due largely to captivity, poor care, abuse, or breeding. Circus elephants are prone to severe arthritis because they are forced to stand, often chained, in cramped cages and boxcars with little opportunity to exercise. People for the Ethical Treatment of Animals (PETA) reports that "foot disorders and arthritis are the leading reasons for euthanasia in captive elephants."[41]

Huge numbers of animals from factory farms and zoos to research labs and circuses show signs of mental illness, post-traumatic stress disorder, depression, and madness, such as repetitive hair plucking, self-mutilation, biting the bars of their cages, pacing, regurgitation and reingestion (repeatedly vomiting and eating it), and repetitive head bobbing. Autistic writer and primatologist Dawn Prince-Hughes describes seeing her own symptoms of exclusion and marginalization in the animals she watched and studied at the zoo: "I would see this kind of behavior with gorillas in captivity. They had nervous tics similar, if not identical, to mine: hair plucking, picking at scabs, scratching, rocking, chewing on themselves, and other repetitive and self-stimulating behaviors. One gorilla spun in tight, fast circles. Another bobbed her head up and down."[42] Such behavior is so common in captive animals that there is actually a diagnosis for it, zoochosis—psychosis caused by confinement.[43] In fact animals in zoos are regularly put on antidepressants and other pharmaceuticals. In her book *Animal Madness: How Anxious Dogs, Compulsive Parrots, and Elephants in Recovery Help Us Understand Ourselves,* science historian Laurel Braitman exposes the widespread use of pharmaceuticals to help animals cope with captivity in zoos, aquariums, and research labs. Not surprisingly, zoos try to keep this information secret, with zookeepers often required to sign nondisclosure agreements. After all, as Braitman writes, "finding out that the gorillas, badgers, giraffes, belugas, or wallabies on the other side of the glass are taking Valium, Prozac, or antipsychotics to deal with their lives as display animals is not exactly heartwarming news."[44] What we do know is that the animal pharmaceutical industry in the United States is booming (it brought in nearly $6 billion in 2010).[45]

All of this raises profound ethical concerns about the ways nonhuman animals are treated—or, more aptly, mistreated—by human beings. It is hard even to begin to consider what disability means in these instances because of how inseparable it is from captivity, abuse, neglect, breeding, and, yes, suffering. What does disability mean for a hen in an environment where her every movement and desire is neglected? What does a physical limitation or difference mean when you are given no opportunity to move in your body, to explore it, because your environment is already limiting everything about you? Perhaps, as with many disabled human beings, these animals' physical or mental impairments are the least of their worries.

Unlike with Mozu or the fox with arthrogryposis, there is no disability empowerment projected here, not in these environments. Because as soon as I imagine these animals embodying their disabilities in ways other than suffering or imagine them fostering new ways of interacting or perceiving, I have imagined them out of the factory farm or research lab. This shows the extent to which the suffering and marginalization of disability is social, built, and structural.

But what happens to these animals when by some stroke of luck they escape or are removed from these environments? I asked Jenny Brown this question. Brown is founder of the Woodstock Farm Animal Sanctuary, author of *The Lucky Ones: My Passionate Fight for Farm Animals*, and a disabled person herself. The Woodstock Farm Animal Sanctuary is home to dozens of chickens, cows, pigs, turkeys, ducks, sheep, and goats who have been rescued from neglect, abuse, and abandonment. Like many other rescue homes for farm animals, the sanctuary cares for a variety of animals who limp, scoot, are blind, or are missing limbs, as well as those who need assistive technologies, including the occasional prosthesis. These disabled and often traumatized animals are rescued from large-scale farming operations as well as from small, family-run farms.

Brown explained that the answer to my question really depends on the extent and variety of the disability. Some disabled farmed animals adapt to their differences on their own or are supported by other nonhuman animals with whom they have bonded. Others are "put down," raising difficult questions about the ethics of animal euthanasia. Brown told me about Emmet and Jasper, two male baby goats who came from a goat dairy operation. They both were diagnosed with caprine arthritis encephalitis, which causes painful arthritic joints that can be debilitating. Jasper was eventually euthanized. Brown wrote me, "After pain meds and rounds of acupuncture we finally let him go because of the severity of his pain and physical debilitation." Jasper's brother Emmet has arthritis in one stifle and barely uses that leg, but he's doing well. Emmet has free rein around the sanctuary, because "when we did put these boys in with the goat herd, they would get rammed and taunted by the other, more dominant goats."[46]

Jasper's and Emmet's stories raise questions about accommodation and access. What are our responsibilities to accommodate and support these animals who we have made disabled? What does accommodation and access, or working to dismantle ableism, even mean for different species?

Brown also told me about Boon, a turkey at the Woodstock Farm Animal Sanctuary who was born with his tongue in his throat instead of in his mouth. Boon has difficulty eating, so the sanctuary staff feed him a few times a day, away from the other birds. There are many examples, such as this, of animals who need simple accommodations to survive. Perhaps they need to eat their meals away from the group or be put in a living space with less dominant animals (even of another species), or perhaps they need to be fitted for some sort of mobility device.

As shows like "My Bionic Pet" attest, animal prostheses are becoming increasingly common. Prostheses have been made for elephants, dogs, cats, dolphins, cows, goats, turtles, alligators, and a variety of birds. At the Woodstock Farm Animal Sanctuary there is Albie, a goat with three legs who can be seen running about every day in the sanctuary's fields, sometimes with a prosthetic leg and sometimes without.[47] Brown, an amputee herself, asked her own prostheticist if he would be willing to make a special prosthesis for the goat, and he obliged. The unique and innovative accommodations that are realized for these animals are all the more intriguing because of how similar they are to various common accommodations made for humans (prostheses, ramps, wheelchairs, and so forth). Yet in an anthropocentric world, accommodating farmed animals takes on a whole other meaning. The Woodstock Farm Animal Sanctuary is in many ways an accommodation in and of itself, as the vast majority of farmed animals don't have access to environments in which they can go about their lives in species-typical ways, let alone thrive—regardless of disability. Instead they are forced into environments that limit and harm them. In this way we return to environment, to the ways in which these animals are debilitated by human domination and exploitation.

The disabilities created in these animal industries, disabilities born of speciesism (the belief in human superiority over other animals) and cruelty, have complicated my understanding of disability. I am left with questions about suffering, a topic that many people invested in a political understanding of disability have rightfully tried to move away from. Disability activists and scholars have worked for decades to challenge the equation of disability with suffering. Many of us have argued that much of the suffering around disability stems from ableism, such as the discrimination and marginalization that disabled people face.

While disability advocates have pushed away from narratives of suffering, it is everywhere within animal ethics scholarship. Animal activists have done a huge amount of work simply to prove that animals *can* suffer, and much more work has sought to explain why human beings should care about this fact. Suffering has become an inevitable part of conversations around animal industries, as well as around disability within these industries, and for good reason. But animals are too often presented simply as voiceless beings who suffer. Exploring their lives through a critical disability analysis can help us to ask who these animals are beyond their suffering. It prompts us to consider how the very vulnerability and difference that these animals inhabit may in fact model new ways of knowing and being. Thinking through these issues also pushes disability scholars and activists to address the uncomfortable question of suffering, opening up avenues of investigation that have too often been neglected by the field.

The title of this chapter is "Animal Crips." To call an animal a crip is no doubt a human projection, but it is also a way of identifying nonhuman animals as subjects who have been oppressed by ableism. Naming animals as crips is a way of challenging us to question our ideas about how bodies move, think, and feel and what makes a body valuable, exploitable, useful, or disposable. It means questioning our assumptions about what a cow or a chicken is capable of experiencing. And it means stopping to consider that the limping fox you see through the barrel of your rifle may actually be enjoying his animal crip life. Animal crips challenge us to consider what is valuable about living and what is valuable about the variety of life.

In the end, it is not only disabled animals who could be called crips. All animals—both those we human beings would call disabled and those we would not—are devalued and abused for many of the same basic reasons disabled people are. They are understood as incapable, as lacking in the various abilities and capacities that have long been held to make human lives uniquely valuable and meaningful. They are, in other words, oppressed by ableism. The able body that ableism perpetuates and privileges is always not only able-bodied but human.

# Part Two

---

## Cripping Animal Ethics

# 4

## The Chimp Who Spoke

BOOEE WAS ONE OF THE BEST-NATURED CHIMPANZEES primatologist Roger Fouts had ever known. He was adored by his caretakers. He was gentle, easygoing, and loved raisins. Booee could learn a new word in American Sign Language (ASL) in an average of fifty-four minutes.[1]

Booee was born at the National Institutes of Health (NIH) in 1967. His mother was a research chimp, and the scientists had not realized she was pregnant, which meant that Booee wasn't targeted for a specific biomedical experiment. When he was a few days old he convulsed, which turned out to be all the reason the scientists at NIH needed to use Booee for split-brain surgery, a new experimental treatment for grand mal seizures.[2]

Roger Fouts tells Booee's story in his book *Next of Kin: My Conversations with Chimpanzees*. Fouts writes, "Doctors opened Booee's skull and severed his corpus callosum, cutting all the connections between his two cerebral hemispheres. Booee was left, in effect, with two separate brains." The recovery was complicated, and Booee had to undergo a second surgery to relieve the pressure on his swelling brain. An NIH doctor, seeing the infant's state and the pain he was in, felt sorry for him and took him home to care for him. As Fouts writes, Booee "fell through the cracks" and NIH never noticed he was gone.[3]

Booee quickly grew too large to live in the doctor's home and in 1970 was sent to Oklahoma to the Institute for Primate Studies, which was run by Dr. William Lemmon, a psychologist notorious in the primatology world for his maltreatment of the animals in his care. It was there that Roger Fouts met Booee and taught him ASL. Fouts had been working with a chimpanzee named Washoe, teaching her ASL and studying her language capabilities, which were nothing short of groundbreaking. He writes, "Many linguists who acknowledged that Washoe was using American Sign Language at the level of a two or three year old claimed she was a kind of 'mutant genius.'"[4] He set out to prove them wrong by teaching ASL to the other young chimps at the institute as well.

Booee had a nickname for Roger. To sign Roger's name, the chimps would tug their earlobes. After a while Booee began simply flicking his fingers off his ear, as if he had shortened Rodger's name to Rodg.[5] Fouts also had a nickname for Booee in ASL: Booee Split Brain. Although Booee seemed to have few noticeable side effects from his brain surgery, Fouts noticed that when pointing Booee would always point in two different directions at once, and when he painted he would always work in two opposite corners of the page. Whatever the effect of the surgery, it did not seem to have interfered with his communication skills: Booee became one of Fouts's most attentive students. In the few short years that Fouts worked with him, Booee managed to learn more than fifty words, with which he would form sentences, ask questions, and comment on the world around him.[6]

The institute was a dangerous place for the animals who lived there, and over time Fouts began to see himself as a sort of "kind jailor" conducting research in a prison. Eventually, to ease his conscience and save Washoe from an unpredictable future, Fouts found a way to leave with her, but not without deep regret that he would have to leave behind Booee and the many other chimps he had taught and loved. There was nothing he could do to save Booee and the others, who were legally Lemmon's property.[7]

In 1982 Lemmon sold Booee and more than two dozen other chimps to the Laboratory for Experimental Medicine and Surgery in Primates (LEMSIP), a New York University–funded research facility. Many of the chimps knew ASL, and two of them, Ally and Nim, were already famous for their language acquisition. Fouts describes how the chimps were said to have continued signing in the lab, asking the unsuspecting scientists for treats and cigarettes and to be let out of their solitary cages.[8] According to *Project Nim*, a 2011 documentary detailing the history of one of the most famous of the signing chimps, Nim Chimpsky, the scientists began pasting signs with basic ASL around the lab to help them learn to communicate with their new research specimens.[9]

Ally and Nim's fame helped spur enough public outrage to have them sent back to Lemmon. Nim was spared from research and sent to live at an animal rescue ranch in Texas. But after the LEMSIP controversy died down, Ally was quietly sold to an even worse research laboratory, White Sands Research Center in New Mexico, which tested cosmetics, drugs, and insecticides on animals. Ally died there many years later, most likely from insecticide poisoning.[10]

The public outcry showed a deep confusion over the ethical implications of animal research. As Fouts writes, "The researchers at LEMSIP didn't care that their newest research subjects could sign GO OUT, SMOKE, and HUG. All they wanted was the chimps' blood. On the other hand, the people protesting the chimps' harsh treatment seemed to care *only* that the chimps could sign, as if that made them somehow more worthy of compassion."[11] In a way the outcry over Nim and Ally at LEMSIP was not about the chimps themselves but about the imprisonment of beings who possessed highly valued "human" traits. People rallied to get these prized human abilities such as language and rationality out from behind bars. Ally and Nim simply went along with them.

Even though Booee knew and used many signs, his abilities were not widely known, and he was not released. When public outcry gave way to celebration after the release of the two famous chimps, Booee's chances of being freed evaporated. He was used for hepatitis C research and was deliberately infected with the virus. Booee spent the next thirteen years living in his cage at LEMSIP.[12]

Aristotle argued more than two thousand years ago that language separated humans from animals. This belief helped lay the groundwork in Western traditions for language to be regarded

philosophically and scientifically both as a uniquely human characteristic and as central to what it means to be human. Aristotle
also held that hearing was necessary for speech, which in turn he
believed was central to thinking, allowing him to suggest that deaf
people lacked thought and intelligence—a legacy that at times has
marked deaf people as animal-like or less-than-human.[13]

It wouldn't be until the sixteenth century that such views
would start to break down, and it wasn't until 1760 that sign language would be taught at the first free school for the deaf.[14] Yet
even as deaf individuals were increasingly recognized as being
capable of language and thus rationality, sign language itself came
to be seen as primitive—an earlier stage in the development of a
more advanced and civilized mode of spoken communication. As
historian Douglas Baynton describes, with the rise of evolutionary theory in the nineteenth century, sign language came to be
viewed as less advanced, an example of primitive language used by
savages and other "inferior peoples." Gestural language was associated with "tribes low in the scale of development," "Indians" in
the Americas, Africans, and other racialized groups, all viewed as
evolutionary throwbacks.[15]

Because it was seen as primitive, even barbaric, manualism (e.g.,
teaching of, and with, sign language), increasingly came under
pressure. Although sign languages had been taught for more than
one hundred years at schools for the deaf in both the United States
and Europe, by the 1880s "oralism" had replaced sign language
in education. Many people claimed that teaching sign language
was actually damaging to deaf students because it kept them from
learning to speak orally, which again was seen as the superior,
more civilized form of language. In much of the latter half of the
nineteenth and first half of the twentieth centuries, individuals
were discouraged from signing and forced to learn to communicate through sound.[16] At many schools for the deaf, children were
made to wear mittens or keep their hands folded on their desks
to keep from signing, and they were considered "oral failures" if
they were unable to learn to communicate through speech.[17]

The supposed lack of sophistication of sign language, which was
used to justify oralism at the turn of the century, is an example
of the ways categories of race, disability, and animality have been

entangled in and co-constitutive of one another. Sign language's gestures and expressions were racialized, associated with people of color who were themselves seen as primitive, rudimentary, and animal. Sign was frequently described with animal metaphors, particularly those referencing monkeys and apes. Its gestures and facial expressions were "monkey-like," and those who used it were accused of making apish gestures and monkey-like grimaces.[18] Deaf people who could not sign or speak were also animalized, seen as lacking language and thus as living in a state of brutishness or mere animal existence. Others argued that gestural language could no more be called a language than expressive animal movements like the wag of a dog's tail.[19]

Some early animal advocates were also persuaded by a supposed relationship between the ways in which animals communicate and the gestures of sign—of course, for very different reasons. Realizing that society was not likely to acknowledge the rights of those who were unable to use language and who were also unable to participate in their own movement for liberation, animal advocates in the late nineteenth century began looking to disability as a parallel struggle to that of animal advocacy. Historian Diane Beers writes, "Increasingly in the United States, the mentally ill and physically handicapped received some ethical and legal consideration despite their inability at times to speak on their own behalf. Activists insisted that animals simply communicated through different means, not unlike those of the handicapped humans."[20] At times advocates resorted to comparing the communication capacities of disabled people to those of animals. Beers quotes one advocate, Henry Childs Merwin, who wrote that "animals translated the 'logic of feelings into the logic of signs; and so far as this particular action is concerned, it is psychologically indistinguishable from that which is performed by the deaf mute.'"[21]

Where gesture was discouraged in human beings, it would eventually be recognized to be a "special faculty" that nonhuman apes used to express themselves.[22] Although research into the sign language capabilities of nonhuman apes wouldn't really take off until the 1970s, the gestural potential of such animals was recognized long beforehand. Given the history of the animalization of deafness and of sign language—and the way that the figure of the monkey or ape has been a powerful container for the merger of racist, ableist, and anthropocentric ideologies—it is little wonder that when researchers began teaching nonhuman primates sign language in the 1970s (only a few years after American Sign Language was recognized by linguists as a complex natural language on par with spoken languages[23]), some individuals found the fact troubling. As one ASL speaker told me, "To some people these studies seemed to say that where spoken language is too complex for other animals to learn, sign language is so simple that even a monkey can learn it." Although the goal of such research was not to show that nonhuman primates were like human signers or even that an ape could communicate in sign language fluently, for some the legacy of comparisons between deaf people and animals and the discrimination it perpetuated existed in tension with the scientific discoveries about animal minds brought about by teaching primates to sign. As visual culture scholar Nicholas Mirzoeff pointed out in a piece on primate scientist Penny Patterson's research teaching Koko the gorilla ASL in the 1970s, such experiments raised compelling questions, but "they may also help to reinforce the idea that it is a primitive language."[24]

With these tensions in mind, perhaps we can begin to reframe the comparison of animal and disability issues, acknowledging the violence caused by such histories of dehumanization, while also taking seriously the need to challenge the role the animal has been forced to play within dehumanizing systems and rhetoric. Animals and disabled people have been compared and conflated in various cultural and historical contexts. As is evident in the quote from Henry Childs Merwin, some advocates for animals have also conflated the abilities and inabilities of animals and disabled humans, which has the problematic effect of flattening out vastly different populations and perpetuating the dehumanization of already oppressed human groups. In contrast to this framing, I am suggesting not that nonhuman animals and disabled humans are uniquely similar, but rather that we must begin to examine the systems that degrade and devalue both animals and disabled people—systems which are built upon, among other things, able-ist paradigms of language and cognitive capacity.

In early research into the linguistic abilities of chimps, research-ers spent years trying to teach them to use spoken language. As great apes lack the necessary anatomical structures for vocaliza-tion, the studies were largely unsuccessful, with the chimps only managing a few basic words such as "mama," "papa," "cup," and "up." These studies were considered failures, and many people thought the question of chimp language was closed.[25] The ableist assumption was that if a chimpanzee were able to use language, it would be in the same way that nondisabled hearing humans do: through sound.

As obvious as it seems now to teach a non-oral language to a gestural species or to people who are unable or less able to use spoken language, the need to match physical, intellectual, cultur-al, and species-specific needs with a form of communication that fits those needs continues to be overlooked. Dolphins have been taught sign language for decades, despite the obvious fact that dolphins don't have hands. Louie Psihoyos points out in the har-rowing documentary *The Cove* that this sort of communication is profoundly one-sided: the dolphins can comprehend human demands but are unable to sign back.[26]

Scientists eventually realized their mistake in trying to teach apes to speak orally, but learning that apes could sign hardly settled the question of whether they were actually using human language. The sign language studies of the 1970s led to heated debates about animal minds and abilities, many of which are still being explored by linguists and primatologists today.

Some linguists argue that although these apes have shown that they are capable of complex communication, their signing should not be considered language because, according to many, they have not been able to grasp grammar.[27] Others claim that chimpanzees like Booee and Washoe are simply being trained to perform scripted responses, like circus animals performing tricks.

Researchers who do believe that apes are using language when they sign accuse the naysayers of a double standard, given that the capabilities chimps demonstrate are often very similar to those seen in young children, where they are clearly recognized as burgeoning linguistic ability. Many primates display creativity in their use of words, even making up new ones, and they commonly initiate conversations with human beings or other apes. There have also been numerous examples of animals learning sign language from one another rather than from a human teacher.

The question of whether primates, or other animals, have their own languages is not the focus of these particular debates. Increasingly, however, such questions are being asked and the incredible communication capacities of a wide variety of animals from prairie dogs to dolphins are being exposed. Yet these communication systems are not acknowledged as "true" language by most scientists—an unsurprising fact. As UC Berkeley gender and women's studies professor and linguistics scholar Mel Y. Chen explains, "Linguistic criteria are established prominently and immutably in humans' terms, establishing human preeminence before the debates about linguistic placement of humans' animal subordinates even begin."[28] The view that language is uniquely human is of course to our advantage.

Whether or not the communication of Nim, Washoe, Ally, Booee, and the myriad of other animals who have complex communication systems can be defined specifically as "true" human-like language ultimately isn't the most important or interesting question. What we need to be asking is why an animal's language or communication abilities alter the way we feel he should be treated. Why should a chimp who knows no ASL signs be sentenced to a life of solitary confinement and experimentation while the signing chimpanzee sparks public outcry calling for his freedom?

Booee was no doubt an emotional creature before he learned his first sign. What was special about Booee's ASL acquisition was not that his use of words suddenly made him an intelligent being with feelings but rather that it confronted us, as human beings, with the fact of his intelligence, his emotional life.

We must ask why language has accrued such power. Chen writes that "language is arguably a major criterion (or even the defining attribute), that separates humans from animals, even among theorists who decry the fact of the segregation."[29] We look down on the ways nonhuman animals communicate—not only assuming a clear hierarchical divide between the way human beings share information and the myriad ways other animals do, but also assuming that this divide is morally consequential.

# 5

## Ableism and Animals

WE NEED TO CRIP ANIMAL ETHICS, incorporating a disability politics into the way we think about animals. It is essential that we examine the shared systems and ideologies that oppress both disabled humans and nonhuman animals, because ableism perpetuates animal oppression in more areas than the linguistic. Indeed, ableism is intimately entangled with speciesism, and is deeply relevant to thinking through the ways nonhuman animals are judged, categorized, and exploited.

Disability studies and activism call for recognizing new ways of valuing life that aren't limited by specific physical or mental capabilities. Implicit in disability theory is the idea that it is not specifically our intelligence, rationality, agility, physical independence, or bipedal nature that give us dignity and value. Many of us in the field argue that life should be presumed to be worth living whether you are a person with Down syndrome, cerebral palsy, profound intellectual disabilities, quadriplegia, autism, or, like me, arthrogryposis.

This is not just some trite declaration of pride or a romantic assertion of the sanctity of human life; rather, we recognize that much of what disabled people can offer society has been undervalued or considered detrimental by a culture invested in certain bodies and certain ways of doing things.

Justifications for human domination over animals almost always rely on comparing human and animal abilities and traits.

We humans are the species with language, with rationality, with complex emotions, with two legs and opposable thumbs. Animals lack these traits and abilities and therefore exist outside of our moral responsibility, which means we can dominate and use them. But isn't it ableist to devalue animals because of what abilities they do or do not have?

Such arguments depend upon assumptions of abled human embodiment as well as neurotypical human intelligence. The term "neurotypical," which emerged from autistic and neurodiversity communities, refers to individuals or traits that are viewed as cognitively normative and species typical. As autistic scholar and animal advocate Daniel Salomon writes, "Neurotypicalism privileges a form of cognitive processing characteristic of peoples who have a neurotypical (non-autistic) brain structure, while at least implicitly finding other forms of cognitive processing to be inferior, such as those natural to autists and nonhuman animals."[1]

Neurotypicalism is a form of ableism, and a recognition of the concept can help us understand the troublingly biased ways we judge animals. The fact that one of the most ubiquitous arguments people use in support of our continued exploitation of nonhumans is that animals are incapable of a myriad of cognitive processes that human beings engage in shows the extent to which speciesism uses ableist logics to function. Presumed to be deficient in human markers of intelligence, animals are understood, to put it bluntly, as stupid. Their lack of various capabilities is often cited as proof of our superiority as human beings and as justification for our continued use of them for our own benefit. As disability studies scholar Harold Braswell explains, "The very same notion of the able individual that marginalizes persons with disabilities also does so to animals."[2] From the belief that man was created in God's image to the belief that human beings are the peak of evolution, our anthropocentric worldview is supported by ableism.

Ableism allows us to view human abilities as unquestionably superior to animal abilities; it propels our assumptions that our own human movements, thought processes, and ways of being are always not only more sophisticated than animals' but in fact give us value. Animals, in their inferior bestial state, can be used by us without moral concern, and those humans who have been associated with animals (people of color, women, queer people, poor people, and disabled people, among others) are also seen as less sophisticated, as having less value, and sometimes even as being less or non-human. In fact, certain abilities and capacities are central to definitions of the human; they are thought to mark the boundaries between humanity and the rest of the animal world. In this way ableism gives shape to what and who we think of as human versus animal.

Ableism also fosters values and institutions that perpetuate animal suffering. The various animal industries that exist in this country (from factory farms to animal research) rely on the public belief that using animals is okay because they lack the capacities that would make their use wrong. These industries also rely on ideologies of nature to justify what they do (perpetuating the idea that it is simply natural to use animals for our benefit, for instance). But even ideas of nature and naturalness are bound up with ableism, because constructions of nature often conflate such things as health, normalcy, and independence with evolutionary fitness or ecological compatibility. Ableist values are central to animal industries, where the dependency, vulnerability, and presumed lack of emotional awareness or intellectual capacity of animals creates the groundwork for a system that makes billions of dollars in profit off of animal lives. The very norms and institutions that perpetuate animal suffering and exploitation are supported by ableism.

None of this is to say that ableism affects animals and disabled people in the same ways. For instance, despite being bound up in systems of scientific discovery and classification in ways that overlap with discourses of medicalization, animals are not pathologized as needing medical interventions to cure them of their animality (at least not in our time and context). And disabled humans are obviously not processed into meat or objects (although they are often objectified). Animals and disabled humans experience marginalization and domination in extremely different ways. My point is that ableism helps construct the systems that render the lives and experiences of both nonhuman animals and disabled humans as less valuable and as discardable, which leads to a variety of oppressions that manifest differently.

In challenging ableism, disability scholars and activists aspire to recognize sameness while valuing differences. Disabled individuals have fought for our equality, our sameness, while also arguing that there is value in our differences and in our limitations. Disability activists do not argue that disabled individuals are valuable *despite* our disabilities; rather, value lies in the very variation of embodiment, cognition, and experience that disability encompasses. Disability may include elements of lack and inability, but it also fosters other ways of knowing, being, and experiencing. This valuing of otherness, of other ways of doing and being, is one of the things that makes disability culture profoundly important to conversations around animal justice—because animals are far more similar to us than we have wanted to think while also being extremely different. Ethologist Marc Bekoff writes, "Variations among species should be embraced and cherished rather than used to justify human dominance," a strikingly similar philosophy to that of politicized disability communities.[3]

Along with unpacking how ableism contributes to speciesism, cripping animal ethics also involves examining the ways in which ableism permeates animal rights communities. For example, disability is regularly used as a fear-mongering trope in vegan campaigns that focus on human health—one of the worst being the PETA "Got Autism" campaign, which plays off of the milk industry's "Got Milk" advertisements to suggest an unsubstantiated link between autism and drinking milk.[4] Such a campaign exploits people's fears and misinformation about autism to boost a vegan agenda. PETA is notorious for such offensive campaigns—which are widely critiqued within animal rights circles—but they are not alone in using such tactics. Case in point is the bestselling book *Skinny Bitch* by Rory Freedman and Kim Barnouin, which attempts to body shame people into becoming vegan by suggesting that eating animals leads people to be fat, diseased, lazy, unhealthy, and unattractive.[5] Author and food scholar A. Breeze Harper, author of *Sistah Vegan: Black Female Vegans Speak on Food, Identity, Health and Society*, writes that mainstream popular vegan books relentlessly present white heteronormative and ableist representations of what being healthy and attractive entails and what ethical eaters should look like. As she writes, "The ethical food consumer in the USA today is expected to consume in a way that reduces their body fat and/or maintains a slim body aesthetic . . . which is implicit in the plethora of ethical consumption oriented popular titles."[6] Such a critique is not limited to vegans and vegetarians—those advocating meat eating employ similar tactics as well, as most diet and fitness books presume a white straight person without disability—but there is something especially offensive about these tactics when they come from a movement that claims to value compassion.

The ableism embedded in animal rights discourse is also evident in a common rallying cry used by animal advocates. To be a "voice for the voiceless" is a sentiment many activists within advocacy communities regularly identify with. However, as Booee's story makes clear, identifying who does and who does not have a voice is no simple matter.

It became common to use the biblical phrase "a voice for the voiceless" to refer to animals after the publication of a poem written in 1910 by American poet Ella Wheeler Wilcox. The phrase can be found in numerous contemporary animal advocacy texts and animal rights campaigns.

*I am the Voice of the Voiceless*
*Through me the dumb shall speak*
*Till the world's deaf ear be made to hear*
*The wrongs of the wordless weak.*

*Oh shame on the mothers of mortals*
*Who do not stoop to teach*
*The sorrow that lies in dear dumb eyes*
*The sorrow that has no speech.*

*From street, from cage, from kennel*
*From stable and from zoo*
*The wall of my tortured kin proclaims the sin*
*Of the mighty against the frail.*

*And I am my brother's keeper*
*And I shall fight their fight*
*And speak the word for beast and bird*
*Till the world shall set things right.*[7]

At the turn of the century this poem was radical in its acknowl-edgment of animal suffering. It is also intriguing as an example of the conflation of animality and disability, which has occurred in some animal advocacy movements. It is sprinkled with phrases that seem to turn animality into a form of disability—animals are dumb (voiceless), weak, and frail. The poem also suggests an unbridgeable divide between those who help and have voices and those who are helped and are voiceless.

The phrase a "voice for the voiceless"—giving voice to a popu-lation that is unable to defend or speak for themselves—inevitably conjures the sentiment in Wilcox's poem: that the voiceless are physically unable to speak or help themselves. It has been cri-tiqued in numerous contexts, including by Indian author and political activist Arundhati Roy, who poignantly writes, "There's really no such thing as the 'voiceless.' There are only the deliber-ately silenced, or the preferably unheard."[8]

Wilcox's phrase and the sentiment are still ubiquitous despite such critiques. Perhaps some advocates still use tropes of voiceless-ness because, as can be seen in charity models of disability, the idea of helping beings who cannot help themselves tends to be more attractive to many people than acknowledging that those who are dependent and vulnerable can also have agency and opinions. Today there are countless organizations and charities intended to help disabled people that don't include a single disabled represen-tative in a decision-making role, for example. The opportunity to express our opinions about our own needs and wants has been such a consistent struggle for disabled people that one of the most common rallying cries of disability rights movements is "Nothing about us without us."

Because of this history of exclusion and charity, some disabled activists are understandably not impressed with the patronizing tone of those animal advocates who wish to be a "voice for the voiceless." Disability activist Stephen Drake writes, "Animal rights advocacy is a cause that operates by defining and advocating for a set of principles which should govern human-animal interaction. It is not the animals themselves demanding this . . . advocates and activists can define the terms of rights advocacy for animals and never have to worry about the animals telling them they got it all wrong or that they want to speak for themselves now."[9]

Drake's is a common critique of animal advocacy, and author and journalist Michael Pollan suggests a similar point in his book *The Omnivore's Dilemma: A Natural History of Four Meals.*[10] How can activists know what animals want? To speak for animals simply reinforces patronizing and paternalistic paradigms. The problem with Drake's and Pollan's arguments is that those who use and exploit animals are making even more drastic choices for them—choices that lead to an animal's imprisonment and death. In virtually all environments where animals are used, they have no freedom and no ability to leave their cages or choose life over slaughter.

Drake and Pollan are also wrong to suggest that animals are not telling us what they want. Roy's phrase "the preferably unheard" is far more apt. Animals consistently voice preferences and ask for freedom. They speak to us every day when they cry out in pain or try to move away from our prods, electrodes, knives, and stun guns. Animals tell us constantly that they want out of their cages, that they want to be reunited with their families, or that they don't want to walk down the kill chute. Animals express themselves all the time, and many of us know it. If we didn't, factory farms and slaughterhouses would not be designed to constrain any choices an animal might have. We deliberately have to choose not to hear when the lobster bangs on the walls from inside a pot of boiling water or when the hen who is past her egg-laying prime struggles against the human hands that enclose her legs and neck. We have to choose not to recognize the preference expressed when the fish spasms and gasps for oxygen in her last few minutes alive. Considering animals voiceless betrays an ableist assumption of what counts as having a voice—an assumption that many disabled and nondisabled people alike often make about animals.

A surprising amount of evidence also points to the fact that animals can and do participate in their own liberation. In 2011 a

German dairy cow named Yvonne made it into the news when she escaped from her farm, sensing her impending slaughter. Yvonne was called a "kind of freedom fighter for the animal-loving German public" by *The Guardian*, because she "outsmarted" her captors for more than three months. She has been bought by an animal sanctuary after stealing many a German's heart. She will never be made into food.[11] She is just one of many domestic and wild animals who have escaped their fates at slaughterhouses, zoos, research labs, and circuses, often by incredible feats.

Historian Jason Hribal's book *Fear of the Animal Planet: The Hidden History of Animal Resistance* looks at dozens of different examples of animals escaping their confinement or attacking their abusive trainers, showing that these events cannot just be brushed aside as flukes, accidents, or examples of nature's unpredictability. Though it may surprise many, his book is extremely convincing. As journalist Jeffrey St. Clair writes in his introduction to the book, "Hribal's heroic profiles in animal courage show how most of these violent acts of resistance were motivated by their abusive treatment and the miserable conditions of their confinement."[12] By looking at the sheer number of calculated escapes and attacks on abusers, Hribal creates a historical record of animals resisting their mistreatment. Many of these escapes are extremely complex: monkeys and great apes scale impossibly high walls, build bridges and even catapults to bypass large bodies of water, ground electric fences to avoid shock, pick locks, and work together to pull off elaborate escape plans that deceive their human captors.

Consider the case of the orangutan Fu Manchu (a racist and orientalist name originating from a series of novels in the 1920s that deserves an essay in its own right).[13] In 1968, a year famous for human resistance, Fu Manchu made headlines for his own attempts at liberation. During that year he and his companions repeatedly escaped from Omaha's Henry Doorly Zoo, completely baffling the head zookeeper, Jerry Stone. Stone threatened to fire his assistants, blaming them for leaving the gate unlocked and allowing the apes to escape. In a *Time* article called "Can Animals Think," author Eugene Linden explained the escape: "First, the young ape climbed down some air-vent louvers into a dry moat. Then, taking hold of the bottom of the furnace door, he used brute force to pull it back just far enough to slide a wire into the gap, slip a latch and pop the door open."[14] But how did Fu Manchu figure out how to pick a lock with a piece of wire? And where did this wire come from, anyway? Stone finally discovered Fu Manchu's secret when he saw a glint of something shiny in his mouth. The ape had found a small piece of wire and had manipulated it to fit perfectly between his lower gum and lip. Fu Manchu would pick the zoo's lock with this little piece of wire and then keep it hidden in his mouth between escapes.[15]

Once free, animals will often do their best to travel as far away from their enclosures as possible or stay stealthily hidden, as Yvonne did. Some are captured within hours, while others live free for weeks or even months until they are spotted miles away crossing a highway or moving through someone's backyard.[16]

Monkeys and apes, with their agile fingers, toes, and limbs, may have an easier time escaping than other animals, although there are many incredible stories of cows and pigs escaping their fates at slaughterhouses even without hands. Many animals resort to attacking their captors, and Hribal repeatedly shows that animals from elephants to tigers to orcas will specifically target trainers and captors who have abused them. Janet, an elephant who had worked in the circus industry for many years, began to rampage one afternoon in 1992 while a group of children were riding on her back. Hribal writes that Janet could easily have killed them by throwing them off, but instead she "paused midway through the melee, let someone remove the children, and then continued her assault on circus employees."[17] Janet's rampage ended with her violently banging a bull hook repeatedly against a wall. A bull hook has a sharpened point at the end like a giant fishhook and is used to stab and hit elephants in an attempt to make them perform.

St. Clair writes, "Each trampling of a brutal handler with a bull-hook, each mauling of a taunting visitor, each drowning of a tormenting trainer is a crack in the old order that treats animals as property, as engines of profit, as mindless objects of exploitation and abuse." And, I would add, in the old order that sees animals as voiceless.[18] When animal advocates describe animals as voiceless, even when it is meant simply as a metaphor, it gives power to those who want to view animals as "mindless objects." In the long run, activists will help animals more if we treat them as active participants in their own liberation—as the expressive subjects animal advocates know them to be—remembering that resistance takes many forms, some of which may be hard to recognize from an able-bodied human perspective.

Yvonne, Janet, Fu Manchu, and the many others like them show that animals are in no way passive in their own struggles. Even the most beaten down and terrorized animals often resist their domination or at the very least express a preference for not being harmed. In 2009 a video went viral of a cow awaiting slaughter.[19] It was taken from inside a slaughterhouse, most likely by an employee, although no details about the camera person or the location are given.

In the video two cows stand in a row in front of a narrow tunnel with tall metal walls on either side. As the video progresses, you learn that the tunnel can only hold two or three cows and that behind them is a closed gate that most likely opens to let in a new set of animals. After about thirty seconds of watching the animals in the tunnel, a man enters the shot. The cows cower and try to move backward. The man approaches the first cow and uses an electric prod on the left of the cow's hindquarters to get her to move forward. As she does a solid metal gate lifts at the front of the tunnel and the cow moves through. We are left watching the remaining cow, who is now alone. The cow sniffs at the gate until something scares or surprises her, and she then walks fiercely backward to the very back of the gate. As time passes she grows increasingly panicked, ears back and body agitated, trying to no avail to find a way out and to turn around. The tunnel is so narrow that all she can do is twist her neck around, and as she does so she looks toward the viewer and we see her eyes and face as she seems to stare directly into the camera—a moment of meeting the gaze of another being who is suffering. Eventually the man enters again and the cow cowers. She is shocked with the electric prod twice on her rear. Having no other choice, she walks forward through the gate and it closes. The camera zooms in on the crack between the ground and the gate and we can make out the cows' hooves. We hear a loud noise and watch as the feet collapse and her body appears on the ground.

I cannot read this animal's actions as anything other than the expression of fear and a desire not to be in that situation. There is no doubt: if she could tell us what she wanted it would be to turn around and leave that tunnel. We are choosing not to hear her.

Ableism manifests itself within animal advocacy movements in a more egregious way as well. One of the most prevalent lines of argument in defense of animal rights is structured around ableist assumptions about cognitive capacity coupled with a rhetorical instrumentalization of disabled people. In 2010 autistic animal activist Daniel Salomon published an article in the *Journal for Critical Animal Studies* called "From Marginal Cases to Linked Oppressions," which drew attention to the problem. In it Salomon critiques animal rights discourse for its neurotypical bias, which not only perpetuates ableism within animal rights theory but also, he argues, actually reinforces speciesism. Although one would assume that theories of animal rights would oppose speciesism, one of the most prevalent animal rights arguments privileges rational thought, which invariably places humans in a hierarchy above nonhumans. As Salomon puts it, "The framing of animal ethics needs to be critiqued; a neurotypical bias remains implicit in the way animal ethics is typically framed, which keeps intact and perpetuates speciesism."[20]

The argument Salomon is critiquing is known in philosophy as the argument from marginal cases. The theory attempts to defend the rights of animals by comparing their mental capacities to those of certain humans. The comparison is problematic both for humans and for animals, flattening varied communities into stereotypes and saying nothing of their differences. It also implicitly ends up privileging capacities that philosophers have long held to be "morally relevant" (such as rationality)—capacities that in the Western tradition of moral philosophy and legal theory are central to deciding who is a "person," someone who has rights or is the subject of ethical duties and obligations.[21]

Although this line of argument has deep historic roots, it was made popular by philosopher Peter Singer in the 1970s and remains a common tactic used by those who are arguing for animal rights.[22] The argument suggests that there is no "morally relevant ability" that all animals *don't* have but all humans *do*. Not all animals have language for instance, but not all humans do either. At its most basic, this argument does not sound particularly problematic; it is a version of the argument I make throughout this book. It can even be understood as anti-ableist, because it emphasizes that there is no one specific ability shared by all humans that gives us value. Nonetheless, the danger of the argument is evident in the very act of deciding which abilities are morally relevant. Morally relevant abilities are those associated with the capacity to reason: self-awareness, language, the ability to imagine a future, and the ability to comprehend death. When the moral relevance of these abilities is taken for granted and left unchallenged, the argument upholds reason as the yardstick of value, implicitly assuming that it is possible to identify beings who are obviously morally valuable—rational human beings with morally relevant abilities. The distinction puts the moral relevance of groups who lack—or are assumed to lack—these specific privileged abilities into question.

Those who use the theory to defend animal rights argue that there will always be some humans (intellectually disabled individuals, infants, the comatose, and elderly people with dementia—the "marginal cases") who don't have certain morally relevant abilities. They say that if we agree that these humans have moral status even though they lack important capacities, then there is no reason why nonhuman animals who have similar capacities to these people should not be granted moral status as well. Although many people use this argument to show that both disabled individuals and animals have moral value and should be granted certain protections,[23] invariably intellectually disabled individuals, infants, the comatose, and elderly people with dementia become lumped together as a single group—the marginal cases—whose lack of abilities is compared to that of nonhuman animals, who are also often and troublingly flattened into a single group. The worth of these groups is then put up for debate. For animals, who are nearly always written out of the debate altogether, this move has some benefits (at least they are being considered), but for intellectually disabled people, it offers little except risk.

Some philosophers object that this is a misunderstanding of the argument: the theory is not saying these groups are like each other but only that members of both groups may lack similar specific morally relevant traits. But to examine only what these groups "lack" invariably erases difference from the conversation. Clearly, two randomly chosen intellectually disabled people are invariably going to be different from each other, as well as being different from a chimpanzee, an octopus, or a human infant. To say that all of them lack a specific trait, even a "morally relevant" one, actually tells us very little. It is for this reason that this argument is always accompanied by an "all things being equal" clause—it is necessarily hypothetical, because intellectually disabled individuals, infants, the comatose, and elderly people with dementia, and animals are obviously all different. Yet, in the very act of using this line of argumentation, these hypothetical groups inevitably become conflated with real populations.

As Salomon suggests, the argument has the truly unfortunate effect of pitting intellectually disabled individuals against animals, implying that if the animals go down, so should the intellectually disabled people. Whether the thinker then concludes that all of these groups are indeed morally relevant, as many theorists do, or that some members of these groups are less morally relevant than rational human beings, the damage has been done. The value of disabled people's lives has been put into question. For a group of people who have won basic rights and protections only within the past few decades, this is a truly offensive and frightening gamble.

Philosopher Licia Carlson, who writes passionately against what she calls the "philosophical exploitation" of intellectual disability in theories such as the argument from marginal cases, vitally asks, "Is it necessary . . . to use the case of intellectual disability in order to make the case against speciesism and to define the moral status of nonhuman animals? . . . Must we view animal interests as being in conflict with the interests of the 'severely intellectually disabled'?"[24] Like Salomon and Carlson, I am convinced that we need not do so. Arguments that compare animals to intellectually disabled people miss the more important point that a focus on specific human and neurotypical "morally relevant abilities" harms both populations. Those of us invested in advancing justice for all species should not be arguing that since we care for intellectually disabled people, we should care for animals. This line of thought is ableist and anthropocentric, as it centers the human as the yardstick of moral worth and implicitly devalues and flattens out intellectual disability. Instead we must argue against the very notion that beings with neurotypical human capacities are inherently more valuable than those without.

Many people point to animal advocates' use of such troubling lines of argumentation to expose the supposed dangers of animal rights. In *The Omnivore's Dilemma*, for example, Pollan refers to Singer's use of the argument from marginal cases to suggest that challenging speciesism may "bring us to an ethical cliff." He also uses it to question the moral judgment of animal rights philosophers.[25] Thankfully, many theories of animal ethics have presented us with alternative arguments for animal liberation that do not rely on, and are often critical of, frameworks that participate in the "philosophical exploitation" of intellectually disabled people, and that challenge the traditional privileging of rational thought. Unfortunately, these frameworks rarely get as much attention, leading the public to continue to associate animal ethics with scholars like Singer and these sorts of troubling arguments.

Feminist animal scholars, for example, have long challenged the ways in which the idea of reason has historically been used to reinforce hierarchical dualisms between man and woman, human and animal. As feminist scholar Cathryn Bailey explains in her essay "On the Backs of Animals: The Valorization of Reason in Animal Ethics," reason has long been "regarded as the very measure of one's level of humanity," whereas anything that emanated from the body, as feelings and emotions were supposed to do, was deemed inferior. Eurocentric conceptions of reason helped establish and support racist and gendered ideologies that rendered some bodies as more physical, more bodily, more of the flesh than white (and, I would add, heterosexual and able-bodied) men. Bailey writes, "It bears emphasizing that the rise of reason was not incidentally associated with the oppression of women and nonwhite men; rather, that oppression itself was part of what legitimized reason. Reason did not first come into existence and then look for a venue to exhibit itself, rather, what much of philosophy came to define as reason only came into being as result of denying and quashing those attributes regarded as feminine or bodily."[26]

Margaret Price and other disability studies scholars have similarly pointed to reason as an ongoing factor in disability oppression. Price writes in her book *Mad at School: Rhetorics of Mental Disability and Academic Life* that "Aristotle's famous declaration that man is a rational animal (1253a; 1098a) gave rise to centuries of insistence that to be named mad was to lose one's personhood."[27]

Price contrasts the so-called rational human with those people who are what she calls rhetorically disabled. Being disabled rhetorically means "that persons with [psychiatric, cognitive, or intellectual] disabilities are presumed not to be competent, nor understandable, nor valuable, nor whole. We are placed in institutions, medicated, lobotomized, shocked or simply left to survive without homes. The failure to make sense, as measured against and by those with normal minds, means a loss of personhood."[28]

Price's statement has heavy implications for nonhuman animals, whose lack of reason is seen by many as de facto justification for denying them personhood, the right not to be killed for someone else's benefit, or even simple compassion. Salomon, Bailey, and others who critique a theory of animal liberation that places so much emphasis on reason question how this privileging of rationality could not simultaneously reinforce animal oppression. Bailey writes that "it sometimes seems as if the contemporary philosophical approach to animal ethics serves as much to define and legitimize reason as to help animals, a kind of legitimacy that could only be wrought on the back of animals."[29]

As Bailey makes clear, the problem is not reason itself but rather the ways in which reason has been held up as separate from and more valuable than emotion, feeling, and other ways of knowing and being. This definition of reason stems from a history of patriarchy, imperialism, racism, classism, ableism, and anthropocentrism, and too often carries these oppressions within it. These issues are particularly important to keep in mind when theorizing liberation for those who do or may lack "reason," such as nonhuman animals and individuals with significant intellectual disabilities.

———

When neurotypical and able-bodied human capacities are used as the measure of a being's value, both nonhuman animals and disabled human beings lose out. The characteristics that humans have used to measure cognitive capacity are no doubt signs of a certain kind of complex cognition, but they are not necessarily the only ways to measure intelligence, let alone value or worth. What's more, the criteria are both anthropocentric, because they reward only recognizably human capacities, and ableist, often leading us to discount the abilities of those with disabilities.

In his book *Rethinking Life and Death: The Collapse of Our Traditional Ethics*, Peter Singer writes, "To have a child with Down syndrome is to have a very different experience from having a normal child. It can still be a warm and loving experience, but we must have lowered expectations of our child's ability. We cannot expect a child with Down syndrome to play the guitar, to develop an appreciation of science fiction, to learn a foreign language, to chat with us about the latest Woody Allen movie, or to be a respectable athlete, basketball or tennis player."[30] His assertion of the things "we cannot expect" from a child with Down syndrome follows a long tradition of experts in science, medicine, and philosophy declaring what can and cannot be expected of various populations. For people with disabilities, these lowered expectations have often meant, among other things, lifetimes of institutionalization and discrimination because experts have said we would never be able to live independently or have a decent quality of life. History has repeatedly been proven wrong. People with Down syndrome have been harmed by centuries of misinformation about what Down syndrome actually is and what should and should not be expected of those who have it. Up until surprisingly recently, institutionalization was considered the only option for people with Down syndrome, and their unstimulating, often abusive institutional environments nearly always led to lowered expectations, lowered IQs, and lowered life expectancy. As Michael Bérubé, whose son has Down syndrome, writes, "I note that in the 1920s we were told that people with Down syndrome were incapable of learning to speak; in the 1970s, we were told that people with Down syndrome were incapable of learning how to read. OK, so now the rationale for seeing these people as somewhat less than human is their likely comprehension of Woody Allen films. Twenty years from now we'll be hearing 'sure, they get Woody Allen, but only his early comedies—they completely fail to appreciate the breakthrough of *Interiors*.' Surely you understand my sense that the goalposts are being moved around here in a rather arbitrary fashion."[31]

Although many people in the twenty-first century would be appalled by the idea of judging a human being's worth by their intellectual capacities, both history and present-day U.S. society is unfortunately rife with examples of such judgments. Disability studies scholar Rachel Adams, who is also the parent of a son with Down syndrome, writes that those with intellectual disabilities are often unwelcome in public space, viewed as discardable, subjected to violence and discrimination, and that "the sight of people with Down syndrome in public may still inspire resentment and loathing."[32]

A poignant example of intellectual discrimination can be seen particularly starkly in the substantial disparities in health care between those with intellectual disabilities and those without.[33] Consider the story of three-year-old Amelia Rivera, whose doctors refused to transplant a kidney from a willing family member because she is "mentally retarded." Amelia has Wolf-Hirschhorn syndrome, which causes physical and mental delays.[34] Without the kidney transplant, she would likely have lived no more than six months. Thanks to the controversy that ensued when Amelia's parents went public with the story, Amelia was eventually given the transplant from her mother and as of the most recent update in 2013 was doing very well. According to a *Washington Post* article about the case, transplant forms often include a box for "mentally retarded" to indicate which cases can be denied.[35] Amelia's difficulty receiving a transplant is not an outlier. For decades individuals with Down syndrome and other intellectual disabilities have had to fight for their right to lifesaving medical treatment.[36] It is hard to read these exclusions as anything other than the use of cognitive capacity as an index of worth.

As Licia Carlson exposes in her important book *The Faces of Intellectual Disability*, the devaluing of those with intellectual disabilities is inextricably entangled with animality. Intellectual "inferiority" has routinely been animalized and dehumanized; as we saw in the racist description of inferior peoples by nineteenth-century geologist J.P. Lesley, such dehumanization has often been represented through merged categories of race, disability, and species. Carlson shows that references to the "animal nature" of the "feebleminded" or "idiots" has persisted for centuries and is still present in today's philosophical discussions. Like those who use sign language, the intellectually disabled have been described as monkey-like and evolutionary throwbacks. Those with intellectual disabilities have been rendered as less than human, and have been routinely subjected to dehumanizing conditions in a variety of institutions.

Of course it is important to point out that it is not only those society identifies as disabled who experience intellectual discrimination. Ideologies of disability and animality have helped pathologize whole populations as intellectually inferior. Nondisabled women and men of color and people of various nondominant cultural and class backgrounds have at times been declared incompetent, and their languages, intelligence, and even ability to feel emotions and physical sensations have at times been denied. From the ubiquitous ways U.S. society privileges particular kinds of academic success and standards of excellence to the disproportionate ways those labeled as needing special ed or as having low IQs are discarded from society and sent into various institutions (a process that is deeply racialized and gendered), intellectual ability and cognitive capacity still play a powerful role in maintaining racialized, gendered, classed, and ableist power structures.

Intellectual inferiority has been so easily animalized because animals themselves have long been understood as intellectually inferior. Anthropologist Hugh Raffles suggests that dehumanization "requires two associations: the identification of the targeted group with a particular type of animal, and the association of the nonhuman in question with adequately negative traits, traits that are always specific to that time and place."[37] Animals have repeatedly been rendered as dumb, deficient, and incapable of meaningful thought in Western philosophical traditions. The association of animals with cognitive deficiency must be challenged, not only because many species exhibit signs of human intelligence, and because animal minds are complex in their own right (in ways that often cannot easily be compared and contrasted with human capacities), but because intellectual capacity should not determine a being's worth and the protections they are granted.

Cognitive capacity is widely accepted as an indicator of a non-human animal's value. Many people won't eat pigs because they have been shown to be at least as "intelligent" as dogs, but they will guiltlessly eat chicken or fish because it is presumed that these animals do not think or have feelings. And nearly everyone has heard a story or two of an outstanding or heroic animal who was spared her fate as dinner because of something uniquely intelligent she did. Remember Yvonne, our famous German dairy cow who outsmarted her captors and so was spared death? Another cow who made the news that year was not so lucky: she escaped but did not manage to avoid her captors, and so she had to wait until "judgment day rolls back around," as one paper lightheartedly put it.[38] It seems this cow just was not smart enough to garner enough sympathy for a pardon.

Nonhuman animals have been victims of centuries of misinformation that negates their abilities. The work of finding out what traits animals share with us is not the only research into animal minds that we should be doing—after all, animals have countless capacities that human beings do not have. Nonetheless it is key, for it exposes the fact that many of the traits we call "human" are instead shared among many species. We do not have an exclusive claim to a broadly defined trait such as empathy or tool use any more than other animals do, even if our forms of empathy and tool use differ.

When we examine neurotypical human standards, it is remarkable how many abilities that we claim to be distinctly human actually belong to many different species. In 1960 Jane Goodall reported that wild chimpanzees were making and using tools. Anthropologist Louis Leakey famously replied, "Now we'll have to redefine tool, redefine man, or accept the chimpanzee as man."[39] Today tool use is evident in a broad range of animals, including primates, dolphins, octopi, numerous kinds of birds, rodents, and fish (some species of which have been observed using rocks to crack open cockles, for instance).[40]

Western science needs to alter radically the way it has thought about animals. In just the past decade we've learned that magpies grieve,[41] prairie dogs can describe through their calls what a predator looks like and whether it has a gun,[42] sheep can remember dozens of faces,[43] and dogs can categorize photographs.[44] Many animals, from rats to wolves to chickens, exhibit signs of empathy and what some argue is a sense of justice.[45] Some species develop specific cultures and pass learned information on to their offspring. Still others are capable of deep bonds resembling human friendship, even across species, and some mourn their dead. In their book *Wild Justice: The Moral Lives of Animals*, ethologist Marc Bekoff and philosopher Jessica Pierce write, "New information that's accumulating daily is blasting away perceived boundaries between humans and animals and is forcing a revision of outdated and narrow-minded stereotypes about what animals can and cannot think, do, and feel."[46] Aristotle argued that one of the things that separated humans from animals was laughter, but we now know we share even laughter with many other primates, as well as dogs and even rats (who seem to quite enjoy being tickled).[47]

Animals are physiologically very similar to us. Consider that fish—one of those catchall categories we give to a huge variety of widely differing species—have physiological reactions to pain similar to human beings, and studies have shown that they react to painkillers as a human would.[48] Some species of fish have been shown to have long-lasting memories, complex social lives, and personalities.[49] Yet our biases against them allow us to withhold even the most minimal of legal protections. Fish die stressful, painful, and drawn-out deaths by such things as asphyxiation, stab wounds, or evisceration (disembowelment).[50] Writer Jonathan Safran Foer points out in his book *Eating Animals* that there is no such thing as a humane death for a fish: "No fish gets a good death. Not a single one. You never have to wonder if the fish on your plate had to suffer. It did."[51]

Another often disregarded animal, chickens, are also far more emotionally complex and social creatures than we have given them credit to be. Chickens are fiercely attached to their families, can complete complex mental tasks, comprehend numeracy, and understand cause and effect, and have been shown to remember the faces and pecking-order ranks of up to one hundred different birds.[52] Chickens have also been shown to plan for the future and pass on cultural knowledge to new generations.[53] They use at least thirty different vocalizations to distinguish between various kinds of threats and are able to navigate by telling where the sun is in the sky.[54]

What is intelligence and how do we measure it? One of the problems with using cognitive capacity as a yardstick of moral worth is that abilities, and the myriad tests humans make to measure abilities, do not necessarily translate across species. Consider for example the classic "mark test," or "mirror self-recognition test," which since it was developed in the 1970s has been the traditional method of measuring self-awareness. The mirror test describes a test in which some sort of mark is surreptitiously placed upon a subject (animal or human) somewhere they cannot see without help. They are then placed in front of a mirror. To pass the test, the subject must recognize that the image in the mirror is not someone else, which they have to demonstrate by noticing the mark and then trying to remove it. Until recently it was thought that nearly all human children older than twenty-four months who are not intellectually disabled would pass the mirror test and that most if not all animals would not. But in recent years new studies have radically challenged the reliability of the test. A 2010 study published in the *Journal of Cross-Cultural Psychology* found that many non-Western children fail to pass the test even at six years old. According to researchers, most of the children tested would freeze, staring at the mirror in seeming discomfort. These children do not fail the test because they are not self-aware but because the test fails to consider cultural and personal differences. The test presumes that all children will react the same way to mirrors, to authority, and to the marks themselves. It doesn't take into consideration innumerable factors that might affect the outcome, including simple embarrassment or discomfort. As an article in *Scientific American* put it, "If the relatively small differences among human cultures can alter mark test results so profoundly, then we have to consider what researchers really learn—and don't learn—when they run the test on an animal."[55]

Despite these complexities, many species of animals have passed the test, including chimpanzees, bonobos, orangutans, gorillas, bottlenose dolphins, orcas, elephants, and magpies. Some species were more difficult to test than others because of their species-specific cultures, though. For example, gorillas were thought unable to pass the mirror test until scientists realized that gorillas have a strong aversion to eye contact and are easily embarrassed. Gorillas would often leave the mirror, go hide, and then try to remove the mark in private. Joshua Plotnik, the head of elephant research at the Golden Triangle Asian Elephant Foundation in Thailand, commented, "The mark test can be difficult to apply across species because it assumes that a particular animal will be interested in something weird on their body. Primates are interested in such things—we're groomers. But elephants are different. They're huge and they're used to putting things *on*, not taking things off of their bodies, like mud and dirt." The test also privileges vision—we really can't tell much about the fact that dogs, for example, fail the mirror test, because we know vision is not their prominent sense.[56]

Clearly measuring the cognitive capacities of animals is no easy matter, which makes it all the more impressive how many human-erected goalposts a myriad of species have met. In fact animals have continuously surpassed what scientists and philosophers have expected of them. As Bérubé aptly put it, "There hasn't been a discovery at any point in the last five hundred years after which we said to ourselves, 'My goodness, animals are stupider than we thought.' Every single discovery has gone in the opposite direction."[57] At the most basic level we know that animals, from lobsters to cows to chimpanzees, are sentient and thus have the ability to feel pleasure, pain, and other sensations and emotions. Sentience has very serious ethical implications because if you can feel and experience, it means you are a being who, as philosophers phrase it, has "interests." You care on some level about what is happening to you; unlike a chair or a cell phone, you can be hurt.

Western science has tried to be objective and avoid anthropomorphizing animals, but it has been unable to avoid measuring animals with human yardsticks. This is a catch-22 for the animals, who are deemed intelligent only when they remind us of ourselves, and yet, if they *do* remind us of ourselves, we often dismiss the evidence with accusations of anthropomorphism. When animals finally do pass our tests and quizzes and exhibit traits that we value as intelligent, the traits are then minimized and new goalposts are erected.

Here is where the limits of such comparisons become evident. These measurements of intelligence have been assigned value by neurotypical human beings and say nothing about other kinds of animal intelligence. Although the work of finding similarities between human beings and animals of other species can be very valuable, philosopher Lori Gruen writes, "When what we are looking for is similarities—how we might share the same general type of intelligence or cognitive skills, the same sensitivities and vulnerabilities, the same emotional responses—we tend to obscure or overlook distinctively valuable aspects of the lives of others." The unfortunate reality is that by focusing on similarities we are still promoting a hierarchy of value—one in which human abilities are the only abilities given worth. Gruen continues, "In our magnanimous embrace of the other, we end up reconfiguring a dualism that will inevitably find some 'other' to exclude."[58]

What kinds of experiences and understandings of the world develop for a creature who perceives it through smell or who communicates through bioluminescence? What sort of intelligence is needed to accomplish extremely complex migrations or to survive in the depths of the oceans? We are just beginning to comprehend the vast array of abilities found on this planet, and human abilities are but a small fraction of them. It is challenging to talk about the intelligence and capabilities that other animals may have that we do not. The anthropocentric lens through which we view the world makes it extremely difficult for us to imagine intelligence and experience beyond our own. However, such limitations should not stop us from attempting to understand and learn from the lives of others.

But what about living beings whose abilities are even more hidden from us, such as insects, plants, mollusks, or microbes? What about the networks of living and nonliving organisms that make up ecosystems? Do they have interests? Do rivers and mountains deserve justice?

By focusing on sentience as the line in the sand dividing those with interests and those without, have animal advocates created yet another hierarchy, another ableist goalpost that organisms must clear in order to have their experiences or existence valued and considered? There are potentially uncomfortable parallels between the way sentience gets thrown around as a prerequisite for moral consideration and the ways other attributes, abilities, and cognitive capacities are set up as yardsticks. Yet, at this point, sentience is one of the only criteria we have to explain why it is more wrong to punch a dog than a rock, a tree, or a cell phone. At the same time, though, the kind of moral consideration that sentience demands should not negate that other forms of life and nonlife also deserve an ethical response, even if of a very different nature. Responding ethically to an individual suffering animal likely looks extremely different than responding ethically to a polluted river, or to the loss of diversity among microbial life. Justice looks different for different kinds of beings.

Questions of sentience are also immensely complex and reveal our lack of understanding about what truly constitutes consciousness. Even vegan animal advocates debate exactly what it is and who has it. For example, in 2010 writer and editor Christopher Cox, a vegan, wrote a *Slate* article called "Consider the Oyster," which argued that it wasn't morally problematic for people to eat animals such as oysters because they most likely are not sentient, given that they lack central nervous systems.[59] In response, Bekoff wrote a passionate rebuttal, "Vegans Shouldn't Eat Oysters," which argued that since oysters are animals, and since humans have been consistently wrong in our assumptions about animals, that the jury is still out on oysters—we should give them the benefit of the doubt.[60]

But the jury could still be out on everything—there are always scientific discoveries to be made, knowledge to increase, and understanding to deepen. For instance, fascinating research on plant behavior has emerged in recent years. Although scientists do not claim that plants can feel emotions, they are exploring the ways plants communicate through electrical and chemical signaling, raising questions about plant intelligence.[61] Perhaps sentience dependent on a central nervous system is only one kind of consciousness.

The questions of the moral status of microbial life, insects, plants, and of the environment as a whole are important and deserve attention. They also each carry their own unique set of ethical quandaries. I worry, though, when these issues are raised in order to excuse the exploitation, commodification, and killing of beings we already know experience and feel their lives, particularly when they end up obscuring the ethical implications wrought by the various multibillion-dollar industries that currently profit off of animal lives. It is true that we do not know with absolute certainty whether plants, or oysters for that matter, suffer or have emotional lives, but we do know that dogs, cows, fish, and chickens all do. We also know that for animals to thrive (including human animals), our environment needs to thrive too, which means that the struggle for animals is inseparable from the struggle for the environment more broadly.

To me, far from proving that animal justice is impossible and silly, the complexity of sentience and moral consideration does not prove either that we need to treat all beings the same or that human exceptionalism is the only realistic framework. Rather, sentience and the vast array of mysterious life and nonlife on this planet show that we need a nuanced understanding of different abilities and the different responsibilities those abilities engender.

As difficult as all these questions are, I find myself drawn to them precisely because of the lack of easy answers. Such questions shatter the idea that this thing we call *nature* can be easily categorized to fit human analysis and needs. Even the seemingly simple question of what, and who, I mean when I am discussing "animals" throughout this book is to me unanswerable. Rather than try to pretend that such taxonomical maneuvers can be cut and dried, I prefer to leave my own definition of "animal" open-ended. Our environments and fellow beings stubbornly refuse our closed definitions.

# 6

## What Is an Animal?

In Franz Kafka's "A Report to an Academy," a great ape is shot (but not killed) and stolen from his home in Africa. The ape is then confined to a cage on a ship, where he begins to realize that the more he acts like a human man, the more likely he'll be able to leave his cage. By the end of the story Red Peter, as he is named by his captors, wears trousers and reports on his acquisition of human language and behavior to an unspecified "academy." Red Peter says, "I'll say it again: imitating human beings was not something which pleased me. I imitated them because I was looking for a way out, for no other reason."[1]

Red Peter becomes a celebrity, performing and lecturing across the country. He acts like a human being, uses human language, and has gained the intelligence of an "average European," an achievement that Red Peter states "has helped me out of my cage and opened a special way out for me, the way of humanity." But still Red Peter is consistently challenged by those who claim his ape nature is not under control—that no matter how much he learns he will never be human.

If Red Peter were real, would he be treated as an equal? Would he be granted basic human rights? Could he be enslaved or sold for scientific experimentation? Western histories of racism and xenophobia would lead us to guess that Red Peter would not achieve equality in human eyes, at least not without a historic battle and debate. His fellow primates, who had not achieved his level of human skill—although his example clearly demonstrated they held the potential to do so—would be even less likely to be granted basic freedoms. Why?

In this hypothetical scenario, the ableism we feel toward Red Peter because of his "lack" of human abilities would likely diminish when he proved himself capable of all things an average person is capable of. But he would continue to experience plenty of discrimination, perhaps because of how he looked and moved, his behaviors and values, and where he was from, but also because of his species.

Speciesism is a belief that human beings are superior to all other animals, condoning human use and domination over animals because we humans rank above them—either spiritually or biologically. Speciesism is manifested when a drug or household product is tested on an animal, when a bull hook is used to make an elephant do a trick, when we visit a zoo and watch animals in cages, when we destroy an animal's habitat to benefit ourselves, and when we send an animal to slaughter or we commodify her body for our own benefit. In the Western tradition speciesism has informed our histories, religions, cultural values, and the stories we tell ourselves about being human. It has also played a central role in how we humans see and treat one another.

Even though Red Peter and the real ape Booee are complex, emotional, and intelligent beings, speciesism allows us to think that since they are still not *human*, we can use them however we wish. But what *is* a human? Is a human an animal? And what is an animal anyway?

In her brief article "On the Animal Turn," historian Harriet Ritvo writes, "Most scholars who specialize in the study of animals believe that human beings fall within that category."[2] Whether among scientists exploring the genetic similarities that unite the animal kingdom, or among those in the humanities examining the emotional, intellectual, and cultural spaces of kinship between humans and other species, it is widely accepted that humans are animals.

However, as Ritvo points out, such an understanding is also persistently contradicted by what she calls "a more common usage" of the term animal, which views animals as lower than and

set apart from the human. Despite the long-standing and ubiquitous understanding across various disciplines that humans are
themselves animals, an unease and distancing remains. Humans
seem to want it both ways: we are animal but we are not. Animal
enough that other species can be used in experiments to model
our own anatomy and physiology. Animal enough that we can
learn about "human nature" by tracking our evolutionary family tree. Animal enough that we can blame the worst of human
behavior on our "animal natures." Yet, we are not animal enough
for most people to want to identify as such. Being an animal
remains an insult. How has such a paradox occurred? How can
we be both animals and not?

In the image *Homo Sylvestris*, a 1699 illustration by the influential
British comparative anatomist Edward Tyson (figure 2),[3] a chimpanzee stands bipedal with a walking stick in his hand. The image
is one of many from the period that represent apes standing erect
with the help of walking sticks. With his wrinkled face, slight
smile, and imperfect posture the ape resembles an old man relying
on a trusted cane as he goes out for a midday stroll.

From the seventeenth century onward, Europeans who came
in contact with anthropoid apes while exploring (and later
colonizing) Africa were perplexed by how to categorize them.
Categorizing the natural world was an obsession of European
explorers, and systems of classification were persistently used to
justify colonialism. Were apes human, but devoid of civilization? Were they proof of a Great Chain of Being, a missing link
between humans and animals? Science historian Londa Schiebinger explains in her book *Nature's Body: Gender in the Making of
Modern Science* that naturalists of the time were generally more
sympathetic in their description of the apes than they were in
describing Africans, "highlighting the human character of apes
while emphasizing the purported simian qualities of Africans."[4]
Such practices worked to legitimize and perpetuate slavery and
colonialism by narrowing the gap between animals and humans
of African descent (as well as many other racialized populations).
One of the human characteristics naturalists focused on in their
discussion of human uniqueness was the ability to walk upright.

Figure 2: *Homo Sylvestris*, an illustration by the comparative anatomist Edward Tyson, made in 1699. The image is one of many from the period that represent apes standing erect with the help of walking sticks.

If apes were to be considered a type of man, then—according to scholars of the day—they too should walk upright on two legs.

Since Plato, erect posture had been seen as a quality that separated humans from animals.[5] Our bodies were said to be drawn upward toward the heavens, as our immortal souls connected us to the angels. In the sixth century Saint Isidore of Seville echoed such thinking, writing that "the human stands erect and looks toward heaven so as to seek God, rather than look at the earth, as do the beasts that nature has made bent over and attentive to their bellies."[6] In Europeans' quest to anthropomorphize the great apes, the animals' failure to walk on two legs became a quality naturalists tried to explain away, either by suggesting those apes who did not do so were sick, or by depicting them conveniently sitting, or, as in the above example, standing with the aid of a walking stick.

If an ape who stands upright (even if with the help of a mobility device) can be seen as more human, what happens to humans who do not or cannot stand upright? Monkey-like posture was one of many simian characteristics used to dehumanize people of color, particularly people of African descent, from the seventeenth century on. Beyond the fact that slouched, curved backs, hunched shoulders, and dangling arms have long been used in racist cartoons and illustrations portraying people of color as monkey- and apelike, numerous historical texts suggest an association between posture and civility, if not humanity. For example, in his influential *History of Jamaica*, eighteenth-century British historian and colonial administrator Edward Long suggests that the colony's white women were being contaminated by their association with slave women, adopting their slaves' purportedly uncivilized and slovenly body language, including their "aukward carriage and vulgar manners" and "aukwardly dangling" arms.[7] We could also look to the writings of Englishman Richard Ligon during his travels to Barbados in 1647; Ligon's racist descriptions of black women presented them as animal-like in both their body shape and posture. He writes, "Their breasts hang down below their Navels, so that when they stoop at their common work of weeding, they hang almost to the ground, that at a distance you would think they had six legs."[8] Ligon's description combines imagery of black laborers bent over working a field with images of fertility, conjuring up a resemblance between black women and dairy cows or some kind of insect with an abundant number of "legs."

Two centuries later Charles Darwin would use posture as a registrar of humanity as well. Posture was particularly significant to Darwin because he believed bipedalism was not merely unique to the human species, but in fact marked the point at which human development diverged from other animals. In his quest to show that evolutionary theory was as important to the development of the human species as to other animals, Darwin turned to racist and ableist stereotypes of "savages" and "idiots," suggesting that these groups were in effect living fossils, examples of intermediate stages of human evolution. One of the traits that Darwin suggested showed that "idiots" were essentially animal-like evolutionary throwbacks was their purported tendency to walk on all fours.[9]

Darwin's interest in bipedalism would be revived in the mid-twentieth century when erect posture, not a large brain or other celebrated human characteristics, would become a deciding factor for anthropologists marking early human status in the fossil record. Upright posture would also be attributed with leading to the development of human tool use and culture.[10] One need only look at the familiar *March of Progress* diagram to see the central place upright posture has held in the way human evolution is often imagined. Since its creation in 1965, the diagram has misleadingly come to represent evolution as a linear progression with "man" as its pinnacle. *The March of Progress* shows a series of figures who grow increasingly erect and bipedal, with the last being a human male of European descent standing upright on two feet—suggesting that the pinnacle of evolution is not only human, but is specifically male, white, and able-bodied.

As we can see in the nearly three hundred years of debate over how to categorize apes and less privileged human populations, the association of animals with negative or positive traits has invariably been bound up with categories of human difference, such as race and disability. In other words, the question of what an animal is has been shaped by changing ideas about what a human is (and vice versa), ideas that have themselves been shaped by political, cultural, religious, scientific and economic factors, and by bigotry.

In *The Animal That Therefore I Am (More to Follow)* philosopher Jacques Derrida writes, "The animal is a word, it is an appellation that men have instituted, a name they have given themselves the right and the authority to give to another living creature." Like many animal studies scholars, Derrida finds the term "animal" lazy and insulting, arguing throughout the work that the name erases the multiplicity of beings that it is supposed to encompass. To explore the naming of animals, he turns to Genesis, reflecting on the way that naming and domination are called forth in the same instance in the story. God makes Adam in his likeness, and commands him to "Subject the fish of the sea, the flying creatures of the heavens, every living thing that crawls on the earth." God then lets Adam (before Eve is created or named) name the animals. Thus man in Genesis is already set apart from the beasts (and, tellingly, apart from woman), and naming is itself integral to this separation.[11]

The project of naming animals is one that "man" would continue. The naming of animals and particularly of categories of animals has been an ongoing activity in Western thought. The obsessive drive to label and categorize nature can be seen in the collections of humans, animals, miracles, plants, and things that from ancient times onward have often been lumped together under descriptions of wonder, and exhibited in cabinets of curiosity or on the stages of the sideshow. These wonders raised questions about whether there was an order to nature, a question intimately tied to another—the question of how to fit humans within this order.

The display of "living curiosities" has occurred in various capacities and configurations at different historical junctures, but the blurring of or enhancing of categories of difference along what we in modern times would refer to as gender, racial, disability, and species lines has been ubiquitous to the art. From medieval "monsters," babies born with horns, ambiguous genitals, body hair, or as conjoined twins, to monstrous races, cannibals, wild savages, and missing links, to exotic animals such as giraffes, platypuses, and chimpanzees, categories of race, sex, disability, and species have been managed and secured through naming and display. The separation of these "living curiosities" into distinct human and animal categories happened slowly over centuries and was aided by the rise of science, philosophical discourse, and taxonomy.

It was not just curiosity that drove this incessant urge to name and classify. Long held to be the center of thought, the church had authority over knowledge production and promoted an understanding of nature and "man's" place within it in particular ways—as closer to the angels than the beasts were, for example. The power of the church eventually overlapped with and gave way to the rise of natural philosophy and science, leaving its mark on these disciplines and shaping their development. At the same time the exploration and eventual colonization of Africa and the "New World" provided political and economic incentives for nature to be ordered in particular ways that privileged Europeans. For example, Europe had a long tradition of identifying monstrous races and body parts in other locations. African and Asian countries were said to have the most occurrences of monstrous races and births and the question of whether such races and physiological features should be categorized as demonic, monsterous, or animal was the subject of much debate. Centuries later, Europeans would still be locating these "oddities" in new places. In the nineteenth and early twentieth centuries, for example, it was common sideshow practice to ascribe non-Western origins to intellectually disabled individuals born in Europe or the United States—thus Jenny Lee Snow and Elvira Snow, two white sisters from Georgia, were billed as "Twins from Yucatan," and William Henry Johnson, a black man from New Jersey, became a "What Is It?" from some faraway jungle.

In the Holy Scriptures, humans were endowed with souls, a concept that has often been intimately tied to the idea of reason. The emphasis on reason can be traced back to Aristotle, who argued that humans are unique in possessing a rational soul. Yet Aristotle did not view beasts as completely separate from man, suggesting that there were three aspects of the human soul: the rational, unique to humans, but also the nutritive, which humans shared with plants, and the sensitive, which humans shared with animals. Furthermore, in a move that would be contested for two millennia, Aristotle placed humans within the category of viviparous quadrupeds, naming humans as animals in his *Historia animalium*, a text that would lay the groundwork for European taxonomy.[12]

Despite Aristotle's influence, humans did not remain in the category of quadrupeds in perpetuity (among other reasons, it was argued that our two legs and upright posture clearly demonstrated the need for a category unique to humans). His hierarchal system of categorization in which humans sat on the top would be developed in the Middle Ages into the concept of *systema naturae* or the "Great Chain of Being." Aristotle's hierarchy had proposed a sort of spectrum of increasingly complex characteristics: at the top was the most lively, mobile, and rational human, followed by less intelligent but sensitive animals. Then there were plants, which were alive, but possessed a limited amount of vitality and mobility. Below plants were stones and minerals, things that Aristotle viewed as lacking life and so as possessing no soul.[13] In contrast, the *systema naturae*, or ladder or stairway of nature, described a more strict hierarchal ordering from God down to rocks and minerals, with humans midway between angels and animals, sharing reason and intellect with the former and body and senses with the latter. Reason was seen as a gift bestowed on man by God that set him apart from animals.

The ongoing investment in reason, perhaps epitomized by the seventeenth-century work of René Descartes (who rejected the idea that animals think or have conscious thoughts), has played heavily into histories of objectification and dehumanization. But reason is not the only characteristic naturalists have looked to in seeking the source of human uniqueness (and superiority). They have also pondered a wide variety of other attributes, including bipedal posture, breasts, hair, and genitals.[14] Each supposedly unique characteristic, whether the shape and size of specific body parts, standards of beauty or culture, or conceptions of language and intellect, has been used not only to separate humans from animals but also to define some humans *as* animals.

In the eighteenth century Carl Linnaeus outraged naturalists by putting human beings firmly within the animal kingdom, under his newly coined term *Mammalia* in his *Systema Naturae*. He further included humans in his category *Primates*, which included apes, monkeys, and sloths.[15] Linnaeus's system of classification is remarkably similar to the system used today. His system was embedded in racialized and gendered debates over the classification of human difference. As Schiebinger has shown, the term mammals linked humans to animals through a distinctly female characteristic: the breast, which was also highly racialized (it was argued by naturalists that breast shape and size corresponded to and legitimized racial hierarchies),[16] whereas Linnaeus's term *Homo sapiens*, meaning "man of wisdom," was meant to distinguish humans from animals through a characteristic assigned almost exclusively to white males: reason.[17] Even when human beings were brought down from the angels to be with the beasts, constructions of human difference were essential to describing what aspects of the human were animal-like (the feminine and nonwhite), and which were still safely unique and superior (the white and masculine).

Human beings' place in the order of nature would be further solidified in the nineteenth century with the birth of Darwinian thought and the rise of evolutionary theory. Darwin would trouble the supposedly stable categories of taxonomy, exposing the relatedness of all organic forms. He would profoundly change the way people thought of species, showing in meticulous detail that species are not immutable, that they are forever shifting. The implications of such a theory were huge. Darwin declared that all plants and animals that have ever existed are related.

Even the knowledge that species are not immutable and that all living things are family was not enough to raise the status of animals and dehumanized humans in many people's minds, however. On the contrary, discrimination toward less privileged people was further propelled by questions of evolution and the drive for missing links it spurred, as can be seen in Darwin's own work. The Great Chain of Being did not die with Darwin, and neither did the desire to search for taxonomic truths (consider the turn to genetics to find distinct boundaries between species), the cult of rationality, the urge to create a hierarchy of beings, or even the obsession with walking erect on two legs.

As a child and teenager I was told numerous times that I walk like a monkey or resemble a monkey when I stand. Now as an adult I never hear such words verbalized, but I am confronted with a barrage of technologies, advertisements, and movie plotlines that suggest that sitting in a wheelchair or not being able to

Figure 3: Disability activist Anna Stonum's altered version of *The March of Progress* replaced the final standing male figure with the International Symbol of Access (ISA). Stonum called the image *ADAPT or Perish*. Courtesy: Mike Ervin.

walk means an end to a full life. It seems walking erect on two legs, whether through rehabilitation or through technology, is the only way to ensure one's immortal "soul of reason" can reach upward toward the heavens, versus staying on earth keeping company with the lowly beasts.

What happens if one rejects this narrative of erectness? In the 1990s disability activist Anna Stonum altered *The March of Progress*, replacing the final standing male figure with the International Symbol of Access (ISA), the familiar wheelchair logo seen on parking signs. Stonum called the diagram *ADAPT or Perish* (figure 3). The altered diagram changes the meaning of the word "adapt," moving it away from evolutionary concepts of fitness and unfitness and toward a cripped understanding of adapting to difference. The word also conjures up the activist group ADAPT, which Stonum was a part of, playfully highlighting the importance of politicization and community for oppressed populations.[18]

Stonum's diagram could be seen as celebrating a sort of cyborgian fantasy of progress—replacing the human with technology. Yet the wheelchair logo represents a person in a wheelchair, not simply a wheelchair.[19] It could also be seen as centering the West: although the ISA has been described as universal and is used internationally, the symbol foregrounds a Western image of disability—wheelchairs are not used universally, nor do they all look alike.[20] At the same time, however, the altered diagram does in many ways succeed in challenging Western notions of progress, dislodging the bipedal European human male as the pinnacle of evolution and replacing him with a symbol of disability, a category of difference that has long been seen as the opposite of progress—as a sign of degeneracy and weakness. Stonum further challenges any easy or linear notion of progress by creating her image out of an already altered version of the diagram, one that begins with a small bipedal monkey versus an ape on all fours.

Despite these subversive changes Stonum's diagram remains anthropocentric, and does not reclaim the animal. The final figure is distinctly human, having shed its apelike posture despite its inability to stand erect.

What would happen if the final figure remained animal? Or was shown with hunched posture in the wheelchair? What if the distinction between human and animal was blurred? Would this blurring of human and ape necessarily be too risky? Or is there any way it could be liberatory for both humans and animals?

Answers to such questions shift across time, culture, and identity. The oppression those of us with physical disabilities in the West face due to our "apelike posture" or inability to be bipedal are totally different from the oppression faced by the women described as and compared to animals in Long's and Ligon's time, or that of the intellectually disabled people Darwin labeled idiots. Yet as we have seen, these comparisons share a genealogy (a connected history), which may open up space for new coalitions across identity, and across species, to challenge classification hierarchies and the oppressive histories they helped legitimize.

What happens if we acknowledge that humans are animals? What happens if we remember that bigotry toward humans has been shaped in part by legacies of speciesism and hierarchical taxonomies that mark humans as above and distinct from animals? If we pay attention to who these diverse creatures are that have for so long been entangled in our categories of difference and our insatiable drive for order, perhaps then we will find more accurate names for all of us.

# 7

## The Chimp Who Remembered

BOOEE SPENT THIRTEEN YEARS living alone in a cage at LEMSIP.

Roger Fouts never forgot Booee, but for years he was helpless to do anything for his former student and friend. This finally changed in 1995 when he was contacted by a producer at ABC who wanted to do an episode of *20/20* on the LEMSIP chimps. Seeing this as a potential opportunity to free Booee, Fouts agreed—but not without grave reservations about the psychological effect this could have on him and Booee if nothing came of it. Fouts recalls his reunion with Booee in his book *Next of Kin*:

> I hesitated for another moment, then entered the room in a low crouch. I approached Booee's cage uttering gentle chimpanzee greetings. A big smile lit up Booee's face. He remembered me, after all.
>
> HI, BOOEE, I signed. YOU REMEMBER?
>
> BOOEE, BOOEE, ME BOOEE, he signed back, overjoyed that someone actually acknowledged him. He kept drawing his finger down the center of his head in his name sign—the one I had given him in 1970, three years after NIH researchers had split his infant brain in two.
>
> YES, YOU BOOEE, YOU BOOEE, I signed back. GIVE ME FOOD, ROGER, he pleaded.
>
> Booee not only remembered that I always carried raisins for him, but he used the nickname he had invented

for me twenty-five years earlier. . . . Seeing him sign my old nickname floored me. I had forgotten it, but Booee hadn't. He remembered the good old days better than I did.

I gave Booee some raisins, and the years just melted away, the way they do between old friends. He reached his hand through the bars and groomed my arm. He was happy again. He was the same sweet boy I met on that autumn day decades earlier when Washoe and I first stepped on to the chimpanzee island at Lemmon's Institute. . . .

Look at him now, I thought. Thirteen years in a hellhole and he's still forgiving, still guileless. Booee still loved me, in spite of everything that humans had done to him. How many people would be so generous of spirit? . . .

As we left LEMSIP, I shook hands cordially with the director, Dr. Jan Moor-Jankowski, as if we were two colleagues who had just transacted some mundane piece of business. I was overwhelmed by shame. I was ashamed of Booee's hepatitis, ashamed of the professionalism of Moor-Jankowski and myself, ashamed of the respectability that hung over all this suffering.[1]

Thanks to a widespread public outcry, Booee and eight other adult chimpanzees were released to a nonprofit animal sanctuary called Wildlife Waystation five months after the *20/20* episode aired.

Like so many others who have learned of Booee's story I was struck not only by his terrible situation but by his sweetness, capacity for forgiveness, and ability to remember the "good old days." Yet the longer I spend with Booee's story, the more I cannot help thinking of Red Peter and the possibility that Booee did exactly what he needed to do to get out of his cage. I'm not doubting Booee's elation at seeing his old friend Fouts—who was likely the kindest human Booee had ever encountered—but rather wondering what would happen if we expanded the possibilities of what Booee could have felt and been trying to achieve during their encounter. Booee acted intelligent enough to impress, and emotional enough to inspire empathy, but he remained nonthreatening, "a sweet boy," who was "guileless" and "forgiving"—the kind of being who would inspire sympathy in humans. What if, like Red Peter, imitating human beings was not something that pleased Booee? What if he did it because he was looking for a way out and for no other reason?

By presenting Booee in a way that was likely to produce the most sympathy—as almost childlike—Fouts too may also have done exactly what he needed to do to free Booee. Both of them needed a way out—Booee from his cage, and Fouts from the conscience-crushing confines of his scientific discipline. Whatever their tactics, they both escaped their fates. In *Next of Kin* Fouts writes that he broke the number one rule of scientists: "Thou shalt not love thy research subjects."[2] I hope more people will continue to break it.

# Part Three

I Am an Animal

# 8

## Walking Like a Monkey

"HEY! YOU WALK LIKE A MONKEY!" The voice comes from a girl who is sitting with a bunch of kids. They are giggling and pointing at me like a freak on a stage. I continue my short walk from my wheelchair to the bench and sit among some of my friends. I try not to let them know I'm mortified.

I'm in kindergarten at a public school in Athens, Georgia. I have friends, but still I regularly get teased for the way I move, especially the way I walk. Kids tell me that I walk like a monkey. Sometimes it's said as if it were a fact. Sometimes they want to make me mad.

Now it's recess, and I'm on the playground with a friend. My power wheelchair is bright red and moves quickly through the dirt.

"Come over here!" some kids yell at us. My friend and I head toward them.

One of them says, "Look. We made a fort."

"It's a club," declares another.

My friend and I look at it. The club just looks like part of the jungle gym to me, maybe with a few sticks added here and there.

"Cool!" both my friend and I say enthusiastically.

One of the girls who seems to be in charge gestures at my friend to come in. My friend walks into the club excitedly.

I park my wheelchair and begin to take a few steps.

"Oh no—" the girl in charge says. "This club is only for people
who can walk. Sorry, Sunny."

I stop. "Why?"

"It's just the rule."

"But I can walk."

She looks at me sadly, as if she has no control over the matter.

"Sunny, you don't walk good enough. It's the rule."

I do my monkey walk back to my wheelchair. My friends are
hanging out under the jungle gym.

"That's a stupid rule," I think to myself.

# 9

## Animal Insults

IN MY LIFE I HAVE BEEN COMPARED to many animals. I have been told I walk like a monkey, eat like a dog, have hands like a lobster, and generally resemble a chicken or penguin. These comparisons have been said both out of mean-spiritedness and playfulness. I remember knowing that my kindergarten classmates meant to hurt my feelings when they told me I walked like a monkey, and of course they did. I wasn't exactly sure why it *should* hurt my feelings, however—after all, monkeys were my favorite animal. I had dozens of monkey toys. My parents recall that my favorite thing as a toddler was to go to our local miniature golf course to see the giant King Kong. But still I knew that when the other children compared me to a monkey, they were not doing it to flatter me. It was an insult. I understood that they were commenting on my inability to stand completely upright when out of my wheelchair—my failure to stand like a normal human being. I understood that being told I was like an animal separated me from other people.

The thing is, they were right. I do resemble a monkey when I walk. Or rather, I resemble an ape, probably a chimpanzee. My standing posture is closest to the second or third figure in *The March of Progress*—certainly not the last. This resemblance is simply true, as is the statement that I eat like a dog when I don't use my hands and utensils. These comparisons have a truth to them that isn't negative—or, I should say, that doesn't have to be negative.

When I ask members of the disabled community whether they have ever been compared to animals because of their disabilities, I receive a torrent of replies. I am transported to a veritable bestiary of frog legs and penguin waddles, seal limbs and monkey arms. It is clear, however, from the wincing and negative interjections, that these comparisons are for the most part not pleasant to remember. One friend shared that while she was growing up her mother told her she had a camel walk. "This was her label for me walking with my hands and legs on the ground—with my bum in the air like a camel hump. It never bothered me, and I'd say I had camel pride." But then she went on to say, "I didn't like being told by my stepdad that I had arms like a monkey."

Perhaps nowhere are histories of disabled people being compared to and treated like animals more unabashedly on display, more brazenly explicit, than in nineteenth- and early twentieth-century American and European sideshows. A populist extension of earlier wonders of the court, sideshows played out the various colonial and scientific dramas of their time. There was Mignon the Penguin Girl, Jo-Jo the Dog-Faced Boy, the What Is It?, the Missing Link, and Krao, the Ape Girl. In the spectacle that was the sideshow, animality was front and center—with the most demeaning of animal comparisons being reserved for people of color and for intellectually disabled people. In the sideshow animality was used to spark the imagination by transgressing common categories and distinctions with theatrics and spectacle, while also legitimizing scientific racism, imperial expansion, colonization, and fear of disability.

The story of Julia Pastrana, billed as "The Ugliest Woman in the World," is one of sideshow history's most harrowing examples of how the melding of pseudoscientific "educational" exhibits with consumable spectacle helped perpetuate the exploitation of people of color and the medicalization of deviant bodies through animalization. An indigenous woman from Mexico, Pastrana was born in 1834, with abundant hair on her face and body. Disability studies scholar Rosemarie Garland-Thomson writes that Pastrana was exhibited "as 'semi-human' with features having

a 'close resemblance to those of a Bear and Orange Outang.'"
She was analyzed by doctors, anthropologists, and scientists who
described her body as "hideous," "deficient," "extraordinary,"
and "hybrid." She was given exhibition names such as "Baboon
Woman," "Apewoman," and "Bear Woman." Scientists and showmen alike would speculate over whether she was human or ape
or whether she might be of African descent (which is where the
racist science of the day imagined that a "missing link" between
the two would be found). Her "feminine figure," small waist,
delicate feet, "remarkably full breasts," and lovely singing voice
were dramatically contrasted to her body hair, beard, and supposedly masculine and apelike facial features. Her gender contributed even further to her objectification, in that she was managed by
her husband, Theodore Lent, a showman who married her after
she became profitable. Lent treated Pastrana entirely as an object,
one he had bought expressly to be put on display.[1]

Pastrana died in 1860 at only twenty-six years of age, several
days after giving birth to a baby boy who also died shortly after
birth. Insisting that their tour go on, Lent had both Pastrana's
and their son's bodies embalmed. Lent toured with them until his
death, and the bodies continued to be exhibited for more than
one hundred years. As recently as 1972, her body toured with a
circus in the United States.[2] She was finally buried in February
2013, 112 years after her death.[3]

As a disabled indigenous woman, Pastrana was marked by iden-
tities that had long been subjects of objectification, study, display,
and animalization. These histories informed the ways in which
Pastrana was animalized in her lifetime and in her death—an animalization that went far beyond a sensational promotional device
and rendered her as someone who could be bought, sold, and
completely objectified for more than a century.

Pastrana's story reminds me just how much my ability and
desire to celebrate my own animal comparisons is a sign of my
whiteness and class privilege. People with disabilities have not
been animalized equally or in the same way. For some people
animal comparisons are not simply insulting—they risk a loss of
personhood.

As Licia Carlson describes extensively in her essay "Philosophers of Intellectual Disability: A Taxonomy" and her book *The Faces of Intellectual Disability*, intellectual disability in particular has been viewed through a paradigm of animality since long before Peter Singer and the argument from marginal cases. Carlson writes, "Foucault has said that madness 'took its face from the mask of the beast,' and in many ways the same can be said of intellectual disability. . . . [There] were more than mere theoretical associations: institutional history of intellectual disability points to numerous instances where the treatment of persons with intellectual disabilities was justified on the basis of their animal-like nature." Carlson notes the historic belief that "retarded" individuals "were insensitive to heat and cold" and so did not need to have their cells heated in the winter: "As late as a few decades ago . . . we find individuals with intellectual disabilities kept in conditions that can only be described as 'subhuman.'"[4]

Consider the example of New York's Willowbrook School, a state-funded institution that housed 5,400 intellectually disabled children. The overcrowded, filthy conditions of Willowbrook shocked the nation when footage of children living in dirt and rags went public in 1972. Abuse was rampant and some of the children had even been used as medical test subjects, deliberately injected with hepatitis. Even before the exposé Willowbrook was described by Robert Kennedy as "a snake pit" and "less comfortable and cheerful than the cages in which we put animals in a zoo." With the passage of important federal civil rights legislation protecting disabled people, the nation has thankfully made headway since the early 1970s.[5] But disturbing stories of people with disabilities kept in dehumanizing conditions still emerge. In 2013 thirty-two intellectually disabled men were found to have been enslaved by an Iowa turkey processing plant for more than thirty years. For three decades these men were forced to live in squalor, at times padlocked into their bug-infested home, and at least one of them even repeatedly being chained to his bed.[6] One can also see troubling legacies of animalization at work in present-day behavior modification therapy for disabled children. In their article "Shocking into Submission: Suppressive Practices and Use of Behavior Modification on Nonhuman Animals, People with Disabilities, and the Environment," scholars D.L. Adams and Kim

Socha report, "Behavioral modification techniques used to train dogs to stop barking, stay, and roll over are the same used in the modification of behavior in students with disabilities."[7]

As these histories show, animalization has also been used as a tool to segregate and police disabled people. We can see this in the "ugly laws" legislation that existed from the 1860s to the 1970s across the United States, which made it illegal for "unsightly" or "disgusting" people to be in certain public spaces. These laws were often intended to get rid of beggars, and at times overlapped with laws designed to clean the streets of stray animals. In her book *The Ugly Laws: Disability in Public*, Susan Schweik, a professor of English and disability studies at UC Berkeley, describes how anxieties about disability, as well as poverty, class, race, gender, nationality, and animality, all intersected in these laws. In some instances, human beggars were compared to stray dogs or other animals, and Schweik suggests that "the threat of unsightly beggars who might spread disease or bite the hand that fed them got phrased at times as a problem of animal control."[8]

The ways disabled individuals move when we "crawl" or "walk on all fours," the ways we sound when we "screech" or "howl" or "make strange noises," the ways we lack control when our bodies relieve themselves at inappropriate times, the way we transgress social etiquette by "eating like dogs," the way we fail to stand erect on two feet—all of these things have been used to confirm disability's perception as an "unruly," "beastly," and "animal-like" state of being.

Is it possible to reconcile my own identification with animals with the brutal reality of human animalization? Is it possible to reconcile an identification with animals given these histories? Is there a way to attend to the fact that animalization has contributed to unspeakable violence against humans, while also recognizing the violence speciesism inflicts on other species?

Scholar Mel Y. Chen writes that when humans are compared to animals, they are not being compared "to that class of creatures that includes humans but quite the converse, the class against which the (often rational) human with inviolate and full subjectivity is defined."[9] Animals make powerful insults precisely because we have imagined them as devoid of subjective and emotional lives that would obligate us to have responsibilities toward them. Animals are a category of beings that in the Western tradition we have decided that we rarely, if ever, have duties toward—we can buy them, sell them, and discard them like objects. To call someone an animal is to render them a being to whom one does not have responsibilities, a being that can be shamelessly objectified.

Animal studies scholar Cary Wolfe writes that "the discourse of speciesism will always be available for use by some humans against other humans as well, to countenance violence against the social other of *whatever* species—or gender, or race, or class."[10] But as Schweik suggests, "Disability studies does not need to replicate this speciesism or repudiate the 'animal' in order to defend the dignity and humanity of people treated like dogs."[11]

Returning to the sideshow we can see the entangled nature of human animalization and speciesism. The sideshow and the modern zoo both emerged in the nineteenth century, a century that saw a proliferation of various spectacular means of display for humans and animals—zoos and sideshows, but also traveling menageries, circuses, museums, world fairs, amusement parks, and ethnographic exhibitions or human zoos. The world's most famous showman, P.T. Barnum, known for his dazzling ability to make entertainment and profit off of human and animal "oddities," was an early target of criticism by animal advocates who saw his disregard for animals as an egregious example of the ways carnivals and zoos hid their cruelty behind a facade of family fun. In 1867 Henry Bergh, founder of the American Society for the Prevention of Cruelty to Animals, began to criticize publicly Barnum's caged menageries and trained-animal acts, which were often larger and more diverse than the collections of many zoos. Historian Diane Beers writes that Bergh "accused the showman of removing animals from their native environments; caging them in small, damp, unventilated pens; and forcing them to perform humiliating acts to 'have peanuts and tobacco thrown at them by gaping crowds.'" In his defense Barnum declared that he loved his animals and, in a familiar argument that is still used today, that the animals had better and safer lives in captivity than they would if they were free in the wild.[12]

The exhibition of humans and animals has a shared genealogy, one embedded in religious, scientific, and colonial practices. From medieval collections of living oddities that represented the strength of the king, to nineteenth-century zoos, sideshows, and world fairs that were meant to display the triumph of Western colonial powers, the display of humans and animals, or so-called "colonial commodities," has long been economically and culturally entangled. Figures such as Carl Hagenbeck, a nineteenth-century German merchant of wild animals, exemplify the shared history of human and animal exhibitions. Hagenbeck captured animals to sell to zoos and showmen like Barnum. He opened his own circus in 1887 and would help revolutionize the design of zoos to be more "natural." He also displayed human beings, removing people from their native lands to be put on exhibit. During his lifetime Hagenbeck put on fifty-four ethnographic exhibitions, displaying people from various colonized communities, both as "natural people" and as "savages," alongside "exotic" animals from the same regions. Many of these people died of smallpox, tuberculosis, or other contagious diseases, or they were unable ever to return home—despite promises—due to cost, or to the colonization and destruction of their home communities.[13]

Between 1866 and 1886 Hagenbeck also exported "around seven hundred leopards, a thousand lions and four hundred tigers, a thousand bears, eight hundred hyenas, three hundred elephants, 70 rhinoceroses . . . three hundred camels, 150 giraffes, six hundred antelopes, tens of thousands of monkeys, thousands of crocodiles, boas and pythons . . . and substantially more than a hundred thousand birds," write Eric Baratay and Elisabeth Hardouin-Fugier in their history *Zoo: A History of Zoological Gardens in the West*. These figures could be doubled, however, since they don't take into account those animals who died during the arduous and months-long journey from their homes to Europe; fatalities are estimated at about 50 percent. Nor do these numbers account for the innumerable animals killed during capture—for every live capture many others were killed.[14] In some cases whole species were completely decimated. For the individual animals who survived, life would be limited to tiny cages, staring humans, grueling performance schedules, and drastically shortened life spans.

What about these animals, who were trapped, taken from their environments, kept in captivity, and trained violently to perform for gawking crowds? What about the animals who still to this day perform with circuses like Barnum & Bailey where rampant violence occurs or who are currently living their lives in zoos with little mental stimulation, performing a human idea of wildness for a perpetual audience? Do they deserve to be treated *like animals*?

It is undeniable that animals have experienced terrible violence at the hands of humans—violence that very often shares a genealogy with the violence humans inflict on one another. What if we saw the terrible acts they have suffered as an example of why they deserve not only our empathy and respect but also our acknowledgment that they are our kin? What if instead of demeaning us, claiming animality could be a way of challenging the violence of animalization and of speciesism—of recognizing that animal liberation is entangled with our own?

Carlson asks whether it is even possible to reassert our animality. She finds power in the idea but also cautions us by asking an important question: "Why is it that certain human faces call forth the face of the beast more readily than others?" She continues, "Can we speak broadly of a 'reassertion of animality' without attending to whose animality has or has not been emphasized and exploited? Without considering the fact that for some, it may be their humanity rather than their animality that needs to be (re)asserted?"[15]

Carlson urges us to remember that for many human beings an identification with animals or animality might not be possible or safe, even if it were in some way desirable. Speciesism doesn't necessarily keep people from wanting to identify as animal; dehumanization does. Perhaps we need to ask how we can assert both our humanity and our animality. How do those of us who have been negatively compared to nonhuman animals assert our value as human beings without either implying human superiority or denying our very own animality?

# 10
## Claiming Animal

PERCILLA BEJANO CONTROLLED HER OWN LIFE. Like Julia Pastrana some fifty years earlier, Bejano had thick dark hair covering much of her body. Born in Puerto Rico in 1911 as Percilla Roman, she was adopted as a young child by showman Karl Lauther, who by Roman's own account treated her "like a daughter" despite putting her on exhibition. She was originally billed as "The Little Hairy Girl," but someone soon suggested the title "Monkey Girl." The name stuck. Like many sideshow performers, Bejano was paired with a trained animal—a young chimpanzee—to enhance the spectacle of her act. Little is known about the chimp except that her name was Josephine and that she rode a bike and smoked cigarettes.[1]

Although Bejano was animalized, she managed her own work and self-image in a way that complicates a purely exploitative narrative. At age twenty she fell in love with Emmet Bejano, a white performer from Florida who was known as "The Alligator-Skinned Man" because of his thick, scale-like skin. Bejano had also been adopted by a showman and grown up in the sideshow. The two eloped. In what I consider one of the most romantic stories of the century, the couple remained together until their deaths more than fifty years later. They went on to exhibit themselves as "The World's Strangest Married Couple," working together through the early 1980s as they led shows across the country, including one that they owned and ran. In a 2002 interview, after the couple had retired, Percilla joked that she might "shave and dye her hair blonde and have a new look." Emmet replied, "You do, and I'm gonna walk out on ya. I love you just the way you are."[2] Emmet died in 1995, and Percilla passed away six years later.

I do not know if the Bejanos embraced or were offended by their animal names, but they controlled their labor and were adamant that they enjoyed the carnival life. In later interviews Percilla Bejano said that she loved what she did and that if she "wasn't so old" she would still be out on the road.

The Bejanos were not an isolated case. Many individuals proudly declared that they enjoyed appearing in sideshows or were grateful for the employment they offered. In 1984 a black disabled man named Otis Jordan was scheduled to make an appearance at the New York State Fair. Like me, Jordan had arthrogryposis and would use his mouth instead of his hands for many daily activities. Due to his small, curved arms and legs, Jordan referred to himself as the "Frog Man" or "Frog Boy" and had been supporting himself by performing in sideshows since the early 1960s. He had managed to get an education in his youth with the support of his family and his two goats, who pulled him in a cart he had designed to meet his mobility needs. But Jordan was unable to find work after graduating. In 1963 he approached a showman at a local fair for a job, and he soon began performing acts where he would roll and light cigarettes with his mouth.[3] Like the Bejanos, Jordan was an active agent in his exhibition, often introducing himself at the beginning of his act instead of having someone else tell his story.

Nearly twenty years later, controversy broke out over Jordan's act when a disabled woman was offended by his performance and went to court to have the sideshow banned. The woman was a disability rights activist and saw Jordan's performance as antithetical to the progress that was being made in the struggle for equality. Jordan fought back and won, passionately arguing for his right to work. As Jordan put it, "I can't understand it. How can she say I'm being taken advantage of? Hell, what does she want for me—to be on welfare?"[4]

In his last few years performing at the Coney Island sideshow,

Jordan was redubbed "The Human Cigarette Factory." I asked sociologist Robert Bogdan, who wrote the book *Freak Show* and who had interviewed Jordan before he passed away, whether the name change was due to the animal comparison. Bogdan told me, "I don't think Otis was sensitive . . . to the link to the animal. Whatever drew a crowd was fine with him."[5]

Although oppression and coercion certainly take many forms—one of which is the lack of alternative employment opportunities for disabled people—it is too simplistic to assume that all freaks were (or are) exploited. Might it also be problematic to assume that all animal comparisons were or are demeaning? Might some performers have reveled in their animal names? Might some freaks have embraced their animal comparisons?

Consider contemporary sideshow performer Mat Fraser. A charming and provocative white man from Britain, Fraser was a thalidomide baby—he has, as he describes them, "flippers" instead of arms. He is a musician, an actor, a performance artist, and a burlesque performer. He is also the self-proclaimed "Sealboy." Disability scholar and artist Petra Kuppers writes that "in the creation of 'Sealboy,' Fraser was searching for his historic role model, his roots, his heritage." By doing so he was "designating the disability experience not as an individual or singular fate, but as a cultural minority experience." By naming himself Sealboy, Fraser claims "freak" and the disability history that goes along with it, including the animalization.[6]

This is not to say that these performers were specifically identifying as or claiming animal—their identification had more to do with claiming a freak heritage (of which animalization played a role) than with animals themselves. Nonetheless they each reassigned meaning to animal insults, evoking wonder and community through their self-assigned animal names.

The Bejanos, Jordan, Fraser, and Pastrana also each experienced animalization in different ways and to vastly varying ends, and these differences often dovetailed with differences in race and ethnicity. As disability studies scholar Rachel Adams reminds us in her book *Sideshow U.S.A: Freaks and the American Cultural Imagination*, "In some cases, to live as a freak means to be accepted into a community unified on the basis of marginality. To be another kind of freak . . . however, means, by definition, exclusion from the community of civilized persons."[7] Perhaps something similar could be said of animal comparisons.

Despite this complicated history, the animal seems to be finding a new place within disability culture. Disabled artists are exploring animal imagery in their work in multifaceted ways, such as the painter Riva Lehrer's many portraits of her aging and disabled dog Zora, which explore themes of vulnerability, interdependence, and companionship,[8] and the photographer and installation artist Laura Swanson, whose inhabitable giant sculpture *Homemade Bull* turns the animal into a place of refuge and learning.[9] Posthumanist scholars such as Cary Wolfe explore how both animal studies and disability studies can challenge the limitations of humanism.[10] The media remind us of the ways disabled and animal bodies are linked through adaptive technology, such as the carbon fiber "cheetah" legs some disabled athletes use to run and the variety of newly available prosthetics for different animal species. Scholars of disability are beginning to take up the question of animality in essays, books, and conferences. One particularly exciting example is the eco-ability movement, a growing group of disability advocates and scholars who are making powerful connections between the oppression of animals, disabled people, and nature. Scholars in the neurodiversity community are also leading the way, actively engaging with controversial questions about the relationship between animal and neurodiverse minds, as well as asking ethical questions about how we should be treating animals. It may be too soon to say that there is an *animal turn* happening in disability culture, but nonetheless we can see a greater acknowledgment of animals, gestures that may ask whether it is safe yet to fully consider them as kin. Will examining animals in relationship to disability remain demeaning, or can we make it enriching, productive, and insightful?

On some level identifying as animal has always felt right to me. As a small child I went through a short period where I would bark like a dog when people spoke to me. I didn't do this out of shyness; according to my parents, I did it because I truly wanted to be a dog. My parents were understandably horrified. Not only did they have to deal with the social implications of having a small child in a wheelchair, but now she was barking, too.

What would it take to claim the word "animal"? If, as I've written, animals can be crips, then can crips be animals?

I'm sitting in a cafe in downtown Berkeley as I write this. I have retrieved all of the objects I need from my bag and arranged them on the table in front of me. To do so, I had to put my mouth on the edge of my computer pad and bite down, wiggling it loose from my bag. I then pulled it out and laid it on the table, reached for my keyboard and did the same. I repeated this a few more times until I had everything I needed.

When I use my mouth instead of my hands in public I realize I am transgressing boundaries, not only of able-bodied etiquette, but of the ways in which one is supposed to inhabit a human body. We use the mouth for language and for eating, yet it is deeply private, an orifice containing germs and breath and slobber. The mouth is sexual. The mouth is animal.

Hands, however, are human. Humans are supposed to have opposable thumbs and dexterous fingers. Like walking upright on two legs, human hands have been said to represent our big brains—as hands make and use tools, they opened the door for human culture to emerge. Hands represent our physical agility and separateness from other species.

I feel animal in my embodiment, and this feeling is one of connection, not shame. Recognizing my animality has in fact been a way of claiming the dignity in the way my body and other non-normative and vulnerable bodies move, look, and experience the world around them. It is a claiming of my animalized parts and movements, an assertion that my animality is integral to my humanity. It's an assertion that animality is integral to *humanity*.

I do not mean this in a metaphorical way. It is not that we are *like* animals or that the *idea* of animals is integral to who we are—although both claims are true. It is that we *are* animals. A fact so boringly commonplace that we forget it—perpetually.

When I rummage through my purse with my face, sometimes getting spit on my cell phone or accidentally ingesting something unpleasant (though not as often as one might think), I remember Otis Jordan and the other freaks I hold as role models who move and use their bodies in beautifully strange and unique ways. I think of my roots, my heritage, and the crip community I call home. *And* I think of animals—pigs who root with their noses, birds who build nests with their beaks, and Bailey, my dog, who like so many other animals likes to make his bed. Bailey enjoys nesting, and since he doesn't have hands, he uses his mouth to create the perfect sleeping pile. He grabs the edge of his blanket in his teeth and pulls it this way and that. Sometimes he'll paw at it, but for the most accurate positioning he uses his mouth. Watching him do this, I feel a visceral understanding of his movements. It is not that I think I know what it feels like to be him, but rather that I recognize we share some similar gestures and perhaps also, despite our sensorial species differences, similar sensations—of taste, of sight, of smell. We are both animals.

# Part Four

All Natural

# 11

## Freak of Nature

THE FULL NAME OF MY MEDICAL DIAGNOSIS is arthrogryposis multiplex congenita. According to the medical field, arthrogryposis is relatively rare, occurring in one out of every three thousand births, but this statistic does not include the many goats, dogs, cows, rats, toads, and foxes who are born with arthrogryposis every day. In cows the condition has its own name, curly calf, and is found often enough on factory farms to have been the subject of the cover article of *Beef* magazine's December 2008 issue.[1]

Cows with curly calf are "destroyed" as a matter of course to prevent further loss of profits to the farms they are born on. As a human born in the twentieth century I was spared such a fate, and instead I was given surgeries and physical therapy as an infant to enhance the range of motion in my feet and legs. For the most part I look back on these medical interventions as helpful. Yet I often wonder what different motions and abilities I would possess if my body had been kept the way it was. What would living in that body have been like? Sometimes these reveries veer toward the sentimental—fantasies of an original body I no longer know. But I also find myself wondering how I would have gotten by if I had not had surgeries that allow me to briefly stand. How would I have adapted if I were that much "more disabled"?

My "naturally" occurring disabled body, compared to my medically altered body, is a point of fascination for me. Yes, it's probably a bit narcissistic, but it has also been a visceral opportunity for me to explore my own ableism and internalized oppression. I am attached to the body I have now: my feet that I can stand on but can never flex; my legs that hold me up, bipedal, but only briefly and with a posture "like a monkey." Would I have learned how to be within that other body as well? Would I have been attached to it—to the way it would maneuver through space and experience the world? Perhaps my own ableism runs so deep that I have projected it onto the "more disabled" body I had as an infant before medical intervention.

I am also drawn to consider these two bodies of mine because they raise questions about nature and what we think is natural. Without these surgeries would my body have been any more natural than it was with them? And what does *natural* mean anyway?

Where or what is my natural body? At what point—if ever— did I have one? My disability was caused by U.S. military pollution in the town where I was born. Everything about my story is typical: the military and its industries secretly dumping toxic chemicals in unlined pits in the ground for decades; the poor, largely nonwhite neighborhoods that were affected; and the fact that the pollution was directly poisoning the lands of the Tohono O'Odham Nation. My body was formed with the help of toxic chemicals, heavy metals, airplane degreasers—the mundane detritus of militarization.

It is hard for me to imagine my "natural" body—I never had a "natural" body to imagine. Because my mother unknowingly drank toxic waste from the faucet in our kitchen, as a fetus I was already being altered by society, by culture, by "man-made" products. Does this make me altogether unnatural?

I realize I am cavorting dangerously close to the cliché of the disabled person wistfully imagining her able-bodied self before or without disability. But what I am actually trying to find is a state of nature—a body without human intervention.

I see my own body as inseparable from human intervention— but what body isn't? In a time when honeybees are disappearing and polar bears are drowning due to humans' impact on the environment, it's easy to appreciate how whole ecosystems are affected by human society. More to my point, however, is the reality that we can never see nature through lenses that are not our own; we can never separate something called "nature" from our human perceptions of it. Even my perception that my imagined pre-surgery body would be more challenging than the one I live in post-surgery is entangled in deeply held assumptions about how a body should naturally look, move, and be in space. But what is this "nature" on which my judgments have been based? And how have I defined it?

The idea of a "state of nature," a nature before or without human culture, is a powerful one. It has informed our philosophical theories, our political systems, and our opinions about which bodies we deem livable and capable of pleasure, and which we deem exploitable, consumable, and edible. But is this thing we call nature actually justifying these judgments and distinctions, or are we?

# 12

## All Animals Are Equal (But Some Are More Equal Than Others)

PETER SINGER IS A UTILITARIAN PHILOSOPHER whose 1975 book *Animal Liberation* is often credited with starting the modern animal rights movement.[1] Although he certainly does not deserve all the credit, there is no doubt that Singer's book helped bring extraordinary attention to the movement. He made animal rights a serious topic of debate in philosophical discourse while simultaneously making it accessible to a broad population. The book has sold hundreds of thousands of copies since its initial publication and has also brought Singer himself into the public eye in a way few philosophers achieve.

As kids interested in animal rights, my siblings and I read many books on animal and environmental issues, but the one I remember most was *Animal Liberation*. I knew who Peter Singer was by the time I was ten. He was one of my heroes growing up and I remember thinking that anyone who would write a book called *Animal Liberation* must be someone I'd like. Imagine my dismay a decade later when I learned that much of the disability community hates the guy.

In an article called "Connecting Disability Rights and Animal Rights—A Really Bad Idea," Stephen Drake of Not Dead Yet (a disability rights group that protests assisted suicide as a form of discrimination) writes, "It's too irrational to expect people who make up the ranks of disability activists to want to build serious bridges with the animal rights community. I can't see us joining hands with a group that holds Peter Singer in such high esteem and at best expressing 'regret' for his writings on disability."[2] In a provocative essay that pushes disability studies to think beyond the human, disability studies scholar Eunjung Kim explained, "Given that the expansion of rights to sentient nonhuman animals in Singer's argument has not necessarily ensured the recognition of some individuals with disabilities as human beings, disability studies scholars have been understandably reluctant to step outside the boundary of human beings."[3]

What has Singer's work done to garner such strong reactions? In many of his books and articles he has argued that some disabled babies should be killed at birth and that some severely intellectually disabled people lacking specific cognitive capacities are not full persons. He has made numerous troubling quality-of-life judgments about living with a disability, insisting that it's "flying in the face of reality" to deny that on average disabled people's "lives are less worth living than the lives of people who are not disabled."[4] By "less worth living" Singer does not mean that disabled people have less of a right to live or that their lives are inherently less valuable; rather he is saying that disabled people have a lower quality of life—that disabled lives are not as satisfying and pleasurable as able-bodied people's lives. Still, this work has understandably led many disabled activists to distrust not only him, but the larger animal rights movement, as many of his ideas are considered foundational to animal rights theory.

It is arguably because of Singer that animal rights and disability rights are nearly always seen as at odds. While his work is celebrated in many animal rights circles, it is often met with ongoing protests by disability activists. Thus any book on the intersection of disability liberation and animal liberation must contend with Singer's work—not just to show that these fields are not incompatible, but that they are extremely relevant to each other.

Singer's arguments in *Animal Liberation* did not require a utilitarian framework (though they worked within one), but his commitment to utilitarianism sheds light on his perspectives on disability.

Utilitarianism is interested in how to minimize suffering and maximize non-suffering or, as philosopher Jeremy Bentham suggested nearly two hundred years ago, how to create "the greatest good for the greatest number of people."[5] If disability is viewed as a negative, as tragic, as lack—which is the dominant view of disability in the United States and elsewhere—then it is easy to see why it would be considered as undesirable, as something to be avoided, within a utilitarian perspective. The creation of a binary between suffering and non-suffering is one of the things that makes Singer, and utilitarianism more broadly, difficult to accept in disability studies and activism.

It's also important to note that, despite often being referred to as the "father of animal rights," Singer does not actually use the language of rights but rather relies on the concept of equal consideration. He writes, "The basic principle of equality does not require equal or identical *treatment*, it requires equal consideration. Equal consideration for different beings may lead to different treatment and different rights."[6] In other words, equal consideration does not demand that we give animals the right to vote or treat them just as we do human beings; rather, it requires that we take their feelings (their "interests") into consideration when making decisions that affect their lives.

Singer argues that the concept of human equality is jeopardized if we base our ideas on anything other than sentience. If we choose any other trait on which to base this belief—be it physical or intellectual—then we run the risk of excluding certain human beings. In *Animal Liberation*, he uses this logic to make an argument that sounds remarkably anti-ableist. He writes, "The claim to equality does not depend on intelligence, moral capacity, physical strength, or similar matters of fact. There is no logically compelling reason for assuming that a factual difference in ability between two people justifies any difference in the amount of consideration we give to their needs or interests. . . . It is an implication of this principle of equality that our concern for others and our readiness to consider their interests ought not to depend on what they are like or on what abilities they may possess."[7] Singer has in fact stated clearly that "the principle of equal consideration of interests rejects any discounting of the interests of people on grounds of disability."[8]

Singer argues that equal consideration ought to be based on sentience, because "the capacity for suffering and enjoyment is a prerequisite for having interests at all, a condition that must be satisfied before we can speak of interests in a meaningful way." However, as we have seen and as Singer explains, nonhuman animals are also sentient. To ignore the interests of nonhuman animals when they are also conscious beings who share the same capacity for having interests that grounds our own equality is nothing short of discrimination—speciesism.[9] Singer therefore concludes that we must acknowledge sentient animals' interests and reconsider the suffering that animals endure for the benefit of humans. This has heavy implications for our interactions with animals, especially those we eat, wear, and use for research.

Since the vast majority of meat and animal products come from factory farms, which are described in unflinching detail throughout *Animal Liberation*, and since these places are exceedingly well documented as bastions of cruelty, Singer advocates a vegan diet. Yet he is clear that he is not arguing that killing animals is necessarily wrong. It is the *suffering* inflicted upon them that he is most concerned about.

Singer does not end his argument at sentience, because if sentience were the only capacity that really mattered morally in terms of a right to life, then it would be as bad to kill a chicken, say, as a human being (as long as both were killed painlessly). Like most people, he has a hard time believing this. Causing the same amount of suffering, whether to a chicken or a human being, is equally bad. Killing painlessly, according to Singer, is a different matter—and it is here where a hierarchy of interests enters.

Animal advocate and philosopher Steven Best explains Singer's argument well, writing that Singer attempts "to distinguish between two different classes of life, not humans and nonhumans, but persons and nonpersons." Best continues, "Defining personhood as the possession of traits like the capacity to feel and reason, self-awareness and autonomy, and the ability to imagine a future, Singer finds cases of humans who are not, by this definition, persons (e.g., the comatose) and nonhumans who are persons (e.g., great apes and possibly all mammals)."[10] Singer suggests that the more cognitively complex a being is, measured by its understanding of death and its sense of itself through time, the more value that being will place on keeping itself alive. It is important to point out that Singer's conception of personhood belongs to a long philosophical tradition—he is not alone in privileging these attributes.[11] Within this framework killing a conscious neurotypical human would be worse than killing a chicken, because humans are rational beings who are aware of death and who experience themselves through time—they have goals and plans for the future that go beyond simply finding the next meal or sexual partner. The loss of a human's unfulfilled dreams adds to the wrongness of her or his death. So while cognitive capacities other than sentience don't play a role in the principle of equal consideration when it comes to suffering, they *do* play a role when it comes to killing.

It follows that if one were able to kill beings who don't have these cognitive capacities without causing them to suffer, it would not be as wrong to kill them as it would be to kill other beings who do—as long as the good consequences of doing so outweigh the bad. This is a complex calculation in Singer's work that involves the feelings and desires of family and community and numerous other factors. For example if the body of the being could be turned into meat and used to feed a number of people, or if the family of the being in question would be happier if the being could die peacefully rather than stay alive, then such factors would have to be taken into consideration and weighed against the harmful consequences of killing the being.[12] In fact, according to Singer, if the being in question were sentient but had none of the attributes of personhood he describes, killing them painlessly and instantly might not be wrong at all. These arguments are widely accepted when it comes to nonhuman animals. Singer's logic is invoked in Pollan's *The Omnivore's Dilemma* to explain why it is not wrong to eat animals who come from what Pollan calls a "good farm": if a chicken simply lives in the now and has no concept of death, what would be wrong with killing her if it were done painlessly?[13] Pollan is presuming chickens don't have these abilities, which is debatable to say the least—Singer himself has changed his view and now thinks chickens do have future-oriented interests.[14]

Of course, some humans also lack the abilities Singer mentions—specifically, infants and some severely intellectually disabled people. He therefore argues that if we are willing to say that animals are sometimes not full persons and that killing them painlessly can be justified, we have to be willing to say the same of human beings who lack the abilities that would make them full persons as well. To be clear, he is not arguing that it is always okay to kill a nonperson, but rather that killing a nonperson is less wrong than killing a person, as long as it is done in a way that does not produce suffering and as long as the killing produces more good than bad.

It is easy to see where this logic can lead and why so many disabled people regard Singer as, well . . . scary.

If Singer had left his argument in its simpler form, with the principle of equal consideration based on sentience, *Animal Liberation* would have been a remarkably anti-ableist book. His argument would have addressed the risks of using cognitive capacity as a yardstick of a being's value. But he didn't. Despite Singer's focus on sentience, in the end he rethrones rationality as the arbiter of personhood by arguing that the life of a full person is more valuable—because of the interests and desires that would be frustrated were it to end—than the life of a nonperson, who couldn't have desires and interests that would be frustrated. Despite the fact that Singer is radically challenging species barriers—human versus nonhuman is not the morally relevant dividing line for him—such an argument clearly has negative consequences for animals who do not have certain capacities. It also clearly has negative consequences for intellectually disabled humans. Within such a framework, these populations invariably become judged and consequentially categorized as less valuable.

Throughout his work Singer discusses a wide range of issues that are relevant to questions of disability, including infanticide and euthanasia. It would take a separate book to do justice to these arguments and the many others that emerge from his work. Instead let me focus on two important questions about his theories: Are the capacities Singer pinpoints adequate for judging one's interests in staying alive? And is it possible to analyze who does or does not have specific capacities? I will show that trying to answer these questions confronts us with a variety of philosophical and political conundrums and pushes us up against the boundaries of our own systems of knowledge. I will start with my second question, focusing mainly on disability.

Perhaps the most urgent problem with Singer's use of disability generally is that he understands it solely through a medical model, in which it is seen as a negative, a biological drawback that needs intervention and should be avoided. The other problem, as disability scholars and activists have pointed out, is that Singer knows very little about the disabilities he's discussing. He rarely includes the voices of disabled people themselves and certainly does not grapple with the perspectives of disability rights and justice communities. Most of his resources on disability come either from the medical establishment or from parents and legislation invested in the medical system. To be clear, Singer is not alone in his limited understanding of disability. As Licia Carlson has pointed out, philosophers have long seen disability—particularly intellectual disability—as a self-evident category that is objectively undesirable.[15]

In his work Singer refers to a wide range of disabilities to support various arguments he makes—spina bifida, cerebral palsy, Down syndrome, "severe intellectual disabilities," anencephaly, hemophilia. He repeatedly assumes that one can predict the capabilities and quality of life a disabled individual has or will have based on such a diagnosis without acknowledging that medical science has repeatedly proven to be extremely bad at such predictions (as we saw in medical professionals' historically low expectations for people with Down syndrome). All of the disabilities listed above are vastly different from one another and each is extremely variable. It is impossible to tell what capacities someone with spina bifida or Down syndrome might have simply based on her or his diagnosis. It is similarly difficult to judge a disabled individual's future abilities at infancy, which is the stage many of Singer's most controversial arguments focus on, as Singer supports infanticide in a certain number of limited cases (for example when a baby is experiencing perpetual pain, or when he believes a child will grow up experiencing immense suffering).

Although Singer often bases his arguments on specific court cases, stories that have made it into the media, and statements by medical practitioners and family members (as well as the rare disabled person), Singer also uses hypothetical situations or an "all else being equal" clause rather than real cases or experiences (something common to many philosophers). A good example of such a hypothetical arose in a debate between Singer and disability rights lawyer and Not Dead Yet member Harriet McBryde Johnson, who turned the conversation into an essay called "Unspeakable Conversations," published in 2003 in the *New York Times Magazine*. Johnson tells the story of a family she knew while she was growing up who took care of an unresponsive family member, a teenage girl. Singer then poses a question: "'Let's assume we can prove, absolutely, that [an] individual is totally unconscious and that we can know, absolutely, that the individual will never regain consciousness. Assuming all that, don't you think continuing to take care of that individual would be a bit—weird?' Johnson replies, 'No. Done right, it could be profoundly beautiful.'"[16] Regardless of one's own views on this particular hypothetical, it's important to point out, as Eunjung Kim does, that Singer's rhetorical move here takes us out of real life because "the absoluteness presumed by Singer is medically impossible."[17] Sometimes the hypothetical nature of his statements is clear, as in the example above, but often it is not. Singer repeatedly uses qualifying phrases such as "all else being equal" or "I will assume that," but the most subtle form of this sort of argumentation is evident in the use of words such as "severe"—the "severely disabled," the "severely intellectually disabled," those with "severe spina bifida"—which he relies on to give shape to the individual or group he is discussing. What defines the category of "severe"? Who decides what counts as "severe"? Am I severely disabled? I certainly have been called so. Should I hope that I am not? Should I defend my intellectual capacities and independent living skills and reject the label out of fear of being associated or confused with those who are "more" disabled than I am? Unlike the porous and broad meaning of "disability"—a word that has come to reflect the potential for community building and solidarity across difference in many disability communities—philosophical and medical framings of "severe disability" presume undesirability, objective tragedy, and potentially a lack of personhood.

Vague hypotheticals are arguments made in a vacuum that sidestep the messiness of consciousness and suffering. Yet by also bringing up specific disabilities and individual cases throughout his writing, Singer dangerously conflates hypothetical examples, medical diagnoses, and murky categories with actual disabled people and populations.

To begin to assess my first question—are the capacities Singer singles out adequate for judging one's interests in staying alive?—it might be helpful to ask another: what if ways of being and experiencing outside Singer's value system were also understood to confer personhood? Singer's work implies that it's not enough to have a sense of time that reaches only as far into the future as the next meal or sexual encounter. But why not? What about animals who prepare for the winter? Or pregnant animals who prepare for birth by building homes or saving food? Or, to ask similar questions for those humans with "severe" intellectual disabilities, what about looking forward to sensations one finds pleasurable? As we have seen, intelligence and emotional complexity take myriad forms. It is presumptuous to assume that certain concepts of the future and death are the *only* capacities that can allow individuals to value their lives. Who's to say there aren't other ways in which sentient creatures might experience themselves as living and dying beings? We know that various animals will go to extreme measures to save themselves from death, including causing themselves extreme pain (such as when an animal gnaws off her own paw to free herself from a trap).[18] It is clear that animals struggle to *survive*, even if they may not know that they could die at any time or that there is such a thing as death.

Disabled scholars and activists have long theorized the idea of "crip time." Crip time means many things to many people and acknowledges that we live at different speeds, that our very sense of time is shaped by our experiences and abilities. Time is relative. Writer and disability activist Anne McDonald describes her sense of time: "I live life in slow motion. The world I live in is one where my thoughts are as quick as anyone's, my movements are weak and erratic, and my talk is slower than a snail in quicksand."[19] Disability fosters a different sense of pacing, of progress, sometimes even of life span. If time can change so drastically for those of us for whom mundane tasks such as getting dressed, preparing a meal, or speaking take longer, then how might time be reconceptualized for those who have profound intellectual differences or for the great variety of animals? It is easy to jump from crip time to what we might call animal time—species whose life spans are only a few hours, days, or weeks, for example, certainly must have a different conception of time than those who live for one hundred or two hundred years. Whereas Singer's conception of time is rooted in Western notions of progress and future-oriented goals, crip time asks us to think about time as variable and changing with our embodiments.

The capabilities that Singer and other philosophers like him espouse as necessary prerequisites for personhood are subjective and embedded in ableist, neurotypical, and speciesist frameworks. That some beings lack capabilities valued by neurotypical humans tells us little about other morally relevant capabilities these beings may possess—capabilities that may be rooted in sensuality, in aesthetics, or in alternative temporalities. Even if certain capacities do make the sentience of some beings more nuanced than that of others, it should not follow that we have the right to take the lives of those we believe to be less "complex."

Where does moving away from a limited definition of personhood take us? I am unwilling to return to the framework of human exceptionalism that says all human life has value while the lives of nonhuman animals do not. Does this mean instead that the lives of all sentient beings are equal? Are we to say that the killing of a human and a chicken are equally wrong? I would rather leave these uncomfortable questions unanswered than embrace theories of personhood that demean the value of intellectually disabled people and nonhuman animals. It is better to acknowledge such uncomfortable spaces—ones that may remain open indefinitely—than to limit our moral understanding simply in order to satisfy some need for hierarchies of values. If our theories lead us to such conclusions, then they are not good enough or complete enough.

As confusing as these questions are, it is not of the utmost importance to me to answer them: to be forced to pit the values of different lives against one another is to take a philosophy of hierarchy for granted. I would rather ask how we can begin to create a world in which choosing between the lives of animals and the lives of humans (whether disabled or able-bodied) is understood as a false dichotomy.

I got a chance to meet with Singer in person in 2012 when he visited Berkeley. Sitting across from the person I had admired so much as a kid was an ambivalent experience, especially since he is quite nice and fun to have a conversation with. Even Johnson wrote that she liked Singer despite herself.[20]

During my time with Singer, I asked many of the usual questions that people ask him: questions about sentience and personhood, about the difference between causing suffering and ending life. I wanted to make sure that I asked him questions that accurately represented his ideas, because it's easy to misunderstand him or to oversimplify his arguments into negative sound bites. I still failed at times, conflating things he had written about different issues or unconsciously exaggerating his positions. He would call me out during these moments, and in turn I called him out when he said something stereotypical or presumptuous about disability.

After this went on for quite a while, I finally asked the question I'd been wanting to ask him for ages: does he think there are any possible positive effects disability can have on society and on individuals? Singer is so attached to his equation of disability with suffering that I wanted to see what would happen if he tried to think about it in other ways.

He seemed intrigued by my question and replied that he thought all people need obstacles to overcome on an individual level, that it builds character and can be satisfying to face challenges, and that perhaps certain disabilities could be satisfying in this way. But as far as disability having a positive effect on the world as a whole, he was more hesitant. Although he thought caring for and helping disabled people could develop certain altruistic qualities in others, he also thought there are already enough people on the planet who need support, such as those living in poverty. "In terms of diversity," Singer said, "I'm not sure. I think it is good to meet people who are different in a variety of ways, but again we have a lot of differences already in the world between people that we need to try and work out . . . so I'm not sure whether there's something distinctive that we get when we have people with disabilities. Maybe there is; maybe there are different things that we perceive. It's something that certainly can be considered."

"Let me ask you this, then, and I'm asking in all seriousness," I replied. "I'm wondering if you think those of us within the disability community who believe disability does have positive aspects, if you think we are just kidding ourselves. Are we just making the best out of a bad situation?"

Singer paused. "I do think there is something in that," adding, "I do think that people have that tendency. . . . But you know, I can't say that for sure. . . . I think it would be arrogant of me to be saying that that's always the case." He continued, "You know, I do ask people when they say something like that, I say, 'Does that mean if somebody offered you a pill that could cure your disability or cure your child's disability and it would cost two dollars and there were guaranteed to be no side effects that you would not use that?' And I think most of them would use it. Virtually all of them would use it. And if so, I think they are saying they are making the best of a bad situation."

"You see, I think most parents would use it, but most disabled people would not use it," I replied confidently.

"So you wouldn't use it?" Singer was clearly surprised.

"There's no way I'd use it!"

"Really?" he asked, even more surprised.

"Disabled people are asked that all the time," I said. "I think the fact that disabled people may answer 'no' is a really complicated thing for able-bodied people to understand."

"So try to tell me more why you wouldn't use it," Singer said, genuinely trying to figure this out.

I hesitated. *What do I find valuable about disability?* I remember thinking. *How do I even begin to answer that?* Here was my big chance to explain to Peter Singer why disability matters. I searched my brain for reasons—things about interdependence and challenging normalcy. But before I could gather my bullet points in my head, the artist in me burst forth with a reply.

"I'm an artist, and so I think about creativity a lot. Being disabled gives you a completely new way of having to interact with the world. . . . For instance, I was never taught by anyone how to use my mouth to do things. There is a certain level of creativity and innovation that goes into every single thing, which some people might find really frustrating, but for many of us who are actually living it, it's a very liberating thing to not have every aspect of your body already defined. . . ." Singer seemed amused but also interested. "I could list numerous reasons why I value disability and other disabled people and why I wouldn't take the two-dollar pill," I said.

I had the distinct feeling that we were like two beings from different planets trying genuinely to make sense of one another.

"But not all people with disabilities are artists or even think of their lives as art," Singer pointed out.

"Yes, but it's not only artists who feel that way. I happen to know a lot of artists, but I think there are many disabled people who value disability for the ways it gives a different perspective on the world."

Singer looked thoughtful. "It's true that Harriet [McBryde Johnson] basically said the same thing—that she was happy. And she was not an artist . . . she was a lawyer."[21]

Why wouldn't I take the $2 pill? Then I could run through open fields! Dance in circles on the beach by moonlight! Run up and down flights of stairs!

In her book *Feminist, Queer, Crip*, Alison Kafer writes that the repetition of the cure question, and "the fact that disabled people are consistently expected to address it, is part of what gives the question its strength, its compulsory and coercive power. It has become inescapable, and the answer is assumed to be self-evident."[22]

Despite ableist assumptions, disability is often incorporated into the lives of disabled people. It does not stop us from living fully. This does not mean that we necessarily enjoy being disabled all the time; it simply means that we live with it. It is not the be-all and end-all of our lives. We do not (or at least many of us don't) live our lives regretting all the things we cannot do, all the barefoot steps on the beach we would have taken were we not disabled.

When I told Singer that disability is creative, I was thinking about disabled dancer, artist, and poet Neil Marcus, who has said, "Disability is not a 'brave struggle' or 'courage in the face of adversity' . . . disability is an art. It's an ingenious way to live."[23]

I love this quote. It resonates with me both as an artist and as a disabled person going about my daily life, trying to figure out creatively how to reach something or to get somewhere. Marcus's statement challenges the idea that disability is simply lack; what's more, it asks us to look for value in ways of living that are not necessarily centered around efficiency, progress, independence, and rationality. Disability studies scholar Robert McRuer provocatively asks, "What might it mean to welcome the disability to come, to desire it?"[24] These sentiments challenge us to see the sensuality, the unruliness, the beautiful potential of living alternative ways of moving through space and of being in time. Disability can be liberating, exhilarating, a place of freedom from the continual work our society demands of us to be "normal."

Such perspectives are not only relevant to those of us with physical disabilities, as the wide variety of autistic pride and mad pride movements attest to, and more effort should be made to understand the creative, aesthetic, and sensual realities of individuals who lack the ability to express themselves through rationality and language. Consider the work of sociologist David Goode, who beginning in the 1960s spent decades observing children who were nonverbal, many of whom were also intellectually disabled. Goode describes working with Chris, a young girl who was deaf, blind, intellectually disabled and who was being institutionalized. Goode understood that he and Chris occupied two different sensory worlds, and decided that to find out what she was experiencing he would need to learn from her. Chris would repeatedly rock back and forth with her head bent at a particular angle, while rhythmically banging a rattle or spoon. After hours of observation Goode surmised that she had some hearing in one ear, and some sight in one eye. To grasp more fully what Chris was doing, Goode covered his ears and eyes attempting to simulate her sensory perception. He then began emulating her rhythmic rocking and banging. Goode found that when he rocked back and forth, it created a deeply pleasurable and stimulating rhythm of light and sound.[25]

Although partaking in such an activity for hours every day may not seem like a particularly enjoyable or meaningful thing to do to many people, the story makes us consider the experiences that people with "severe" intellectual disabilities can have—experiences that no doubt can be deeply pleasurable and meaningful, even as they remain hidden or even unknowable to the rest of us. Such a story could challenge assumptions that disability is only suffering and lack. The private nature of some experiences of people with disabilities, which vary widely, make arguments about quality of life and personhood fundamentally problematic to me.

As Harriet McBryde Johnson expressed so thoughtfully in her conversation with Singer, it's important to examine closely these issues of quality of life and suffering, because such ideas have a profound impact on the way people understand disability. As shocking and extreme as Singer's ideas may seem to some, they are rooted in widely held beliefs that disability is an inherently negative state that should be avoided. Kafer writes, "If disability is conceptualized as a terrible unending tragedy, then any future that includes disability can only be a future to avoid. A better future, in other words, is one that excludes disability and disabled bodies; indeed, it is the very *absence* of disability that signals this better future."[26] Singer is a particularly vocal proponent of the idea that disability is a negative experience that causes suffering, which understandably has led him to be a target of criticism from the disability community. Yet his ideas simply take common beliefs about disability to their natural conclusions. As Johnson suggests, the ubiquity of such opinions makes it difficult to pinpoint Singer's views as particularly horrible and single him out as some kind of monster. She writes, "If I define Singer's kind of disability prejudice as an ultimate evil, and him as a monster, then I must so define all who believe disabled lives are inherently worse off. . . . That definition would make monsters of many of the people with whom I move on the sidewalks, do business, break bread, swap stories and share the grunt work of local politics. It would reach some of my family and most of my nondisabled friends."[27]

Singer is able to make many of his arguments because many of his views already are widely shared by our society and medical establishment. He cites work by dozens of doctors to support the medical and quality-of-life claims he makes about certain disabilities, but he fails to recognize the biases medical professionals tend to hold against disability. He writes, "Many doctors and theologians, including those who are quite conservative in their moral thinking, agree that when a patient's prospects of a minimally decent quality of life are very poor, and there is no likelihood of improvement, we are not obliged to do everything we could to prolong life. For example, if a baby is born with severe disabilities incompatible with an acceptable quality of life, and the baby then develops an infection, many doctors and theologians would say that it is permissible to refrain from giving the baby antibiotics."[28]

But what exactly is an acceptable quality of life and who decides? Remember Amelia Rivera, the young girl who was denied a kidney transplant because of her intellectual disabilities? Was her quality of life "unacceptable"? Although Singer would likely not have supported that decision, as Amelia's parents were clear they wanted her to have a transplant, her story points to the dangers of relying on the medical establishment's views on disability and quality of life. Doctors, theologians, and parents of disabled children often have very different answers to questions of quality of life than disabled people themselves do. When it comes to infanticide, Singer and medical professionals usually discuss especially difficult situations involving infants born with large parts of their brains missing or with disabilities that cause extreme amounts of pain and drastically shortened life spans. The particularities of such cases are complicated and admittedly far from clear-cut. I should note that, perhaps in contradiction to some disability activists, I do not always disagree with Singer about conclusions he draws about ending life. Like Singer, I am not convinced that life is always the most compassionate choice in some cases. Although many of his conclusions are undeniably offensive and dangerous, for me, it is largely *how Singer argues*—his rhetorical use of stereotypes about disability, his assumptions about suffering, and his commitment to rationality as the only tool capable of defining personhood—that I seek to challenge here. Singer and the medical establishment whose work he relies upon repeatedly stray from the subtleties of particular cases, betraying their prejudice against things as various and broad as intellectual capacity, use of a wheelchair, dependency on other people (needing help with eating and toileting, for instance), life on a ventilator, and so forth. In this way, such quality-of-life arguments move beyond extreme cases of infant distress, as we saw in Singer's opinions on having a child with Down syndrome and of disabled people's lives as "less worth living." In such examples, he is not making a case about life and death—he is clear that his work is not in any way suggesting ending the lives of kids and adults with disabilities. Rather, in these moments, he is using the association of disability in general with a lesser quality of life to build the framework of his larger arguments. In my opinion, the reliance on that association is one way in which Singer goes very wrong.

Disability activists tend to cringe at the phrase "quality of life," as it has too often been linked to an ableist justification for the death of disabled individuals. When nondisabled individuals talk of wheelchairs, catheters, needing help with toileting, "diminished" intellectual capacity, or a general "lack of independence," they are basing their assumptions on imagined, rather than lived, experiences. It is difficult, if not impossible, to separate any of these experiences' inherent negativity from the negative cultural and social symbols they have become. Is needing help to wipe your ass inherently horrible? As someone who did need this sort of help as a child and who has countless friends who continue to navigate that need with dignity and humor as adults, I don't think so. In my own experience, it began to be uncomfortable for me only when I realized other people found it embarrassing, when it felt like this help was becoming burdensome to those providing it, and when I (wrongly) assumed it meant I could never be independent, move away from home, or have a partner. As in my case, it is the stigma around being a burden and needing help that is so often the issue, rather than the help itself. Given the power to choose who provides one's care, and when one is assured that it need not be embarrassing or shameful, the effect of such close care on one's quality of life becomes far more nuanced.

Johnson poignantly asks, "Are we 'worse off'?" She writes, "I don't think so. Not in any meaningful sense. There are too many variables. For those of us with congenital conditions, disability shapes all we are. Those disabled later in life adapt. We take constraints that no one would choose and build rich and satisfying lives within them. We enjoy pleasures other people enjoy, and pleasures peculiarly our own. We have something the world needs."[29]

Even when disability impacts one's quality of life, it is then a disturbing leap to argue that person's life is less satisfying and pleasurable than one without any disability. At the same time, none of this is to say that conversations about quality of life are never useful—the point is that we need to examine these issues with great care and individual attention, while being mindful of what assumptions, stereotypes, and prejudiced opinions underpin our positions.

In an article on Singer, Steven Best quotes disability rights activist Sarah Triano, saying that she is "absolutely confounded by the fact that Singer can so brilliantly make an argument for a social model of animal rights, but cannot seem to apply the same logic to disability. Is it impossible for him to imagine that certain humans might actually be subjected to the same kinds of oppression as animals?"[30] While Singer can clearly understand animals as living in an oppressive and discriminatory environment, he is unable to see that his arguments about disabled people's lives being less worth living are themselves born of discrimination. Best writes, "If in describing the suffering of animals Singer calls for their liberation, not their euthanasia, why then, Triano wonders, does he advocate killing infants sure to experience suffering in their lives rather than advocate social changes that might minimize their pain?"[31] This is one of the most contradictory aspects of Singer's work. He is explicit that just because a view seems like "common sense" or is widely held about animals does not mean the view is ethical or shouldn't be questioned. Yet "common sense" views are exactly what Singer uses to defend his thoughts on disability.

One of the most frustrating things about Singer's work is the way he puts disabled people on the defensive: we have to prove to him and his supporters that our lives are just as worth living as able-bodied lives. Yet Singer is not obligated to prove that our lives are less satisfying, because he has an ingrained culture of ableism, and what numerous disability scholars have called a system of compulsory able-bodiedness, on his side. Arguments that describe disability as a negative, a drawback, or something to be cured rely on the idea that it is simply "natural" and "normal" to think disability is a bad thing—it is "common sense," and everyone knows it. As Fiona Campbell writes, "Regimes of ableism have produced a depth of disability negation that reaches into the caverns of collective subjectivity, to the extent that the notion of disability as inherently negative is seen as a naturalized reaction to an aberration."[32]

I see my own defensiveness in my conversation with Singer. I was not content to say that some of us would not take the $2 pill—I said "most." But surely there are a lot of disabled people who do not enjoy being disabled, would laugh at calling it creative, and would no doubt be overjoyed at the thought of a cure— not necessarily because of ableism and internalized oppression, but because of loss, pain, or personal desires. What I should have told Singer is that it's fine if some people do not want to be disabled . . . but that doesn't mean we all do.

But even this response gives these questions far too much power. The cure question—as well as an overemphasis on suffering, an assumption that suffering negates fulfillment—has the effect of creating a false dichotomy between disability pride and medical intervention. Kafer argues that it is compulsory able-bodiedness and able-mindedness that is of concern, not "individual sick and disabled people's relationships to particular medical interventions," and that "a desire for a cure is not necessarily an anti-crip or anti-disability rights and justice position." She clarifies that she is not talking about cures but "speaking here of a curative imaginary, an understanding of disability that not only expects and assumes intervention but also cannot imagine or comprehend anything other than intervention."[33] The fact that many individuals desire cures, do not want to be disabled, or suffer a great deal from disability is not the issue. What needs to be challenged is the ingrained and ubiquitous assumption that these things mean that disability is objectively undesirable and that such feelings are the only reasonable response to disability.

Trying to prove whether disability is bad or good, whether it causes suffering or not, is ultimately a hopeless game, and it distracts from more important questions about vulnerability, variability, and what kind of world we want to live in. As we've seen, disability is also not only a lived experience, it's an ideology and a political issue that requires critical engagement. Disability is part of the reality of living in a body—*any* body. Disability should be understood, as Kafer writes, "as political, as valuable, as integral."[34]

Disabled scholars and activists have had to invest a lot of energy in dispelling certain stereotypes about tragedy and suffering, as these oversimplified tropes have played an essential role in naturalizing disabled people's inequality. After all, as feminist movements have long taught us, labeling something as personal rather than political is an excellent way for those in power to deny discrimination and inequity. These tragedy narratives are tools of oppression and abuse. They are the stories that convince us that we are not valuable and don't deserve jobs, education, romantic companionship, or a place in society. Striking a balance between admitting hardship and denying disability can be extremely challenging, as the supposed tragedy and undesirability of disability leads directly to discrimination. Disabled people are too often left in a quandary: they can compromise themselves by denying their own struggles or risk fanning the flames of ableism.

Compounding this dilemma is the simple fact that most of us can't easily separate and label our suffering and experiences. Disabled author and poet Eli Clare writes, "On good days I can separate the anger I turn inward at my body from the anger that needs to be turned outward, directed at the daily ableist shit, but there is nothing simple or neat about kindling the latter while transforming the other."[35] The inevitable tangle of external ableism, discrimination, and oppression with internalized ableism, pain, sadness, and loss makes disability a challenging, if not impossible, experience to unpack. It is crucial when considering disability to leave room for pain, which is an essential experience for many disabled people, and for the mourning that can come with living in a disabled body or mind. It is, however, also important to continually question why we feel the way we do and to remind ourselves that suffering and mourning are not unique to disability.

To use a personal example, early on in my relationship with my partner, David, I was sometimes embarrassed and saddened that I could not hold his hand when we went on strolls together. At first this emotion might seem rooted in my physicality—my arms and hands are simply too weak to do this. Sure, we could make some sort of contraption that would keep my hand near his, but no piece of adaptive technology would let me hold his hand, palm to palm, spontaneously, whenever we chose. I mourned this. But at a certain point I realized that this scenario was not solely personal and was not the simple product of my body's "lack of function." How would my notions of how a couple is "supposed" to interact differ if he and I had grown up in a culture where images of disabled or interabled couples were abundant, if we had seen people strolling together the way we do, with him leaning his elbow or hand on my shoulder and me leaning my head on his arm in return? Would I have felt the same loss, or would I have felt more confident that the way my body expresses affection is a valid one?

Our personal lives are deeply entangled with our sociopolitical world, so much so that even private moments of mourning and loss can't be isolated from the social environment. At the same time, it would be a form of denial to imagine that none of my challenges stem from my body, a denial that limits my ability to explore the implications of my physicality theoretically, politically, and artistically. Disability is not something that simply happens to me, as a strict social model of disability would have it; disability is, rather, an integral part of who I am, both in my creativity and in my challenges. By acknowledging the disability within my body, I am not only realizing my limitations, I am also allowing myself to examine my disabled body as a creative site with the potential for new ways of interacting with and understanding the world. It is important that disabled people take ownership of our suffering, of our moments of "undesirability," and tell our own narratives, because we should be able to suffer without the able-bodied world framing and stereotyping our lives. We all suffer, but suffering does not negate our other experiences.

It must be pointed out however, that as much as an overemphasis on suffering is clearly problematic, so too is a denial of suffering. The capacity to suffer is one shared across human difference and species. Suffering can be a place of empathy, of recognizing another's struggles. To deny someone's capacity to suffer is an act of extreme violence that humans have too often enacted on humans and on other animals.

What would happen if disability communities took back and reclaimed suffering, holding on to all we have learned about the dangers that lie within a discourse of suffering while simultaneously recognizing suffering as a place of potential empathy across difference? Disability studies scholar Susan Schweik shared with me her memories of Judith Greenwood, a disabled animal activist who attended UC Berkeley in the 1980s and passed away shortly thereafter. Schweik credits her with pioneering disability studies before the discipline even existed, saying, "I vividly remember Judith talking about her experience of being tortured—experimented on—by scientists and by doctors. It gave her a fire in her belly to prevent any being from being experimented on. She just had a complete connection . . . an understanding based in shared sentience, shared capacity, shared suffering."[36] An emphasis on suffering can perpetuate pity and stereotypes, but it can also inspire empathy and ignite this sort of passion for solidarity.

When I asked Singer if disability can offer anything positive to the world, his reply imagined disability as something negative that can potentially teach people about struggle, about overcoming, and about care. It is a common sentiment that suggests the only positive potential of disability is as a teaching opportunity for able-bodied individuals on how to be more compassionate. What this narrative misses is that disability can help all of us ask bigger questions about culture, politics, independence, productivity, efficiency, vulnerability, and the possibility of empathy and solidarity across difference—including across species. Disability asks us to question our assumptions about who counts as a productive member of society and what sorts of activities are seen as valuable and worthwhile. Disability asks us to question the things we take for granted: our rationality, the way we move, the way we perceive the world. It can present new paradigms for understanding how and why we care for one another and what kinds of societies we want to live in.

The late historian and disability studies scholar Paul Longmore described the value systems that have emerged from disability communities: "Beyond proclamations of pride, deaf and disabled people have been uncovering or formulating sets of alternative values derived from within the deaf and disabled experience. . . . They declare that they prize not self-sufficiency but self-determination, not independence but interdependence, not functional separateness but personal connection, not physical autonomy but human community."[37] These "values" of disability grow ever more important in our increasingly precarious world. I envision them extending beyond the human, creating paths of liberation that celebrate the interdependence, agency, and community—not only of humans, but of humans, animals, and the environment.

The question still lingers: how can disability movements be expected to build bridges with animal rights movements? My first response is to point to the criticism Singer's work has garnered from animal advocates and to recognize the alternative conceptions of animal justice laid out by feminists in particular.[38] My second is to call on disability movements to consider their own fear of difference.

It has been suggested to me numerous times that disability movements are resistant to animal issues not only because of the ableism voiced by Singer and others but because of their own speciesism. I think this is undoubtedly true, as is evident in many of the responses to Singer that have been voiced by disabled people and their allies. For example, Harriet McBryde Johnson brilliantly challenges Singer's arguments—she combats assumptions about quality of life with incredible wit and finesse—while at times she also basks in her lack of concern for animals, asking her assistant to make sure the sheepskin that she has draped on her wheelchair is visible. She later informs Singer that she would rather not learn about animal suffering. Johnson explains her resistance to animal issues this way: "As a disability pariah, I must struggle for a place, for kinship, for community, for connection. Because I am still seeking acceptance of my humanity, Singer's call to get past species seems a luxury way beyond my reach."

I find Johnson's lack of concern for animals troubling. Denying someone else's justice because you do not yet have your own is never a good idea. I am also convinced we cannot have disability liberation without animal liberation—they are intimately tied together. What if, rather than dismissing or disassociating from the struggle of animals, we embraced what political theorist Claire Jean Kim calls an "ethics of avowal," a recognition that oppressions are linked, and that we can be "open in a meaningful and sustained way to the suffering and claims of other subordinated groups, even or perhaps especially in the course of political battle"?[39] Compassion is not a limited resource.

Perhaps the most striking proof of the linked nature of disability and animal oppression is that the things in Singer's arguments that make it ableist also make it speciesist. By holding up particular capabilities related to rationality as the registrar of personhood (and of the protection from being killed that personhood offers), Singer's arguments reinforce not only a hierarchy of ability but also a hierarchy of species. Within this framework, species whose capabilities resemble (neurotypical) human capabilities are granted more protections. Those whose capacities we don't understand, or whose qualities are debatable, are then at risk of continued exploitation, ownership, and death. It's an anthropocentric framework that tries to solve complex problems of consciousness and personhood by delineating blurry differences between suffering and killing and by emphasizing the value of reason.

Contrary to what one might think of work by the "father of animal rights," Singer's writing is regularly used to justify commodifying and killing animals. His work has popularized an emphasis on suffering, which has narrowed animal ethics conversations to a focus on lessening egregious cruelty instead of challenging the systematic causes of animal exploitation and asking what animals need to flourish. With tens of billions of animals living life in terribly brutal conditions, it is not surprising that so much of the conversation within animal ethics has focused on suffering, of course, and I do not want to minimize the importance of raising awareness about animal cruelty. Nonetheless, the focus on suffering has its pitfalls. It offers only a limited understanding of animals as beings with interests, allowing people to continue to devalue animal lives. It also fails to challenge the multibillion-dollar industries that benefit from animal exploitation.

Animal welfare, largely viewed as the most popular and mainstream branch of animal ethics advocacy and philosophy, has been strongly influenced by Singer's theories around suffering. At the risk of generalizing a multifaceted term that can include both radical and conservative conceptions of human/animal relations, animal welfare in general sees animals as beings who must be treated responsibly because they can suffer but whom we can still use for our own benefit. Most Americans believe in some form of animal welfare, as can be seen in Gallup polls in recent years that consistently show that more than 94 percent of Americans say animals deserve some protection.[40] Those who advocate for animal welfare recognize that animals are sentient beings who can feel pain, but they do not necessarily believe in challenging anthropocentrism, the status of animals as commodities that can be bought and sold, or the killing of animals for human pleasure. The amount of suffering that an animal can endure before it is deemed unnecessary remains widely debated. Animal welfare legislation mainly focuses on making animal industries less cruel in targeted ways: banning gestation crates for pigs, for instance, or giving veal calves enough space in their pens to lie down and turn around. Such legislation, as minor as it can be, is nonetheless hard to get passed. Although recognizing animal suffering is crucial to improving how we treat them, focusing only on suffering leads us to ignore that animals may in fact value *living* itself.

At a certain point in the conversation between Singer and Johnson, he asks her how she can "have such high respect for human life and so little respect for animal life." She retorts, "People have lately been asking me the converse, how you can have so much respect for animal life and so little respect for human life." After a brief exchange in which Singer begins to tell her why in his view animals deserve our concern, Johnson replies, "Look. I have lived in blissful ignorance all these years, and I'm not prepared to give that up today."[41]

Singer, of course, can reply the same. Why shake up his perfectly logical, impeccably reasoned theories when he could just live in ignorance of disability?

# 13

## Toward a New Table Fellowship

In September 2010 I agreed to take part in an art event at the Headlands Center for the Arts in Marin County, California. The Feral Share was one part local and organic feast, one part art fund-raiser, and one part philosophical exercise.[1] I was invited to be part of the philosophical entertainment for the evening, serving as the vegan representative in a debate over the ethics of eating meat. I was debating Nicolette Hahn Niman, an environmental lawyer, cattle rancher, and author of *Righteous Porkchop: Finding a Life and Good Food Beyond Factory Farms*.

David and I got to the event as soon as it started but spent the first forty minutes or so sitting downstairs by ourselves while everyone else participated in the art event, which took place on an inaccessible floor of the building. Our only company was a few chefs busily putting the finishing touches on the evening's meal: a choice of either grass-fed beef or cheese ravioli.

David and I had been warned prior to the event about the lack of access, but we began to feel increasingly uncomfortable while we sat there waiting. The disability activist in me felt guilty that I had agreed to partake in an event that I could not participate in fully. My innocuous presence, as I quietly sat downstairs in my wheelchair, made me feel as if I were condoning the discrimination that was built into the physical space of the art center, as if my presence were saying, "It's OK, I don't need to be accommodated—after all, being disabled is my own personal struggle."

Our alienation was heightened when David and I were given our meal. As the only two vegans in the room, we were made a special dish by the chefs (some of whom were from Alice Waters's famous Berkeley restaurant Chez Panisse) that consisted mainly of roasted vegetables. I was about to expound to a room full of omnivores the reasons for choosing veganism, and I felt keenly aware of how this food would be read—as isolating and different, as creating more work for the chefs, and as less filling than the other dishes. I entered into the debate with a distinct sense of being alone in that room not only because I was the only visibly disabled individual, but also because I knew that David and I were the only ones without animal products on our plates.

Pollan writes in *The Omnivore's Dilemma* that what troubled him the most about being a vegetarian was "the subtle way it alienate[d] me from other people."[2] People who write about food often spend a surprising amount of energy deciphering how much social alienation they are willing to experience for their ethical beliefs. Countless articles in popular magazines and newspapers addressing the "challenges" of becoming a vegetarian or vegan focus on the social stigma one will face upon "going veg"—the eye rolling, the teasing comments, the weird looks. Jonathan Safran Foer writes that we "have a strong impulse to do what others around us are doing, especially when it comes to food."[3]

It is difficult to ascertain what role these articles play in marginalizing the vegetarian experience when there are so many more pressing issues that confront individuals who might otherwise choose to try to become vegetarian or vegan, such as the lack of healthy affordable food in low-income neighborhoods, often largely inhabited by people of color, and a government that subsidizes and promotes animal and sugar-heavy diets over ones with vegetables and fruits.[4] Yet rather than focus on these serious structural barriers, many articles on vegetarianism and veganism often present the challenge of avoiding meat and animal products as a challenge to one's very own normalcy and acceptability.

In the United States today, animal activists are regularly represented as overly zealous, as human haters, and even as terrorists, while vegetarians and vegans are often presented as spacey, hysterical, sentimental, and neurotic about food. Vegetarian foods

become "freaked," and meat alternatives are often described as
the results of lab or science experiments. Many animal protein
alternatives are not traditionally American, and the marginalization of these foods by casting them as somehow weird or unnatural works both to solidify an American identity ("real" Americans
eat real meat) and to exoticize the other. The abnormality of those
who do not eat animals is perhaps best exemplified by the name of
a popular vegan podcast and book, however: *Vegan Freaks*. That's
how many vegans feel mainstream culture perceives them.[5]

It's not that there are no challenges to becoming a vegetarian or vegan, but the media, including authors of popular books
on food and food politics, contribute to the "enfreakment" of
what is so often patronizingly referred to as the vegan or vegetarian "lifestyle." But again, the marginalization of those who
care about animals is nothing new. Diane Beers writes in her
book *For the Prevention of Cruelty: The History and Legacy of Animal
Rights Activism in the United States* that "several late nineteenth-
century physicians concocted a diagnosable form of mental illness to explain such bizarre behavior. Sadly, they pronounced,
these misguided souls suffered from 'zoophilpsychosis.'" As Beers
describes, zoophilpsychosis (an excessive concern for animals)
was more likely to be diagnosed in women, who were understood
to be "particularly susceptible to the malady."[6] As the early animal
advocacy movement in Britain and the United States was largely
made up of women, such charges worked to uphold the subjuga-
tion both of women and of nonhuman animals.

As this history suggests, not so very long ago Hahn Niman and
I would not have been invited to speak with any sort of authority on these topics simply because we are women. Hahn Niman
and I are also both white, however, and that reflects the reality
that racism is still largely an underaddressed issue within animal
ethics conversations. Although historically middle- and upper-
class white women have made up the bulk of the animal advocacy movement, it was not until the mid-1940s that they began
to achieve positions of leadership within it. People of color have
been even less likely to be included in these conversations, let
alone be recognized as leaders within mainstream animal advocacy movements. It unfortunately comes as no surprise that this

legacy of patriarchy and racism still deeply affects conversations around animal ethics, sustainability, and food justice. In 2012 the scholars Carol J. Adams, Lori Gruen, and A. Breeze Harper were driven to write an open letter of complaint to the *New York Times* for forming a panel that consisted solely of five white men to judge a contest for the best arguments defending meat eating. Over and over again, the people who are given conference speaking slots, publication opportunities, and media attention on these topics are white and male. Adams, Gruen, and Harper write, "The fact is that ethical discussions about eating animals are permeated with sexist and racist perspectives that have operated as normative."[7]

Because ableism has been rendered as normative and naturalized, disability and disabled people also have been largely left out of these conversations. The disability community has long had a strained relationship with the animal advocacy community, epitomized by the ongoing debates with philosophers such as Peter Singer. But even in less dramatic ways, disabled individuals and the various issues that affect us have been mostly excluded from the animal welfare and sustainability movements, whether because of the movements' obsession with health and physical fitness or a lack of attention to problems of access to different kinds of educational and activist events.

As I sat in that inaccessible space at the Headlands, waiting downstairs for the debate to begin, feeling like a freak in both my body and my food choices, I thought about Michael Pollan and the numerous other writers who speak of "table fellowship," or the connection and bonds that can be made over food. Pollan argues that this sense of fellowship is threatened if you are a vegetarian. Would I have felt more like I belonged if I had eaten a part of the steer who was fed to the guests that night? Of his attempt at going vegetarian, he writes, "Other people now have to accommodate me, and I find this uncomfortable: My new dietary restrictions throw a big wrench into the basic host–guest relationship."[8]

Pollan feels "uncomfortable" that he now has to be "accommodated." It is a telling sign of his privilege that this is a new experience for him. Disrupting social comfort and requesting accommodation are things disabled people must do all the time. Do we go to the restaurant our friends want to visit even though it has steps and we will have to be carried? Do we eat by holding forks in our hands, versus holding forks in our mouth or using no fork at all, to make ourselves more acceptable at the table—to avoid eating "like an animal"? Do we draw attention to the fact that the space we have been invited to debate in is one of unacknowledged privilege and ableism? For many disabled individuals, the importance of upholding a certain politeness at the dinner table is far overshadowed by something else: upholding our right to be at the dinner table even if we make others uncomfortable. Pollan assumes you can make it to the table in the first place. I looked around at the audience I was about to speak to and thought about those who were not at the table: people whose disabilities, race, gender, or income too often render them invisible in conversations around animal ethics and sustainability.

Safran Foer asks a simple question in his book *Eating Animals*: "How much do I value creating a socially comfortable situation, and how much do I value acting socially responsible?"[9]

My debate with Hahn Niman was like many other conversations between vegans and those who advocate for the consumption of sustainably raised meat: we debated the environmental consequences of both veganism and sustainable omnivorism, discussed whether veganism was a "healthy" diet, and spent a long time explaining why animals may or may not have a right to live out their lives free from human slaughter. Hahn Niman and I passionately agreed about the atrocities of factory farms, and we both understood animals to be sentient, thinking, and feeling beings, often with complex emotions, abilities, and relationships. Where Hahn Niman argued that it is possible to kill and eat animals compassionately, however, I argued that in almost all cases it is not and that the justifications for such positions are not only speciesist but ableist.

The debate was only an hour long, and I had previously decided that trying to talk about disability as it relates to animal issues would not be possible. But after being in that inaccessible space, I felt compelled to discuss it. I felt a responsibility to represent disability and animal issues to the best of my ability—to represent a model of disability I politically agreed with in the hope that some of the marginalization I had experienced would be acknowledged by others.

Throughout the debate I had tried to explain how my perspective as a disabled person and as a disability scholar influenced my views on animals. I spoke about how the field of disability studies raises questions that are important to the animal-ethics discussion. Questions about normalcy and nature, value and efficiency, interdependence and vulnerability, as well as more specific concerns about rights and autonomy, are central to the field. What is the best way to protect the rights of those who may not be physically autonomous but are vulnerable and interdependent? How can the rights of those who cannot protect their own, or of those who cannot understand the concept of a right, be protected?

I described how the animals that humans exploit are often disabled themselves. I spoke about how animals continue to be judged negatively when they do not possess certain human traits and abilities. I tried to share what I could about disability studies. But as the debate ended, I felt a sense of defeat creep over me— not over my presentation of animal issues, but of disability issues. I had a strong feeling that the disability politics I had articulated would be misunderstood: instead of people considering their own privilege as human and nondisabled, I would be seen as using my disability to boost animal issues.

The very first person that came up to speak to me introduced herself as the mother of an intellectually disabled child. She was both impressed with me, in a sort of super-crip way, and worried for me—like someone trying to save my soul. "This doesn't help your cause," she kept saying. "You don't have to compare yourself to an animal."

I understood where she was coming from. Individuals with intellectual disabilities have not been treated well by Singer's branch of animal ethics discourse. As Licia Carlson writes, "If we take seriously the potential for conceptual exploitation and the current marginalization of intellectual disability in philosophy, we must critically consider the roles that the 'intellectually disabled' have been assigned to play in this discourse."[10] I tried to explain that I was not really meaning to compare myself to an animal but was rather comparing our shared oppressions. Disabled people and nonhuman animals, I told her, are often oppressed by similar forces, but to me being compared to an animal does not have to be negative—after all, we are all animals.

She told me she did not want to compare her disabled child's situation to an animal's situation and that they were not related. Her child was not an animal. I was doing a disservice to myself and others by making these connections.

The woman never got mad at me, as I assume she would have with an able-bodied person saying what I was saying. Instead she seemed sad for me, as if I lacked the disability pride and confidence to think of myself as anything more than animal.

If I had demanded accommodation instead of politely following social etiquette and making others feel comfortable, would my confidence as a disabled human being have come through differently? If I had arrived at the event insisting on my body's right to access, would the confidence I have in my embodiment have been so unmistakable that even discussing my relationship to and affinity with animals would have been recognized as a gesture of my love for disability? Perhaps my behavior would have been seen as disruptive, perhaps it would have made others uncomfortable, but by demanding accommodation I would have insisted on a different kind of table fellowship.

The inaccessibility of the space framed my words that night and led me to focus on the ways in which animal oppression and disability oppression are made invisible by being rendered as simply natural: steers are served for dinner and disabled people wait downstairs.

# 14

## Romancing the Meat

IN *ANIMALS MAKE US HUMAN: Creating the Best Life for Animals*, Temple Grandin writes, "I vividly remember the day after I had installed the first center-track conveyor restrainer in a plant in Nebraska, when I stood on an overhead catwalk, overlooking vast herds of cattle in the stockyard below me. All these animals were going to their death in a system that I had designed. I started to cry and then a flash of insight came into my mind. None of the cattle that were at this slaughter plant would have been born if people had not bred and raised them. They would never have lived at all."[1]

Slowfood USA's "US Ark of Taste" program lists "over 200 delicious foods in danger of extinction," many of which are heritage breeds.[2] As Josh Viertel of Slowfood USA told NPR, "You've got to eat them to save them!"[3] Their tagline reads, "Saving Cherished Foods, One Product at a Time."[4] In many ways the "eat them to save them" logic of Slowfood USA is the pinnacle of consumer activism. By eating heritage breeds—by literally consuming individual beings who are transformed into products—we are not only helping small farmers, supporting local agriculture, and promoting biodiversity, but even saving the animals themselves.

Grandin wants to justify animal slaughter in general (including by the largest producers), and Slowfood USA wants to support small farmers. But in both cases the paradigm presents domesticated animals as being dependent on their very own exploitation in order to live. If humans don't eat them, these animals won't exist—they will go extinct. Grandin and Slowfood USA use the extinction argument toward different ends, but both argue that by eating animals we are doing them a favor.

When I moved to the Bay Area for graduate school in 2006 I assumed, as many people do, that it would be a safe haven for vegetarians and vegans. I was disappointed to learn that, despite the region being home to numerous excellent plant-based restaurants, my perception wasn't quite true. The Bay Area is also the home of author Michael Pollan, after all, who at the time seemed to be singlehandedly responsible for countless born-again omnivores. The Bay Area is also home to many local farmers such as Nicolette Hahn Niman and her husband, Bill, who are giving people alternatives to factory-farmed animal products; restaurants such as Chez Panisse, which cook those alternatives; a new, young, and fashionable generation of butchers and hunters; and even at one point a print quarterly dedicated to the subject of meat and art. Many in the area seem to have come to believe that vegetarianism and veganism are outdated solutions, ones advocated for in previous decades but now shown to be too simplistic and romantic for those who care about the environment in the twenty-first century. And the Bay Area is not alone. Across the country there has been a move away from the dichotomy of carnivore and vegan to a new middle ground: the conscientious omnivore.

The backlash against industrial meat has been brewing for many years and for many reasons. Ever-increasing awareness of the industry's horrendous impacts on the environment and on human and animal welfare is making it harder even for the most ardent omnivore to consume meat without guilt. Many people are not opposed to eating animals in general, however; they are simply opposed to eating industrially raised animals. Conscientious omnivores believe it is possible, and preferable, to eat meat the old-fashioned way—from small, sustainable, and local farms, produced by farmers who love their animals. "Local," "grass fed," "sustainably produced," "humanely raised," and "free range" are just a few of the benevolent-sounding phrases that greet conscientious shoppers in the meat, dairy, and egg aisles. Many of these products tout smiling pigs and happy farmers in green pastures on their packaging. For many people who care about the environment and animal welfare, choosing to eat "humanely raised" meat seems to honor traditional farmers and diets while also solving the ethical problems of environmental degradation and animal suffering.

Although I am very glad that an increasing number of people are waking up to the horrors of factory farms, the logic behind what has alternately been called "the new meat movement," "the humane meat movement," "the grass-fed meat movement," or simply "happy meat" (this last one usually said by fed-up vegans), is troubling. The conscientious omnivore's argument for animal consumption no longer relies on pesky goalposts that animals potentially could reach. Instead proponents of this position agree that many animals are complex and emotional beings but don't see this as an argument against eating meat or against commodifying animals for other purposes—just as an argument against causing egregious suffering. Their justification for using animals lies elsewhere, in nature.

"Nature" is one of the most common and compelling rhetorical tools used by those who justify animal exploitation and commodification. Arguments range from nuanced discussions of sustainable farming to popular declarations that animals eat other animals and that nature is simply "red in tooth and claw." Hahn Niman writes, "Clearly it's normal and natural for animals to eat other animals, and since we humans are part of nature, it's very normal for humans to be eating animals."[5] Pollan argues that vegans and vegetarians "betray a deep ignorance of the workings of nature" and accuses vegans of wanting to "airlift" humanity and all other carnivorous animals out of "nature's 'intrinsic evil.'"[6] British farmer Hugh Fearnley-Whittingstall deems vegans and vegetarians unwilling to admit basic facts when he reminds us that animals will never be "immortal."[7] Farmer Joel Salatin informs vegans that killing is inevitable by saying, "It is a profound spiritual truth that you cannot have life without death. When you chomp down on a carrot and masticate it in your mouth, that carrot is being sacrificed in order for you to have life."[8] These statements reflect the feeling I first confronted

during my years at Berkeley: a general sense that vegans are
naive—and are going against nature.

Conscientious omnivores argue that the relationship between
farmer and animal is symbiotic, a product of evolution that cannot simply be stopped, as it is central to who we are as a species.
Pollan explains, "To think of domestication as a form of slavery
or even exploitation is to misconstrue that whole relationship—to
project a human idea of power onto what is in fact an example of
mutualism or symbiosis between species."[9] In evolving with us,
domesticated animals helped shape who we are as a species (and
we in turn shaped them). This evolutionary relationship cannot
simply be abandoned. To try to escape this reality through veganism or vegetarianism is to deny the complexity of being part of a
larger ecosystem, and in fact, of being an animal in relationship
to other animals.

During my first few years in California, at the height of my
time painting from the photographs of the chicken truck, I was
struggling with the nagging feeling that I should become vegan.
Because I found this idea challenging and did not want to do it
immediately, I immersed myself in the vegan/omnivore debate
in order to gain a clearer understanding of the issues. Despite
my initial reluctance to renounce all animal products, the arguments for humane meat never sat well with me. Even then I was
troubled by the way conscientious omnivores presented a specific
relationship between farmer and animal as naturalized—as an
inevitable consequence of biology, species, and evolution. Many
years later, and I now believe even more strongly that such a relationship cannot exist. In presenting "symbiosis between species"
as something purely biological and depoliticized, conscientious
omnivores neglect to consider that the way we interpret such relationships, and the values we glean from them, are undoubtedly
political and embedded in power dynamics.

The way we view animals has been informed by centuries of
religion, politics, economics, social relations, and so forth. When
we consider just how much our understanding of nature has
shifted over even just the past few decades, let alone centuries,
or how much it shifts with cultural difference, it becomes clear
that we have always viewed nature through our own value sys-

tems and power structures. As Alison Kafer writes, "Our ideas about what constitutes 'nature' or the 'natural' and 'unnatural' are completely bound up in our own specific histories and cultural assumptions."[10]

Some proponents of the humane meat movement might respond that they know this—that they long ago disavowed the idea that nature is something "out there" separate from human culture. Others may say they already know our morality should not be based on nature. Pollan in fact argues this: "Do you really want to base your moral code on the natural order?" he asks, reminding his readers that "Murder and rape are natural, too."[11] But such statements are persistently contradicted by a reoccurring emphasis in these arguments on essentialized and depoliticized notions of biology, symbiosis, human evolution, and domestication (categories that are themselves defined by, and meaningful only to, humans).

Ableism is used to justify animal exploitation by presenting animals as incapable, but as I've researched over the years I've also realized it operates within humane meat arguments as well, by perpetuating the naturalization and normalization of animal oppression. When humans exploit, commodify, and harm animals, it is portrayed not as political, not as exploitation, but just as "the way things are." Whether through popular arguments about a biological need for meat or through more sophisticated theories about evolution and symbiosis, "nature" continues to be used to legitimize animal slaughter.

Appealing to nature as a justification for an ethical belief is a fallacy, one that has recurred in various cultural and historical contexts to justify conservative power structures. This is not to say that we shouldn't look toward the ecological for ways of being and living sustainably. Rather, our interpretation of nature cannot be separated from human culture and biases, especially because we inevitably understand nature through a long and pervasive historical paradigm of human domination over animals. The way we view animals is not "natural," just as the category of animal itself is not natural.

Even if nature were objectively separate from human thought and culture, as Pollan pointed out, it would not follow that it then should become our ethical model for living. John Stuart Mill argued over a century ago that "nature cannot be a proper model for us to imitate. Either it is right that we should kill because nature kills; torture because nature tortures; ruin and devastate because nature does the like; or we ought not to consider what nature does, but what it is good to do."[12] Despite their attachment to doing things "naturally," conscientious omnivores seem to agree with Mill to some extent: many choose humane meat as they believe that we have a moral obligation to kill animals humanely, even though humane slaughter is hardly natural.

Other animals with no alternative sustenance, often with specific dietary requirements, and with varying cognitive capacities for empathy do not seem to be appropriate role models for our ethical lives. We are animals that have evolved to recognize other beings' subjectivity, experience empathy, and make ethical choices. If a desire for meat is part of "human nature," it must be remembered that it is also part of "human nature" to question the way we live, to think about justice, and to change our habits to reflect the development of our moral lives. This doesn't make us better or more evolved than other animals—we all have different abilities, and one of those is the power to consider these sorts of ethical matters.

Yet Mill also missed an important part of the picture. Although it is undeniably true that "nature" does "kill" and "torture," it is also cooperative, compassionate, and just. An increasing amount of research is beginning to show just how many the social interactions among various species are affiliative rather than divisive or violent. Nature may be brutal, but it is also far more complex than a dog-eat-dog world. Marc Bekoff and Jessica Pierce write that the "consumption paradigm . . . has monopolized discussions of the evolution of social behavior. The predominance of this paradigm in ethology and evolutionary biology is both misleading and wrong, and momentum is building toward a paradigm shift in which 'nature red in tooth and claw' sits in balance with wild justice."[13]

People often see certain values as the consequence of our "natures": if we understand nature to be competitive and ruthless, then we would be denying our own natures to try to be otherwise. The act of eating animal flesh is seen as a way of coming to terms with our "animal natures," and many stories in the mainstream media focus on people resisting the supposed romanticism of vegetarianism (its desire to "airlift" humanity out of "nature's intrinsic evil," to quote Pollan again), by eating a grass-fed steak or by killing their own chickens or rabbits. These narratives suggest that we must overcome our naive and sentimental empathy for individual animals to grasp something greater: the cycle of life and death.

Of course we could just as "naturally" get in touch with our inner empathetic herbivore. It is true that we would still be causing death—while "masticating a carrot," say—but vegans are not opposed to death. We are opposed to the commodification and unnecessary killing of animals for human pleasure and benefit.

People also argue that it is better to eat animal products than not because such products are natural—they are the same foods our grandparents, and theirs before them, ate. But as Woodstock Farm Sanctuary founder Jenny Brown so unappetizingly points out in her book *The Lucky Ones*, doing things "naturally" is often a far more complex task than many omnivores think.

> First a worker "milks" the semen out of a bull—meaning he or she masturbates him. Then, the dairy farmer who purchased that semen pushes his arm up a cow's vagina to artificially inseminate her. A calf begins to grow, and eventually the cow's body begins to manufacture a food suited perfectly to that calf. . . . But instead of having her calf's mouth on them, the mother's teats are fitted with synthetic-lined metal cups. Her milk is sucked through tubes into a large vat. Because her teats are clamped repeatedly by a machine . . . she endures painful chafing and mastitis—an infection in her udder—which often leads to pus draining into the milk. Meanwhile, the cow has most likely been administered hormones and genetically manipulated so that she will produce up to ten times the amount of milk she would produce naturally. As a result, her body is under constant stress, and she is at risk for numerous health problems, which causes the farmer

to add antibiotics to this "natural" cocktail. Then, instead
of nourishing a newborn, that milk is taken to factories
where it is separated, analyzed for fat content, pasteurized
to destroy enzymes and microorganisms, sucked into an
electric churn via a plate heat exchanger, separated again,
and churned again. . . . Viola! "Natural" butter.[14]

Brown's details of butter production are only part of the story.
The description says nothing about dairy cows' shortened lives
(they are sent to slaughter for meat after living only a fraction of
their normal life spans), the cyclical nature of the process (cows
are kept in a continuous cycle of pregnancy, birthing, and lac-
tating), or the fate of their calves (who are separated from their
mothers when only hours or days old, the males to be made into
veal and the females headed to the same fate as their mothers).
Some of the details may vary on the most humane family-run
farm, but in general the story is the same: the cow is impregnated
by humans, has her calf—and the milk she specifically produces
so she can nurse that calf—taken from her, and is killed after only
a few years of life. How can a process that involves such profound
exploitation of a being's reproductive system be understood as
"natural," let alone justifiable?

However, the desire to be "natural" runs deeper in people than
choosing what to put in their mouths. The humane meat movement's conceptions of nature betray strikingly conservative ideas
about independence, labor, productivity, and value. Consider
a controversy that broke out in 2012 at Green Mountain College over the slaughter of the school's two working oxen, Lou
and Bill, who had tilled the school's land for nearly a decade and
were beloved by the community. The board of Green Mountain, a school known for its environmental and sustainable mis-
sion, voted to slaughter the two oxen for food when one of them
became disabled. The decision was made after Lou stepped into
a woodchuck hole, aggravating an injury in his leg. As the assistant manager of the farm told the *New York Times*, "His quality
of life is rapidly deteriorating, and this is the logical time to use
him for another purpose." Because the oxen worked as a pair,
and were both old, the school wanted to slaughter Bill as well.

Although numerous sanctuaries offered to care for the two oxen, Green Mountain continued to insist that Lou would be better off dead. The use of the ableist rhetoric of "quality of life" allowed the school to sound compassionate—supposedly having Lou's best interests at heart—while simultaneously emphasizing his work value and productivity. This is a common phenomenon: when animals can no longer earn their keep by working, their bodies must be put to work in another way—as meat. "It makes sense to consume the resources we have on campus," said the farm's director, Mr. Ackerman-Leist, who pointed out that the farm's purpose is to produce food in a humane and sustainable way, not to shelter animals. "We have to think about the farm system as a whole."[15] As the controversy became increasingly heated and public, the school decided to "euthanize" and bury Lou, but not without emphasizing the amount of meat that was wasted by not slaughtering him for food. According to the school's official statement, Bill was spared and left to live out his days at the school.[16]

Disability was used to justify Lou's killing, but ideologies of nature played a role as well. Feminist and environmentalist Marti Kheel argued nearly thirty years ago that environmentalists often betray a preference for the whole, the "biotic community," over the individual, creating a hierarchy of value that places more or less importance on different parts of nature.[17] Species and eco-systems are valued, while individuals are not. Wild animals are valued more than domestic animals. This view celebrates both the autonomy of non-domesticated species from human beings and a species' contributions to the larger whole of nature while suggesting that focusing on the well-being of individual animals, especially domesticated animals (who are often disdained for being dependent and unnatural, and are sometimes viewed as damaging to the larger biotic community), is naive and sentimental. This tendency is still evident in mainstream environmental movements, and pervades contemporary conversations about sustainable animal farming. Respecting the "farm system as a whole" required that people put aside their love for Lou and Bill, for example, and accept their slaughter as natural—an inevitability one must recognize in order to have a mature understanding of sustainability and the workings of nature.

Is it possible to value the ways in which various species contribute to keeping the larger environments thriving without erasing the value of individual animals' lives? Kheel thought so, arguing that this nature hierarchy has been perpetuated by centuries of patriarchal perspectives celebrating the value of abstract thought over care and relationship. In this hierarchy relationships to individual animals are devalued, and the broader "biotic community" is revered. Kheel's goal was to show that pitting these parts of nature against each other is unnecessary and rooted in patriarchal thinking. As is clear in Lou and Bill's story, and in the emphasis on autonomous wild animals over dependent unfree ones, this hierarchy has also been perpetuated by ableism.

The idea that some dependent individuals are less valuable and more justifiably exploitable because they are supposedly unable to contribute to society at large has historically been leveraged against disabled human beings as well. The philosophical tradition of the social contract can help shed light on why dependency in both humans and animals is so looked down upon, as it has helped shape Western concepts of care and contribution, privileging mutual advantage over other, less clear-cut forms of support.

In her book *Frontiers of Justice*, philosopher Martha Nussbaum shows how the tradition of the social contract has failed to provide justice for disabled people, nonhuman animals, and people living in less privileged nations. The social contract is a theoretical idea that emerged during the Enlightenment as an attempt to explain why individual, free, and rational people would choose to come together to govern themselves with laws in a society. The social contract framework suggests that people who were roughly equal in strength and cognitive capacity chose to leave a "state of nature" and govern themselves for mutual advantage.[18] Nussbaum argues that this profoundly influential theory nonetheless does not address disability, species membership, and nationality, as it "assumes that in a 'state of nature' the parties to this contract really are roughly equal in mental and physical power."[19] She points out that this assumption ignores physical and intellectual asymmetry between the disabled and able-bodied and between humans and nonhumans, as well as inequality between those who are born into wealthy nations and those who are not.

Nussbaum similarly shows how the social contract tradition's reliance on the idea of mutual advantage falls short when addressing disability and species membership, because disabled individuals and animals don't necessarily offer mutual advantage per se and in fact may occasionally offer a disadvantage. She argues that a more complete theory of justice must challenge this tradition and include more complex reasons for cooperation than advantage, such as love, compassion, and respect.

An interesting parallel to the idea of the social contract is available in the co-evolution theory that Pollan, Fearnley-Whittingstall, and other authors use to justify eating animals—what Pollan calls "mutualism or symbioses between species." According to this theory, human beings and domesticated animals have entered into a contract with each other that, like the social contract theory, is based largely in mutual advantage. This contract is a co-evolutionary pact that assigns humans the responsibility to care for these animal species in exchange for their services and flesh. To be vegetarian or vegan would mean abandoning those animals who are most dependent on us. Leaving them to their own devices, insist the proponents of this theory, would be a fate far worse than the dinner table.[20]

These theorists go on to say that if we look at matters in evolutionary terms, domesticated animals are doing remarkably well. Their populations are high and spread all over the planet, and they have another species—humans—providing them with food and shelter. The relationship of domestication and the killing that goes along with it are argued to be just as beneficial for animals as it is for humans. After all, if we didn't eat them, they wouldn't exist—they are, as Grandin explained, dependent on their own slaughter for their existence. Of domesticated animals Pollan says, "From the animals' point of view the bargain with humanity turned out to be a tremendous success, at least until our own time. Cows, pigs, dogs, cats, and chickens have thrived, while their wild ancestors have languished."[21] According to this line of thought, to stop eating animals would be to turn our back on this relationship and send these dependent, domesticated creatures out into the wild only to die of starvation or be brutally killed by other animals.

The idea that the enormous number of farmed animals constantly living and dying is somehow a boon to these species is a ludicrous misuse of the concept of evolutionary success. Yes, there are billions of animals on Earth that would not exist without farming, but these animals live in the most oppressive of environments from the day of their birth until the day of their slaughter. Bred as engines of profit for an unabashedly violent and immoral industry, these animals are kept from fulfilling even the most basic of their desires. How is that situation a boon or any kind of moral good?

Of course, Fearnley-Whittingstall and Pollan's point is that factory farms and the violence they cause are a terrible breach of our co-evolutionary contract, which is why Pollan permits the caveat "at least until our own time." This is a contradictory argument, however. Both authors cite high populations as proof that these species have become successful with our help and that the social contract between us is working, but in the same breath they declare that factory farms—which are the very reason for such high populations—violate the contract. Fearnley-Whittingstall says of factory farms, "This isn't husbandry. It's persecution. We have completely failed to uphold our end of the contract. In the face of such abuse, the moral defense of meat eating is left in tatters."[22]

The only reason there are so many domesticated farmed animals on the planet is that humans are constantly breeding them. If a species' evolutionary "success" is really what matters and justifies our exploitation of them, how can Fearnley-Whittingstall and Pollan argue against factory farming practices and for small, sustainable, local farms, which would inevitably lead to a drastic reduction in these species' populations if they became the norm?

A more pertinent critique of their arguments can be found in Nussbaum's challenge to the social contract and the power asymmetries in a so-called state of nature. To argue that animals were on a level playing field with human beings when this co-evolution contract was formed ignores the obvious fact that humans and animals have differing and highly varied mental and physical capacities. This bargain was not made between beings "roughly equal in mental and physical power," but between powerful human beings and more vulnerable animals. It is clear that this contract was written by the more powerful human beings to support their own interests: under it, humans benefit both as a species and as individuals, whereas animals "benefit" (if that word can be used at all) only as species, not as individuals. The question also remains as to how these animals agreed to this contract in the first place. Did they have a choice or were they denied the possibility of refusing the negotiation altogether?

Fearnley-Whittingstall and Pollan argue that on some evolutionary level the animals have agreed to be slaughtered, because animals tend to stay around human encampments even when there are no physical fences; thus, despite the inevitability of being killed, a relationship with humans must be worthwhile to them—worth even their own deaths. But not all fences are physical, as we humans know too well. One need only look at the history of male domination over women to see various psychological and economic fences at work in the rampant and insidious nature of patriarchy. One cannot argue that the domesticated animal chose slaughter any more than one could argue that generations of women chose patriarchy. Human domination is the system domesticated animals live under because there is no other system available to them.

Even if we accept this evolutionary contract and its symbiotic relationship between humans and domesticated animals as an accurate description of animal farming, we must still reevaluate what it is that animals have agreed to. Is it possible that on these "humane" farms, slaughter is actually a breach of contract between interdependent beings who are supporting each other? After all, these animals do far more for us than provide us with meat: if raised sustainably they help soil retain moisture, provide nutrients for our crops, and not least enrich our lives as friends and companions. According to Hahn Niman, Fearnley-Whittingstall, Salatin, and Pollan, we could not grow food sustainably without these farmed animals (which it should be pointed out, does not mean that the slaughter of animals is necessary, if true, only that access to their poop and their ability to graze is).[23] But instead of appreciating our mutual relationship, we charge them an extraordinary price: we breed them as we deem fit; eat their children; and then, when it suits us—such as when their dependency becomes burdensome—we kill them. This evolutionary bargain is clearly unequal.

Concepts of dependency play an important role in these arguments. Consider a quote from Fearnley-Whittingstall suggesting that it is our responsibility to kill animals because they are domesticated and thus will always be dependent on us:

> Of all the creatures whose lives we affect, none are more deeply dependent on us—for their success as a species and for their individual health and well-being—than animals we raise to kill for meat. . . . This dependency would not be suspended if we all became vegetarians. If we ceased to kill the domesticated meat species for food, then these animals would not revert to the wild. . . . The nature of our relationship would change but the relationship would not end. We would remain their custodians, with full moral responsibility for their welfare.[24]

Fearnley-Whittingstall argues that since we would still have a responsibility to these animals if we didn't slaughter them, we should eat them. He is not alone in such views. Historian and science writer Stephen Budiansky, whose book *The Covenant of the Wild: Why Animals Chose Domestication* helped popularize the co-evolutionary argument Fearnley-Whittingstall and Pollan use, presents us with an absurd and troubling image of human "excess kindness" and animal "degenerates":

> One may argue that domesticated animals are degenerates that through dependency and excess kindness from humans have become weak and ever more dependent on the crutch of human care. But calling them "degenerates" does not somehow mean they are less worthy of our consideration. If anything, their degeneracy . . . argues for an even greater responsibility on our part.[25]

Budiansky makes clear that domesticated animals' dependency, and their "degeneracy," is directly linked to how we humans have bred animals for traits that are often "troubling" for the animals, but "economically desirable" for us—traits that are linked to physical vulnerability and incapacity. For Budiansky, however, this is not unjust, as he argues that their "degeneracy" is in fact what has led to what he sees as these species' evolutionary success. Like Fearnley-Whittingstall, Budiansky views the dependency of domesticated animals on human care as an argument for raising, slaughtering, and eating them.

Dependency has been used to justify slavery, patriarchy, imperialism, colonization, and disability oppression. The language of dependency is a brilliant rhetorical tool, allowing those who use it to sound compassionate and caring while continuing to exploit those they are supposedly concerned about.

In many ways the thinking behind the humane meat movement is a philosophy built on the idea of interdependence. Domesticated animals and human beings have evolved together to be interdependent—animals help human beings, and we in turn help the animals—or so the argument goes. The interdependence theories of the new meat movement nonetheless still reward the independent at the expense of the dependent and the stronger at the expense of the more vulnerable. In contrast, disability communities have long recognized that interdependence is not a mutual-advantage calculation. Instead a disability perspective on interdependence recognizes that we are *all* vulnerable beings who will go in and out of dependency and who will give and receive care (more often than not doing both at once) over the course of our lives. What disability can bring to the humane meat conversation is a much-needed analysis of what it means to be accountable to beings who are vulnerable.

Kafer writes, "Visions of nature are often idealized and depoliticized fantasies, and disability plays an integral, if often unmarked, role in marking the limit of these fantasies."[26] Such visions of nature are evident in humane meat arguments, which betray a romanticization of a natural state of things that leaves out certain bodies and histories, including the disabled body. Narratives drawn from such essentialized visions of nature value strength, autonomy, productivity, and independence—the same patriarchal values that have historically fueled the oppression of more vulnerable bodies. This nostalgia for "how things used to be" and celebration of "how things are in nature" ignore how poorly some have fared compared to others.

As historian James McWilliams writes, "Pre-industrial farms were marked by radical and highly exploitative dependencies, environmental degradation, and highly abusive power relations codified in many cases by law. It's interesting, to say the least, how young people in particular have embraced the agrarian myth without appreciating the nature of these underlying historical realities."[27] Histories of racism, colonialism, and patriarchy have conveniently been erased from this idealized fantasy of preindustrial agriculture, while ableism and speciesism have simply gone unquestioned. Disabled, old, or vulnerable animal bodies, like those of Lou and Bill, are understood as having no use or value except as meat. If those bodies are human, they are often left out of the imagined agrarian utopia, with its emphasis on normative notions of health, fitness, and self-sufficiency. TV dinners, fast-food restaurants, and the decline of the home-cooked meal are subjected to countless critiques, and we are glibly warned that "the revolution will not be microwaved."

The reality is that not having to do everything from scratch, spending an eternity on the farm or in the kitchen, has been undeniably liberating for many people. Journalist Emely Matcher writes in an article on gender dynamics within what she calls the "food movement" (and specifically Pollan's work) that the "movement, with its insistence on how fun and fulfilling and morally correct cooking is, seems to have trouble imagining why women might not have wanted to spend all their time in front of the stove."[28]

It also seems to have a hard time imagining that some people can't do such domestic work even if they wanted to. Feminist disability studies scholar Kim Q. Hall points out the complexity of some people's relationship to fast food in her talk "Towards a Queer Crip Feminist Politics of Food," which she gave at the 2012 Society for Disability Studies conference.[29] Hall contrasts the wry humor of disabled activist and scholar Harlan Hahn, who joked that if every culture has its own cuisine, the cuisine of disability culture is fast food, with Pollan's book *Food Rules: An Eater's Manual*. Hahn was alluding to the fact that cooking is a difficult if not impossible task for many disabled people, and that disabled people are also disproportionately low-income, making fast food a regular choice of those with disabilities. But, Pollan's book *Food Rules* states, "It's not food if it arrived through the window of your car."[30] In another vein, at an event titled "Food, Justice and Sustainability," food justice activist Nikki Henderson pointed out that although fast-food restaurants are clearly problematic, they have provided accessibly priced foods to countless low-income people and are some of the only public spaces that include playgrounds, which can be a lifesaver for an overworked parent.[31] Both Henderson and Hall are extremely critical of industrialized agriculture and fast-food restaurants, as am I, but they also recognize that a radical change in our food system must not shame those who are on the front lines of food inequity. Too often we are confronted with a food movement that seems to care only about the well-being of those who can afford to pay for, or who have the privilege of growing their own, healthy food.

Can we crip sustainability? The point is not to shield our current agricultural methods and unsustainable food system from critique, but rather to ask how we can develop a sustainability movement that includes more bodies and more radical value systems. As a disabled person I realize that efficiencies such as microwaves, fast-food restaurants, and precooked meals help disabled, elderly, and low-income individuals who are pressed for time get by. I also know that the agricultural industry is responsible for vast amounts of human and animal illness, disability, and environmental destruction. I don't want the food my disabled family eats to be linked to animal, human, and ecological devastation and cruelty, but I also don't want food that is accessible only to those with fat wallets or so-called self-sufficient bodies. Can we acknowledge that not all people have the income, time, or desire—let alone ability—to be self-sufficient eaters, while simultaneously continuing to challenge the many abuses and inadequacies of our current industrialized food system? Can we create a movement where animals are recognized as more than dependent bodies that can be exploited and commodified? A more radical vision for a sustainable future needs to encompass values that aren't simply good for the environment and the individual consumer's health but also challenge historical paradigms of hierarchy and oppression, including ableism and speciesism.

Thankfully the sustainability movement is not monolithic and ubiquitously uninterested in such issues. Countless activists, community organizers, and farmers are far more nuanced in their considerations of the inseparability of environmental issues and complex social issues. For example, national and international food justice and food sovereignty movements are leading the way in demanding affordable, healthy, and sustainable food, justice for food workers, and the right of communities to control their own food systems. Such movements do not always address disability issues, and rarely do they promote veganism or vegetarianism, but with their emphasis on community control and empowerment, a focus on those who are the most vulnerable, and a vision of a more just future, such movements hold radical potential for anti-ableist and anti-speciesist frameworks. And there are some organizations that are making these connections. For example the Food Empowerment Project, an Oakland-based vegan food justice organization, connects issues of access to food, justice for farmworkers and low-income communities, racism, disability, abuse of animals, and environmental concerns. The Food Empowerment Project not only challenges food movements to think intersectionally (and to take animal suffering and veganism seriously), it also challenges animal advocates to think intersectionally as well, for example, pushing vegans and vegetarians to broaden their conceptions of the traditional vegetarian goal of being "cruelty free," to include the human costs of growing, picking, and processing plant-based food (they look at child slavery in the production of chocolate, and the extremely poor working conditions of field-workers who grow our produce).[32]

What I have attempted to examine here is a particularly well-publicized and privileged branch of the sustainability debate, a segment of the movement that—perhaps due to its many crossovers with those who would identify happily as "foodies"—has been particularly vocal in dismissing veganism and justifying animal consumption based on fundamentally ableist understandings of dependency, independence, and nature.

My criticisms of the new meat movement have not meant to deny the validity of its members' farming methods, knowledge of various ecosystems, or the importance of thinking about the biotic community or "farm system as a whole." Rather, I'm denying that their view of nature is the sole, unbiased one. "Humane" farmers' accounts are often taken as authoritative descriptions of animal behavior and romanticized as the ultimate human-animal interdependent relationship. But the reliance on farmers—such as Joel Salatin, Fearnley-Whittingstall, Hahn Niman, and the many others who actively participate in this debate—as experts on animals and nature is troubling. While these "experts" have great knowledge about certain aspects of animal minds and behavior, they are also biased in their views, not least because they profit off of these populations. A farmer is trained to see in a certain way, dependent on specific paradigms of nature. Too often farmers don't look for signs of intelligence, compassion, individuality, emotion, or a drive for life in animals, or even see those animals as beings who can suffer. Of course there are exceptions—many farmers know their animals individually—but even they can have a hard time resisting more oppressive mainstream perspectives. Consider Salatin, a passionate believer in sustainable farming who has become a leading voice in the humane meat movement. He understands that animals are capable of suffering and feeling pleasure, so he opposes factory farming just as much as any vegan. During their short lives, the animals on his farm seem to be genuinely content. But when asked by Pollan "how he could bring himself to kill a chicken," Salatin replied, "That's an easy one. People have a soul, animals don't. It's a bedrock belief of mine. Animals are not created in God's image, so when they die, they just die."[33] Even Salatin, a farmer praised for his compassionate treatment of animals, is caught in the old paradigm of species hierarchy and unable to imagine that animals may have souls—or that perhaps neither humans nor animals have souls. It's hard to see how Pollan then could claim that human ideas of power don't play a role in the relationship between humans and domesticated species, when the question of the soul has been integral to defining the categories of human and animal for millennia.

Troublingly, some of the very people who are leading the conversations around animal advocacy are profiting from the continuation of these oppressive systems. One of the most telling examples of this phenomenon is Temple Grandin.

Grandin's popularity is unquestionable. She is the author of numerous bestselling books and the subject of academic articles, documentaries, and even an HBO movie starring Claire Danes. Whenever there are accusations of animal cruelty on farms or slaughterhouses, you will likely see Grandin being interviewed as an expert on animal welfare and humane treatment. As an expert on cows and slaughter and a person with autism—a disability that is profoundly stigmatized in the United States—she is an unlikely and powerful American icon.

Grandin is best known for her books exploring her experiences of autism and her understanding of animal cognition. Her work as one of the first autistic people to speak publicly about being autistic is extremely influential. When Grandin first emerged as a public figure in the 1980s her ability to describe her sensory experiences and explain how she thinks (she has said that she is a visual thinker and "thinks in pictures") was groundbreaking.

Grandin has written that autistic individuals perceive and process information in certain ways that are similar to that of some nonhuman animals, and the fact that she supports animal consumption despite having these special insights into animal minds is often taken as the ultimate justification for eating animals. If Temple Grandin, a woman who says she thinks like a cow, supports eating meat, how could there be anything wrong with it?

But Grandin's view of the roles domesticated animals play in our lives is hardly unbiased. She designs slaughterhouses, consulting for huge corporations such as McDonald's and Burger King.[34] She has said that she does this work out of love: since the animals are going to be slaughtered anyway, the least she can do is make their deaths more humane.[35] Predictably, her argument has its critics. As Jim Sinclair, another autistic animal advocate, puts it, "If you love something, you don't kill it."[36]

Grandin believes she has a cognitive connection to nonhuman

animals, and she also understands her own experience of marginalization to be connected in some ways to animal oppression. But her conception of the ways in which autistic and animal minds are similarly misunderstood ultimately stops short of asking challenging questions about how disabled human beings and nonhuman animals are oppressed and exploited by neurotypical and ableist paradigms, questions that we saw for example in Daniel Salomon's critique of the argument from marginal cases and the emphasis on neurotypical thought processes in animal advocacy movements. By not pointing to intersectional violence and oppression, Grandin risks feeding into ableist stereotypes that uncritically associate autistic people with animals. She also satisfies the public's desire to have a clean conscience while eating at McDonald's.

Salomon, for his part, is protective of Grandin to a degree, arguing that some animal activists unprofessionally attack her character with stereotypes about autism—namely, that she holds the views she does because she is autistic and therefore "cannot empathize"—but he is also critical of Grandin's views of both autism and animals, as groups whose oppression Salomon sees as interlocking.

Grandin is not (and should not be represented as) an unbiased party when it comes to animal welfare; nor is she the only autistic individual with opinions on these issues.

Humane meat is an oxymoron, and its advocates know it. Read as Pollan tries to overcome his hesitation and shame in hunting a wild boar in *The Omnivore's Dilemma*; see newspaper stories on the new meat movement describing people trying to get over their uneasiness about killing and eating animals; listen to the Nimans' grief when sending their animals to slaughter; hear Grandin recall the horror she felt when seeing animals go to their deaths in a system she herself had designed.[37] Conscientious omnivores often struggle to overcome their own empathy toward animals.

I agree with those who support sustainable animal farming about the horrors of factory farms and the importance of environmentally sustainable agricultural practices. But commodifying and slaughtering animals for food is not natural or righteous—even if it's done on a small family farm or in a factory system designed to minimize cruelty. There are better ways to be humane.

# 15

## Meat: A Natural Disaster

FOR THE FIRST TIME IN HUMAN HISTORY our planet has reached a concentration of four hundred parts per million of carbon dioxide, an amount that scientists have long held to be a tipping point into environmental catastrophe. It is widely accepted that one of the leading causes of this disaster is industrialized animal agriculture. As temperatures rise, global food shortages increase, and natural disasters take countless lives around the world, we must ask ourselves whether a taste for animal flesh is worth the increasing environmental devastation it has helped create.

In 2006 the United Nations released the report *Livestock's Long Shadow* that went on to be widely cited and receive a flurry of media attention; it was met with both horror and denial. It estimated that "7,516 million metric tons per year of $CO_2$ equivalents ($CO_2e$), or 18 percent of annual worldwide GHG [greenhouse gas] emissions are attributable to cattle, buffalo, sheep, goats, camels, horses, pigs, and poultry"—more than the exhaust emitted from all transportation sectors (which is responsible for about 13 percent).[1]

A 2009 report showed things were even worse than the United Nations had thought. Environmental researchers Robert Goodland and Jeff Anhang from the organization World Watch Institute "concluded that over 51 percent of greenhouse gases (GHGs) emissions come from livestock." Their report makes an urgent plea for replacing animal products with alternatives, which they say "would be the best strategy for reversing climate change," because it would "have far more rapid effects on GHG emissions . . . than actions to replace fossil fuels with renewable energy."[2] About 37 percent of human-induced methane comes from livestock. Methane warms the atmosphere far more rapidly than $CO_2$ (over a twenty-year period it is somewhere between twenty-five to one hundred times more destructive[3]), but its half-life is only about eight years versus at least a hundred for $CO_2$. That means ending industrialized animal agriculture would have an immediate and dramatic effect to slow the pace of climate change.[4]

An earlier 2008 Carnegie Mellon University study already had showed that avoiding red meat and dairy for just one day a week achieves more greenhouse gas reductions than eating a week's worth of local food.[5]

More than 99 percent of the meat Americans eat comes from factory farms,[6] and our cheap meat habit is spreading at an unprecedented rate around the globe. In 2007 global meat consumption was at about 270 million metric tons and "growing at about 4.7 million tons per year."[7] Meat production worldwide has tripled since 1980, and predictions suggest it will double by 2050.[8] In many countries where meat used to be a luxury, it is now the centerpiece of every meal. The consequences of such an increase are unimaginable as humans and the animals we raise for food already now make up 98 percent of the world's mammalian zoomass, compared to 10–12 percent at the beginning of the industrial revolution.[9]

The meat industry is a $140 billion a year industry that occupies nearly a third of the land on the planet.[10] It is a leading cause of rainforest destruction (animal agriculture is responsible for 91 percent of the destruction of the Amazon[11]), and water pollution and waste (20–33 percent of the world's freshwater consumption is caused by animal agriculture[12]). The UN reports that since "there is now a global shortage of grassland, practically the only way more livestock and feed can be produced is by destroying natural forest."[13] In another sector, we are facing the total collapse of all fished species in the next fifty years.[14]

Countless articles, books, and scientific studies have already elaborated on this crisis—a crisis that environmentalists, scientists, and numerous outspoken omnivores agree is a disaster of epic proportions. But the environmental consequences of these industries can be felt on a far more intimate level as well. Our current food system is not only brutalizing billions of animals and contributing to the destruction of the planet, it is also harming people's health and contributing to mass starvation (consider the fact that 50 percent of the grain we grow worldwide is fed to the animals we eat).[15] Such disturbing facts point to the reality that food and environmental justice is inextricably connected to disability rights and justice.

In her book *Disability and Difference in Global Contexts*, Nirmala Erevelles addresses a perceived tendency within disability studies to romanticize and universalize the experience of disability. Disability scholars, activists, and artists—myself included—tend to fiercely embrace disability and see it as holding radical potential for creativity and alternative ways of being. Consider disability scholar Robert McRuer's question from earlier in the book: what might it mean to welcome or desire disability? Erevelles recognizes the value in this embrace of disability and its possibilities while also criticizing the failure to expose the systemic violence of capitalism that leads to disability. She asks, "How can acquiring a disability be celebrated . . . if it is acquired under the oppressive conditions of poverty, economic exploitation, police brutality, neocolonial violence, and lack of access to adequate healthcare and education?"[16]

Erevelles's question is vital to conversations about environmental destruction and agricultural practices, because industrial farming and the toxicity it unleashes in our communities are leading causes of illnesses, disabilities, and health concerns, which are more likely to impact low-income individuals—who, as we have seen, are already at increased risk of acquiring an illness or disability.

Factory farms and slaughterhouses are disproportionately located in low-income communities. So-called hog factories, for instance, produce huge amounts of air and water pollution that largely comes from the manure lagoons—huge pools of pig shit—always and necessarily present at these farms. The Food Empowerment Project reports, "Residents who live near these factory farms often complain of irritation to their eyes, noses, and throats . . . and increased incidents of depression, tension, anger, confusion, and fatigue."[17] These sites have been reported to have higher concentrations of dangerous groundwater nitrates and hydrogen sulfide, and "runoff from factory farms—containing a wide range of pathogens, antibiotics, and toxic chemicals—can permeate aquifers and contaminate surrounding groundwater sources."[18] Along with other health concerns, there are strong correlations between these pollutants and higher rates of asthma.

Yet despite all the evidence of industrial meat production's environmental and humanitarian harms, many people suggest that vegans aren't helping to change the world's food production systems, whereas conscientious omnivores are.

Safran Foer writes, "There isn't enough nonfactory chicken produced in America to feed the population of Staten Island and not enough nonfactory pork to serve New York City, let alone the country."[19] Labels such as "cage free," "free range," "natural," and "organic" often say nothing about the animals' treatment, and the industrialized operations behind them have simply managed to find loopholes for their products. These products become little other than part-time, feel-good conscience alleviators. When small-scale and sustainable farmers actually do succeed, their products are necessarily exorbitantly priced.

Conscientious omnivores excuse such high costs partly by pointing out that even sustainable meat should be eaten in moderation. But the movement also praises and glorifies animal products, casting doubt on whether getting people to eat less meat is really in line with its image. Trendy, socially conscious events serve sustainable animal products, while articles praise their mouth-watering taste, accompanied by glamorous photos of young hipster butchers and "compassionate" farmers. All of these articles mention that we need to be eating less and better meat, but it doesn't take an advertising expert to see that what is being sold are the animal products—not lentils and cabbage.

Increasing the availability and popularity of humanely raised and sustainably produced animal products does little to kick America's cheap meat habit, and it contributes to the growing international fetishization of meat as a class signifier. It is also debatable whether such products could ever be adapted to a national—or international—scale solution. Articles on the new meat movement never ask if all of the United States' animal products could be grown locally, and they never mention what the vast majority of Americans who can't afford these products would consume if all factory farms shut down: they would become vegan. To be clear I am not saying that sustainable farming can't work because it won't feed the world—in fact I argue it is the only thing that will work. But how much meat, eggs, and dairy can be produced under truly ecologically sustainable and humane conditions is another question.

Small family farms that try to treat their animals humanely and raise them sustainably are often caught in a catch-22, finding themselves unable to expand their businesses without lowering their sustainable and humane standards. This is what happened to Niman Ranch, which was a leader in sustainability for many years. Many restaurants sport signs reading, "We proudly serve Niman Ranch," and it's one sign that meat from small farmers appears to have become more widespread and accessible. But as the *San Francisco Chronicle* reported in 2009, "In nearly 30 years of existence, despite becoming the darling of high-end chefs and turning the brand into a household name, Niman Ranch never did turn a profit."[20] That year Niman's chief investor merged the company to keep it from going bankrupt, and Bill Niman himself was ousted from the company he had founded. Niman has since vociferously criticized the company for not keeping to his standards and has said he will no longer eat Niman Ranch's products. In a world with nearly 7 billion people, a growing number of whom want access to cheap meat, it is hard to imagine how these small family-run businesses could ever replace industrialized animal farming without inevitably morphing back into a similar system.

The question of how to grow food in a just way is relevant to vegans and omnivores alike. There is no doubt that access to healthful vegan foods is also a privilege and that the industrialized, crop-based agriculture that produces much of it also raises serious environmental and ethical concerns. For example, agricultural field labor is some of the worst-paid and most dangerous work in

the United States. The majority of workers are low-income people of color, who often are paid less than the national minimum
wage. A large but unknown percentage of these individuals are
undocumented and/or underage laborers.[21] The National Institute for Occupational Safety and Health reports that agriculture
ranks as one of the most hazardous industries in the United States
and that "agricultural workers experience increased rates of respiratory diseases, noise-induced hearing loss, skin disorders, certain
cancers, exposure to toxic chemicals and heat related illnesses."[22]
Every year ten thousand to twenty thousand agricultural workers
are diagnosed with "pesticide" poisoning, and the Food Empowerment Project reports that "long-term exposure to agricultural
chemicals is associated with severe health effects such as cancer,
neurological disorders including Parkinson's and Alzheimer disease as well as infertility and reproductive complications."[23]

Low-income individuals are also the least likely to have access
to healthy and environmentally sustainable food, whether vegan
or animal-based, and they are the most likely to live in neighborhoods affected by pollution caused by industrialized agriculture.
Given the fact that disability is statistically linked to low incomes,
people with disabilities clearly are among those who are least likely to have access to healthy foods, either vegan or animal-based.
According to a 2009 report prepared for the U.S. Department
of Agriculture, about 2.3 million people live more than a mile
away from a grocery store and don't own a car.[24] These people are
mostly in low-income neighborhoods predominantly made up of
people of color. Their food choices are often limited to fast-food
restaurants, liquor stores, and small convenience stores. Wealthy
neighborhoods have three times as many supermarkets on average
as poor ones do, while predominantly black neighborhoods have
four times fewer grocery stores than white neighborhoods and a
more limited selection of products.[25]

Access is only part of the problem. The cheap food available
to low-income individuals often makes them sick and can lead
to disability. While sugar is arguably the leading cause of food-
related health conditions, industrialized meat and animal products
are notoriously bad as well, leading to many diseases and health
concerns, including coronary and cardiovascular diseases, diabe-

tes, and various cancers.[26] In 2015 the World Health Organization released a study that concluded that processed meat causes cancer and that red meat "probably" causes cancer. The report placed processed meat into its Group 1 category, placing it beside tobacco smoke, asbestos, and alcohol.[27]

However, it is the people living near and working in these industries who are often most at risk of being harmed. Industrialized agriculture manufactures not only animal disability but also human disability. As with plant-based agriculture, the meat industry hires largely low-income people of color, many of whom are undocumented immigrants.[28] These industries are eager to hire individuals they know are unlikely, or unable, to demand better treatment, seek safer conditions and health care, or report cruelty.[29] Remember the thirty-two disabled men enslaved in an Iowa turkey processing plant mentioned previously?[30]

A slew of articles and books have emerged over the years that have brought to light the brutal reality of meatpacking work on employees. Books like Eric Schlosser's *Fast Food Nation* and Gail Eisnitz's *Slaughterhouse* have exposed meatpacking as the most dangerous occupation in the United States. Schlosser writes, "The meatpacking industry not only has the highest injury rate, but also has by far the highest rate of serious injury—more than five times the national average, as measured in lost workdays."[31]

Given how low-paying, dangerous, and grueling these jobs are, they have some of the highest rates of worker turnover—for meatpacking plants it's 100 percent annually.[32] The average plant hires an entirely new workforce every year.[33] Eisnitz writes that "a worker's chances of suffering an injury or an illness in a meat plant are six times greater than if that same person worked in a coal mine."[34] Eisnitz reports that over the course of her extensive investigative reporting she "heard of workers being crushed by cattle; burned by chemicals; stabbed; breaking bones; and suffering miscarriages and fainting from the heat, fast pace, and fumes."[35] Schlosser writes that the list of accident reports filed by the Occupational Safety and Health Administration for meatpacking jobs "sound more like lurid tabloid headlines than the headings of sober government documents" with employees losing limbs in meat grinders, getting crushed by falling carcasses, and being burned by hot vats of animal fat.[36] But both Eisnitz and Schlosser found that the most common injuries came not from accidents but from the standard practices that made up the jobs. Whether due to bagging intestines, trimming meat, dismembering cows, or bleeding pigs, the most commonly reported injuries in the meat industry are repetitive stress injuries. A Human Rights Watch report titled *Blood, Sweat and Fear: Workers' Rights in U.S. Meat and Poultry Plants* concludes, "The single largest factor contributing to worker injuries is the speed at which the animals are killed and processed."[37] Facilities often operate twenty-four hours a day, seven days a week, killing hundreds or even thousands of animals every hour. One worker said, "The line is so fast there is no time to sharpen the knife. The knife gets dull and you have to cut harder. That's when it really starts to hurt, and that's when you cut yourself." It's not unusual for a worker to make up to forty thousand repetitive cuts during a single shift. Employees experience chronic pain throughout their bodies, in their backs, shoulders, wrists, arms, and hands, but they are "scared silent," because they know they will lose their jobs if they complain.[38]

These workers also are exposed to a number of harmful gases and regularly inhale particulate matter, which is an innocuous phrase for such things as "dry fecal matter, feed, animal dander and skin cells, feathers, fungi, dry soil and bacterial endotoxins."[39] In pig confinement operations, nearly 70 percent of workers experience "one or more symptoms of respiratory irritation or illness."[40] Virgil Butler, an employee at a chicken processing plant, said, "If you stayed there very long you were going to get hurt. It wasn't a matter of if, it was a matter of when."[41]

Studies showing that employees of industrial farms and slaughterhouses experience high rates of psychological trauma make explicit the connection between animal suffering and human suffering. Workers whose job it is to kill animals have to watch them struggle for their lives. One former kill floor manager attests, "The worst thing, worse than the physical danger, is the emotional toll. . . . Pigs down on the kill floor have come up and nuzzled me like a puppy. Two minutes later I had to kill them—beat them to death with a pipe. I can't care."[42]

Butler worked at Tyson's Grannis slaughter plant in Arkansas for many years. He was known as "the best chicken killer in the state." In an interview with *Satya* magazine, he described his job,

> When I first started killing, it really bothered me. It bothered me because the chickens were hanging there in those shackles, helpless, and couldn't run away. . . . And it really bothered me when I missed one and heard the poor bird go through the scalder alive, thrashing and bumping against the sides of it as it slowly died. I worked to become really good at killing so that I wouldn't miss so many. I did become really good, but at a steep price. The more I did it, the less it bothered me. I became desensitized. The killing room really does something to your mind—all that blood, killing so many times, over and over again.[43]

Eventually Butler decided he did not want to kill any longer. In 2002 he contacted People for the Ethical Treatment of Animals (PETA) to expose what was happening at the plant. He spent the next four years advocating for animals and raising awareness about the exploitative practices of the meat industry before unexpectedly passing away in 2006.

The *Blood, Sweat and Fear* report explains, "In an industry where profit margins are slim and volume is everything, workers are endlessly pressured to kill more animals in less time. Rather than regulate line speeds for the interest of worker safety, line speed is limited only by federal sanitation laws."[44] Both Schlosser and Eisnitz confirm this policy and culture of speed, repeatedly describing how simple things such as bathroom breaks or taking a pause because of a sudden injury or illness cause people to lose their jobs. Workers are fired for taking doctor-prescribed sick leave, reporting their injuries, and complaining about animal cruelty. A 2016 report from Oxfam found that some poultry workers in the United States are resorting to wearing diapers as they are denied bathroom breaks.[45] These industries are also notoriously good at leaving injured workers without medical coverage, worker's comp, or any sort of compensation or livelihood.[46] After they are fired, these disabled and often undocumented workers find it

difficult if not impossible to find new work or health care. Eisnitz writes, "Drained of their usefulness to the slaughterhouse,
[disabled workers] are cast aside, reminders of a system that places
nearly as little value on human life as it does on animal life."[47]

From the dairy cow who has become lame due to confinement and over-production of milk to the worker with repetitive
stress injuries to the polluted and damaged environment, animal
industries produce disability. Farmed animals and employees of
factory farms and slaughterhouses are usually seen as at odds,
with workers relying on animal exploitation for their livelihoods
and animals being hurt and killed by these very people. But the
vulnerability of humans and animals in these industries exposes
just how utterly discardable and replaceable these industries think
humans, animals, and the environments that support them are.
This vulnerability across species creates powerful opportunities
for solidarity between workers, animals, environmentalists, and
all of us who want to challenge the meat industry's disregard for
life.

Pollution is a disability issue. Industrialized agriculture, factory
farms, and meatpacking plants are disability issues. Toxic waste,
economic inequality, climate change—all of these are disability issues, not only because all of them can cause disabilities and
make life harder for humans and nonhumans with disabilities, but
because ideologies of disability are central to how these injustices
are produced, represented, and dealt with. Disability and illness
are often warning signs for environmental damage—that the air,
soil, or water isn't safe, or that governments, corporations, and
industries are wreaking havoc on specific populations. As Erevelles asks, how can I celebrate disability as creative and valuable
when it is so deeply linked to suffering? The workers, consumers,
and exploited animals affected by industrialized agriculture have
had their bodies battered, poisoned, debilitated, dismembered,
and made ill by these entities. Isn't it offensive even to suggest
that their disability may not be a bad thing?

The hardest question philosopher Peter Singer posed to me
when we sat down together in Berkeley was whether my belief
that disability is not simply a negative experience in need of a cure
means we should take the warning labels off alcohol and other

things that cause "birth defects." If disability adds to the world, then why shouldn't we let pregnant women take thalidomide?[48] These questions were the most difficult to answer not because I didn't have a response but because of how hard they hit home for me, someone whose body was shaped by military pollution, and how utterly different my and Singer's understandings of an acceptable answer are. His question is not dissimilar to Erevelles's question about the difficulty of celebrating disability that results from poverty and oppression. But Erevelles also asks another question, reframing Robert McRuer's sentiment: "Within what social conditions might *we* welcome the *disability* to come, to *desire* it?"[49]

After September 11, when war was first declared against Afghanistan and the Bush administration warned that anthrax and other chemical warfare was being used against innocent Americans, I began wearing a homemade badge on the back of my wheelchair that said, "The U.S. Military and Its Garbage Made Me Disabled." I wore it as a way of protesting, a way of resisting the fear-mongering that enabled the United States to invade other countries, a way of saying, "Let's look at how our own country is poisoning people." Other people read it differently, telling me things like "I'm sorry to hear that" or "Well, you're sure handling it well!" I took it off when I realized that even those who read it as a criticism of our military also read it as a criticism of my body. What the badge probably should have read is "The U.S. Military and Its Garbage Made Me Disabled, and I Love My Body"—but the underlying sentiment is a bit too complex for a badge.

Erevelles's question resonates with one I have long struggled with in my own life: how can we criticize the systems that often lead to disability while simultaneously allowing disabled people to experience their bodies in empowered ways—or at least in ways that are not defined by oppression, discrimination and the able-bodied world? As Eli Clare asks, "How do we witness, name, and resist the injustices that reshape and damage all kinds of bodies—plant and animal, organic and inorganic, non-human and human—while not equating disability with injustice?"[50]

Like factory farms and slaughterhouses, war manufactures disability in the form of PTSD, wounded soldiers and civilians, and the lingering impacts of war's toxins—both purposeful, such as

Agent Orange and depleted uranium, and incidental, such as airplane degreasers buried in unlined pits in the ground. After people are harmed there are often no systems set up to help them figure out how to live their lives, let alone how the best way is for those lives to be interdependent and for institutions to support that. People who have become disabled by war largely end up impoverished, stigmatized, and unable to find work, health care, or community support. Then these disabled people are made into symbols of the horrors of humanity.

When disabled activists and scholars acknowledge that disability offers something valuable to the world, it does not mean we think we should actively disable people or celebrate when people acquire disability. Whether from war, slaughterhouses, agriculture, industrial pollution, chemical poisoning, accidents, disease, poverty, or a lack of social services, disability often results from terrible injustice; even when its source is more benign, it can still be traumatic. But acknowledging this pain does not negate the value that can come from the experience of disability. If the extent of my understanding of my body were simply "The U.S. Military and Its Garbage Made Me Disabled"—if my disabled friends thought of themselves only as representative of injustice— the world would be emptier, with fewer possibilities of alternative ways of being, communicating, moving through space, loving and caring for one another, building community, and, significantly, challenging the very injustices that gave and give us shape. Disability is too complex to write off as simply bad or good, but the industries and systemic inequalities that create it can be far more clear-cut.

# Part Five

---

## Interdependence

# 16

## A Conflict of Needs

DISABLED AND INCURABLY ILL for Alternatives to Animal Research (DIIAAR) was ahead of its time in so many ways. A group of animal activists active in the 1980s, DIIAAR was made up of people who identified as disabled and who explored animal issues through a lens of disability. Even now, as interest in the intersections between disability and animal advocacy is growing, DIIAAR is still the only animal activist group I know of to frame their activism in relation to both disability and animals. The fact that the group's founder, a disabled woman named Dona Spring, lived and worked in Berkeley while I was in school there made my belated discovery of DIIAAR bittersweet. For many years DIIAAR's office was located only a few blocks from my first apartment, though I didn't know about the group at the time. Spring died in 2008, the year I graduated.

Although I didn't know about DIIAAR then, I was growing increasingly committed to disability advocacy and identifying more and more strongly with disability culture while I was in Berkeley. At the same time I was confronting animal rights issues through the artwork I was making in school. I began to wonder how I could reconcile my own needs as a disabled person with the ethical issues around animal use that I was learning about through the research for the art I was making—oil paintings of animals in factory farms, like the painting of the chicken truck. After delving deep into the debate between vegans and conscientious omnivores, and after learning about egg and dairy production, I felt even more strongly that I wanted to become vegan. But I also felt that I was having a hard enough time trying to eat well as someone for whom even the most basic cooking presented serious challenges. If I had known Dona Spring at the time, I would have found out she was also confronting her own set of ethical contradictions.

DIIAAR was formed in response to an issue that has often positioned disabled individuals at odds with animals: animal research. Spring, her partner Dennis Walton, and activist Polly Strand founded the group in the mid-1980s to show that "disabled people did not want animals experimented on and tortured on their behalf."[1] In Lindsay Vurick's 2008 documentary *Courage in Life and Politics: The Dona Spring Story*, Spring says, "Since I myself have a disability and do use medications that have been tested on animals, I felt a responsibility to research whether or not this was really necessary to test these products on animals, because the thought of it was horrid to me. . . . There's something so contradictory about people wanting to relieve the suffering of people at such a horrid expense of suffering of animals." DIIAAR, she explains, was formed "to get people to try to understand that our own health advances, although they have been based on animals in the past, do not have to continue in that vein."[2]

Spring was a beloved Berkeley City Council member and an activist and leader for human rights, the environment, and animal rights. A fiery woman with arthritis, she used a wheelchair throughout her entire political career, which spanned more than seventeen years. She was an important voice in Berkeley politics and held a government post longer than any other Green Party member in U.S. history.[3] Out of an ongoing concern for animals, Spring was a vegan for much of her life.[4]

During the 1980s animal advocacy movements were growing and making significant headway in exposing the atrocities that took place behind closed doors—including those of scientific research facilities. In response to this threat, the American Medical Association (AMA), the largest association of medical doctors and students in the United States, devised a plan to combat the animal advocacy movement by capitalizing on infighting within it, and by criminalizing animal activists. Many of their tactics attempted to spin the conversation, changing phrases such as "Animals in Research" to "Advancing Biomedical Research" and decrying animal activists for obstructing scientific and medical progress.[5] The AMA's plan was not supposed to be shared with the public, but in 1989 a document titled "Animal Research Action Plan" was leaked to animal advocacy groups.[6] It stated, "To defeat the animal rights movement, one has to peel away the outermost layers of support and isolate the hardcore activists from the general public and shrink the size of the sympathizers."[7] One way to do that was to pit animals against disabled people.

The AMA helped promote a group called Incurably Ill for Animal Research (IIFAR),[8] a pro–animal research group of disabled and ill people. The role of IIFAR was to find disabled and ill individuals who were willing to testify on the benefits of animal research. The AMA supported IIFAR because one of the tactics stated in their plan was to use emotional appeals and heart-wrenching personal narratives to gain support for animal research and to present animal activists as dangerously anti-science and anti-progress.[9] At first this approach was controversial within the scientific community because it was seen as unscientific and too much like the tactics of the anti-vivisection movement, which often uses graphic images of animals undergoing disturbing experiments in their campaign literature. But the AMA's strategy was to "combat emotion with emotion," which meant contrasting the "fuzzy animals" of the anti-vivisection movement with what the AMA called "healing children": ill kids who had benefited from medications produced through animal research.[10] Initial reservations were overcome once the scientific community realized the efficacy of these tactics, and soon posters began to appear with images of young children pleading for animal research to help find cures for their illnesses. One such poster shows a little white girl holding a teddy bear and a toy cat. The top reads: "It's the animals you don't see that really helped her recover"; at the bottom is: "We lost some animals. But look what we saved."[11]

The campaign was not limited to posters: disabled and ill people gave interviews on television and testified in court. One of the AMA's goals was to work with organizations like IIFAR to publicize court cases in which someone could benefit from animal experimentation.[12] In one such case, a disabled child was brought in front of the Virginia state legislature in 1989 to plead with the court not to interfere with research that could bring cures.[13] The law that was eventually passed, in part thanks to this child's testimony, allowed for any pound animals without identification to be provided for animal research.[14]

At the same time, the late 1980s and 1990s were a period of passionate disability rights activism, much of which sought to raise awareness about the exploitation inherent in poster-children campaigns and telethons. From the 1950s onward, organizations such as the Muscular Dystrophy Association (MDA) held yearly star-studded fund-raisers that offered hackneyed portrayals of disability, playing on pity to raise money for cures. Although less acceptable now thanks to disability activists, the telethon was a symbol of American values and charity for many decades.

Many of telethons' harshest critics were former poster children who called themselves "Jerry's Orphans"—playing off Jerry Lewis's MDA campaign "Jerry's Kids."[15] Disability activists such as Mike Ervin, Cris Mathews, and Laura Hershey argued that telethons perpetuated damaging myths and stereotypes about disability through fear-mongering, infantilization, and pity.[16] Far from helping disabled people, this kind of representation actually helps perpetuate stigmatizing myths about disability that lead to marginalization and discrimination. The campaigns presented disability as pitiable, always in need of a cure, and as a barrier to a full life.

Like Jerry Lewis and the MDA, IIFAR and the AMA soon found themselves in opposition to disability activists. With Dona Spring leading the way, DIIAAR criticized IIFAR and the AMA on numerous media programs, including *The Oprah Winfrey Show*. DIIAAR's message was similar to the anti-telethon protesters': disabled people's experiences should not be generalized, stereotyped, and exploited. Disability and illness cure narratives used to promote animal research capitalized on the public's fear of disability and perpetuated the idea that disability drastically decreased one's quality of life. According to these narratives, disability and illness could be made bearable only by being cured, which in turn was possible only through animal research. DIIAAR grew out of disabled people's urgent need to tell a different story about disability and to express their own opinions about animal experimentation, which many found abhorrent and unjustifiable.

The U.S. Department of Agriculture estimates that 1.04 million animals are used for research every year in the United States. If this number seems surprisingly low it's because it excludes all birds, reptiles, amphibians, and agricultural animals used in agricultural experiments, plus an estimated 100 million mice and rats.[17] In addition, countless animals are bred for research but then "discarded" because they do not fit specific health, sex, or age requirements. Lawyer and animal advocate Gary Francione writes, "Federal estimates of animals that are discarded for these reasons are as high as 50 percent."[18] These discarded animals are not covered by anticruelty legislation.[19] Millions of animals, including tens of thousands of primates, cats, and dogs, are used for animal testing, much of which cannot be considered medically "necessary."[20] Some animals, like Ally the chimpanzee, are used for horrific toxicology tests for cosmetics, pesticides, and household products. Others are used in military research and so-called educational experiments in schools and universities across the country.

For decades, the use of animals in research, even for medical purposes, has been hotly debated. Many scientists argue that animals make poor models for human health due to species differences. Treatments often do not translate across species, and even high-quality studies too often produce unreliable results.[21] For example, various treatments for HIV have been effective in primate studies, despite not working in humans. Cancer studies have also been unreliable, with both causes and treatments proving hard to predict across species. Perhaps the most notorious example of the failure of animal testing though, was in the 1960s, when thalidomide was given to animals with few notable side effects. It was then given to pregnant women for nausea. Thousands of children were born with limb disabilities due to the drug.[22]

Many scientists argue that more accurate alternative technologies are now available, such as advanced computer modeling methods and in vitro studies based on human cells and tissues.[23]

Even back in the 1980s, DIIAAR knew that alternatives already existed (including in vitro options), and demanded that more resources be directed toward their use instead of animal testing. They argued that investing in alternatives would not only help the animals, it also would help disabled and ill people in need of treatment. In fact one of Dona Spring's repeated messages was that animal research could have a damaging impact on ill and disabled people when treatments tested on animals did not work as expected in humans, causing severe side effects or making their conditions worse—which she believed is what happened to her when she took an anti-arthritic drug that had been tested on animals.[24] DIIAAR was not against the search for cures; rather they recognized that claiming to advance the health of disabled and ill individuals at animals' expense was manipulative and misleading. The members of DIIAAR were also aware of their complex position as disabled people who had benefited from past animal experimentation. Where IIFAR saw disabled people as dependent on the continuation of animal exploitation, DIIAAR asked how this relationship could be challenged.

Since two of DIIAAR's founders are now deceased (activist Polly Strand passed away in 2003), it is difficult to find concrete information on the group, including how many members they had, what years they were active, and how the group ended. Dona Spring's partner Dennis Walton, who had also been with DIIAAR since its inception, kindly agreed to talk to me for this project and search his records for information on DIIAAR. Unfortunately most everything has been lost over the years, except for some of DIIAAR's old stationery with their logo (figure 4). The black-and-white logo uses a simple version of the International Symbol of Access, but with a heart on the chest and four silhouettes in the wheel: a monkey, a dog, a cat, and a rabbit. The image transforms the standard disability symbol into one that advocates for animals.

DIIAAR's greatest strength was that it entered difficult spaces of conflict and contradiction. Criticizing animal research as disabled people who had themselves benefited from animal testing, and challenging other disabled people who believed animal research was the only way to bring cures, DIIAAR went straight into some of the most heated areas of potential conflict between

Figure 4: The logo of Disabled and Incurably Ill for Alternatives to Animal Research (DIIAAR). The image transforms the standard disability symbol into one that advocates for animals. Image Courtesy: Dennis Walton.

the animal rights movement and the disability rights movement, instead creating opportunities for solidarity. DIIAAR recognized that part of the struggle for disability and animal liberation is acknowledging where the needs of animals and disabled people have historically been at odds.

During the last few years of her life, Spring faced yet another ethical dilemma placing her own needs in opposition to animal needs. As she grew increasingly ill and less mobile, her body began rejecting plant protein. Spring reluctantly began to consume small quantities of seafood in order to survive.[25] Where some people may have taken the contradictions Spring faced as evidence that holding on to one's animal ethics position is impossible or romantic, she mobilized the dilemmas and contradictions she lived into powerful activism. Her work leads me to ask how those of us invested in trying to figure out how to live ethical lives can embrace the inevitable contradictions we face, as productive spaces of inquiry and activist work.

One evening in 2007 I went for drinks with a few disabled animal activists. Although not the sole reason, this meeting prompted me to finally commit to being vegan. Talking to other disabled animal advocates forced me to acknowledge that I was participating in systems of animal commodification and suffering simply for my own convenience. I began investigating what I could change in my own life to make being vegan possible. I also began an honest effort to separate my own attachment to animal foods from my actual physical limitations.

At the time I thought of veganism largely in relation to my diet and other consumer choices. It was rooted in a love and respect for animals and was a logical extension of being vegetarian. (Because contrary to common perceptions, chickens used for egg production and cows and goats used for milk, and their continual supply of offspring, are always slaughtered for meat—except in the rarest of occasions when they are kept as companions or for some other special purpose—and in many ways have more brutal lives than animals used solely as flesh.) Over the years, however, veganism has come to mean something different to me, and I am now critical of the way veganism is framed as a "diet" or "lifestyle choice" that emphasizes individual health, fitness, and purchasing power. Throughout these pages, I have sought to show that ableism and speciesism are inextricably linked and that anti-ableist thinking has to contend with and challenge anthropocentrism. As we have seen, people justify eating animals—and using and killing animals more broadly—with ableist standards that create hierarchies of value based on mental and physical abilities. People also justify it through ableist conceptions of the natural and of dependency, which suggest that there is a depoliticized thing called "nature" that determines what kinds of bodies and minds are exploitable and killable, and that excuses using those who are weaker and dependent for our own benefit. When animal commodification and slaughter is justified through ableist positions, veganism becomes a radical anti-ableist position that takes seriously the ableism embedded in the way we sustain our corporeality—socially, politically, environmentally, and in what we consume. In other words, veganism is not just about food—it is an embodied practice of challenging ableism through what we eat, wear, and use and a political position that takes justice for animals as integral to justice for disabled people.

Food does play an important role, though, because animal commodification for consumption is one of the leading causes of the devaluation and objectification of animal lives. As feminist scholar Carol J. Adams has shown, animals metaphorically and physically must be turned into objects to be eaten.[26] This commodification allows us to separate a living being with her own life experiences, desires, and emotions from the slab of meat or even the cup of milk in front of us, and it is perpetuated by the ableism that structures our society. Of course countless objects we use in our daily lives are produced through violence and exploitation, from our computers and our clothing to many of the vegetables we consume. Why, one might ask, are we focusing on animal objectification and not human objectification? I think the question misses the fact that oppressions are not mutually exclusive: they are entangled and interlocking, as is so clear when we look at slaughterhouses themselves, where, as we have seen, animal and environmental destruction are wrought on the backs of largely low-income people, who are funneled into such undesirable jobs due to class, disability, and immigration status.

I am not trying to make a universal claim for veganism, as such arguments too easily gloss over important complexities, such as legacies of Western domination and the devaluing of differing perspectives and worldviews that have been part and parcel of it. But I am saying that we must take seriously the idea that disability liberation cannot happen when our environments, the species who share those environments with us, and the individual animals who live their lives entangled with ours continue to be seen through ableist and anthropocentric lenses that view them as things we humans can own and control—as discardable, fungible, and killable. Veganism is an embodied act of resistance to objectification and exploitation across difference—a corporeal way of enacting one's political and ethical beliefs daily.

Before becoming vegan, I was living in a delusion of independence, painstakingly cooking and cleaning for myself or, more often than not, forgoing the work by eating precooked meals or eating out. I would also rely on my nearby family, roommates, or partner for much of my food. Sometimes I did not eat enough and went hungry. When I was first trying to live independently, I went through months of being malnourished. I was ashamed to ask anyone for help accessing food.

Thanks to my disabled friends and community, and my politicization around disability, I finally realized that I needed a personal attendant. Because I lived in California, which recognizes more than most other states the importance of in-home care for disabled, ill, and elderly individuals, I eventually received support to hire someone to help me. This person cooked me healthy vegan meals and prepped my vegetables if I wanted to cook for myself. I discovered a number of small things I could do to make eating easier—the healthy foods I can snack on in a pinch, the lentils and rice I can safely cook in a rice maker, the joys of being a crip with a microwave. Yet because of the difficulties I faced in the seemingly simple act of feeding myself, I know how hard it can be for some people to eat a vegan or vegetarian diet. How do we as disabled people make sure we are eating healthy, plant-based meals when many of us have a difficult time making sure we are eating at all?

Cripping animal ethics means many things to me, including acknowledging that some people may be politically vegan in the way I have described but unable to sustain themselves on vegan food. This is true for people who have little to no control over their food choices, such as those in prisons and nursing homes, but also for those disabled people who rely on other people (sometimes people they were unable to choose) for their care and meal preparation. Or perhaps, as with Dona Spring, eating a vegan diet is too extraordinarily difficult, if not impossible, due to extreme health issues. I see this as a social model of veganism, a recognition that usually the biggest challenges to being vegan are not simply personal but structural—social, political, and economic.

Dozens of mainstream health organizations and countless highly respected studies confirm that for the vast majority of people being a vegan is safe and healthy when it is based on whole foods (rather than vegan doughnuts and soy dogs). The World Health Organization (WHO), the American Dietetic Association, the Physicians Committee for Responsible Medicine (PCRM), and the British Medical Association all recognize this fact, supported by the Oxford Study and China Study, among others.[27] As the American Dietetic Association states, "Appropriately planned vegetarian diets, including total vegetarian or vegan diets, are healthful, nutritionally adequate, and may provide health benefits in the prevention and treatment of certain diseases. Well-planned vegetarian diets are appropriate for individuals during all stages of the life cycle, including pregnancy, lactation, infancy, childhood, and adolescence, and for athletes."[28] For a large number of us, eating a plant-based diet is simply a matter of recognizing the violence animal commodification wreaks not only on animals, but on human beings and our environments. For others, including some people with disabilities, it is not so easy.

Cripping animal ethics means acknowledging that veganism as a diet is not as easy for some as it is for others, but that there are countless other ways one can challenge anthropocentrism, speciesism, and violence against animals. You can avoid animal products in other arenas, raise awareness about the violence of animal industries, participate in movements for animal liberation, protest the systemic economic exploitation of nonhumans, and you can bring an intersectional animal liberation framework into your other activist work. An expansive understanding of veganism leaves room for people like Dona Spring who embody a sort of disabled vegan praxis, a commitment to animal justice even in the face of contradiction.

Those of us who can refuse to eat animals and animal products

should do so. Critics of animal ethics and veganism too often justify meat eating by insisting that some people's health or circumstances depends on it. This argument uses other people's political
and economic struggles and serious health concerns as an excuse
to resist change. Increasing demand for healthier plant-based foods
and putting pressure on our government to stop supporting and
subsidizing animal products will make healthy plant foods more
accessible for everyone. This is not about wealthy or healthy people patting themselves on the back for doing something "good";
this is about the privileges of ability and access. It's about taking
responsibility for the cruelty and environmental destruction that
our food choices create for others.

Because I acknowledge these realities, some animal activists
may accuse me of privileging the needs of disabled and ill individuals over those of the animals they are consuming. This is a
legitimate criticism. My goal here is not to reify speciesism but
rather to acknowledge that right now, in this messy world, some
of us are in a better position to challenge animal exploitation
through our food choices than others. As Spring said, "Our own
health advances, although they have been based on animals in the
past, do not have to continue in the vein."[29] Cripping veganism
means working toward the goal of animal and disability liberation
while recognizing that our varying abilities enable us to work at
different speeds and in different ways.

# 17

## Caring Across Species and Ability

FEMINISTS HAVE LONG RECOGNIZED the importance of inter-dependence. Whether critiquing the ways in which caring for "dependents" has historically been made the burden of women, especially women of color, or drawing attention to an ethic of care—the ways in which caring should play a vital role in our conceptions of justice—feminists have a long tradition of under-standing humans (and often nonhumans) as interdependent beings who rely on one another. But while feminist theory has devoted much attention to what it means *to care*, less has been said about what it means to be *cared for*.

I have had a complex relationship to care. As a disabled person I espouse a philosophy of interdependence, of which care is a vital component, while simultaneously resisting the narrative that care—especially in the form of goodwill or charity—will some-how allow me to live a more liberated life. Being cared for can be stifling, if not infantilizing and oppressive, as of course can be the role of the caregiver. In her article "Building Bridges with Acces-sible Care," disability scholar Christine Kelly writes, "Theoretical work in disability studies implicitly and explicitly positions care as a layered form of oppression that includes abuse, coercion, a history of physical and metaphorical institutionalization, and a denial of agency."[1] Historically disability rights advocates have declared that we do not want to be cared for; instead we want rights, services, and an accessible society that does not limit our involvement and contributions.

Over the years there has been an emergence of feminist disability studies scholars and others who have tried to bridge these complications and build a theory of care that recognizes both the value and the oppressive histories of being both cared for and a caregiver. One of the aspects such work considers is what those who have historically been viewed as in need of care—those who have been labeled as dependents or burdens—contribute to their relationships, society, and the larger world.

Theories of care and interdependence also manifest themselves in a number of ways within conversations around animal advocacy, as we have seen most often in animal welfare debates. Domesticated animals' dependency on human beings for survival is frequently used to reconcile our responsibilities to care for animals with our continued use of them for our benefit.

In contrast, a feminist ethic of care regarding animals views animals and humans as entangled in interdependent relationships, recognizing that animals are often vulnerable and dependent but that they are not here for our own benefit or pleasure. This departs from rights theories with their rule-based principles in favor of what Carol Adams and Josephine Donovan describe in their book *The Feminist Care Tradition in Animal Ethics* as "situational, contextual ethics, allowing for a narrative understanding of the particulars of a situation or an issue."[2] A feminist ethic of care toward animals also avoids privileging such traits as rationality, autonomy, and independence—attributes that have historically been used to oppress and mark boundaries between deserving and undeserving beings. Adams and Donovan point to paying attention as an important part of creating more just relationships with animals. They suggest that attention needs to be directed not only to the individual animal, but to the systems that cause animal suffering.[3]

Within a feminist ethic-of-care framework, dependency does not justify oppression; it is rather an argument against it. Adams and Donovan explain, "Domestic animals, in particular, are for the most part dependent on humans for survival—a situation requiring an ethic that recognizes this inequality."[4] While many animal advocates have historically viewed animals simply as vulnerable victims in need of protection—seeing themselves as a "voice for the voiceless"—a feminist ethic of care offers a liberatory framework that has the potential to complicate conceptions of dependency by paying attention to domesticated animals' agency as vital participants in and contributors to our shared world.

Adams and Donovan emphasize the importance of paying attention to "what the animals are telling us—rather than to what other humans are telling us about them."[5] This is no easy task, but, as we saw with Yvonne the dairy cow who escaped slaughter, Janet the abused and rampaging circus elephant, and the many other animals who masterfully challenge their confinement and abuse, animals do speak to us—voicing their preferences and desires. An ethic of care asks how we can learn to listen to animals, and how we can help and care for them without the paternalism and infantilization that allows for them to be seen as voiceless. In a similar vein, philosopher Lori Gruen's work on empathy across species challenges us to consider how our empathetic responses to nonhuman animals can help us not simply to sympathize with their suffering but to consider what an individual animal wants, needs, and is communicating.

Gruen writes, "Being in ethical relation involves, in part, being able to understand and respond to another's needs, interests, desires, vulnerabilities, hopes, perspectives, etc. not simply by positing, from one's own point of view, what they might or should be but by working to try to grasp them from the perspective of the other."[6] These sentiments have important parallels in disability theory and activism that centers justice for people who are nonverbal with intellectual disabilities. Disability scholars, such as philosopher Eva Feder Kittay, have in fact said similar things—arguing that to understand the needs and wants of those who are nonverbal and intellectually disabled we need to be attentive to people individually, being in a position to recognize their particular sounds, gestures, and patterns, instead of generalizing based on diagnosis.[7] This sort of close and personal attention to difference is a crucial step in moving conversations about animal and disability liberation away from limited narratives of suffering and dependence to more radical discussions about creating accessible, nondiscriminatory space in society where humans and animals can thrive.

It is generally accepted that disabled people are dependent. We are dependent on caregivers for our physical well-being and often dependent on the government for our economic well-being. It is also generally accepted that animals are dependent. Domesticated animals are dependent on human beings in obvious ways: they rely on us for feeding, shelter, health care, and often even birthing and intercourse aid. Wild animals rely on us as well, albeit very differently: they are dependent on human decisions that involve their habitats, their food sources, whether they as individuals can be hunted or culled, and increasingly even whether their species will survive into the future.

My libertarian grandmother once told me I should be grateful for everything I get as a disabled person, because I'd "die in the woods" if left to my own devices. In a "natural state" there would be no question of my complete and utter dependence: I would quickly starve unless someone kindly decided to share their berries with me or (as my grandmother would have it) gave me some meat.

These are fighting words for a grandma—she was quite a character—but her basic thesis is widely accepted. The notion that disabled people have no place within nature and survive only thanks to other people's goodness is widespread. Yet my grandmother missed the fact that my able-bodied siblings would also eventually die in the woods if left alone with no human support or tools. They might make it for longer than I would, but odds are they would still go pretty quick.

Domesticated animals are similarly understood as utterly dependent, and unfit for the wild. Environmentalists, animal welfarists, and animal advocates have all portrayed domesticated animals as tragically, even grotesquely, dependent. Disabled people and domesticated animals are among those who have to contend with society's stereotypes about what it is to be unnatural and abnormal, as well as assumptions about the indignity of dependency. In many ways we have been presented as beasts and as burdens.

Dependence often becomes an excuse for exploitation, in part because it has extremely negative connotations—no one wants to be dependent. But the truth is that all of us *are* dependent. Human beings begin life dependent on others, and most of us will end life dependent on others. We humans rely on each other for services such as clean water, waste management, and electricity. We rely on a massively complex food system to feed us. Those who grow their own food still rely on water service, human-made technology, and human labor. Even the most self-sustaining people, who make their own clothes, grow their own food, and make their own tools and shelter, nearly always rely on others for some kinds of basic goods or services or at the very least for companionship.

In America, there is a strong emphasis on independence and self-sufficiency. The United States is romanticized as the country where everyone has the opportunity to become independent. Independence may be a value prized beyond all others in this country, especially when couched as "freedom," and for disabled people this means that our lives often are automatically seen as tragic. But how true is that view? Disability studies scholar Michael Oliver, like many other disability theorists, argues that dependence is relative: "Professionals tend to define independence in terms of self-care activities such as washing, dressing, toileting, cooking and eating without assistance. Disabled people, however, define independence differently, seeing it as the ability to be in control of and make decisions about one's life, rather than doing things alone or without help."[8]

The difference between the way many disabled people see dependence and how much of the rest of society views it lies in the emphasis placed on individual physical autonomy. In many ways independence is more about individuals being in control of their own services (be they electrical, medical, educational, or personal) than it is about individuals being completely self-sufficient; this is true not only for the disabled population but for everyone.

The negative consequences of dependency are largely human-made, whether through economic disenfranchisement, social marginalization, imprisonment, or societal, cultural, and architectural barriers. In many ways society's treatment of disabled people is merely a more pronounced form of the conditions faced by other populations. The point is not that nondisabled people and disabled people are equally dependent, but rather that the dichotomy between independence and dependence is a false one. Someone who is quadriplegic, for example, is not physically autonomous in the same way a nondisabled person is, but that does not necessarily make this person dependent. If this person has little to no access to assistant services, accessible housing, or transportation, she will at worst spend her life locked away in a nursing home or at best be subject to the whims of her family or volunteer caregivers, with very little recourse to change her situation. Yet if this person has access to the social services she needs to choose who assists her and an accessible environment in which to live and work, then her life becomes one of interdependence rather than dependence. The distinction may seem minor, but to many disabled people—a population constantly labeled as dependent and burdensome—any reminder to everyone else that they are far less independent than they think and, more important, that we are all actually interdependent, becomes vital.

Granted, not all disabled people can be self-directing. Michael Bérubé writes, "Autonomy and self-representation remain an alluring ideal even (or especially) for people with disabilities."[9] He points to the fact that there are individuals who rely on others for all aspects of their survival and lack not only physical independence but the ability to make choices about their lives.

All of us exist along a spectrum of dependency. The challenge is to understand dependency not simply as negative, and certainly not as unnatural, but rather as an integral part of our world and our relationships. Because disabled people are seen as burdens, our contributions to our families, communities, and cultures are often overlooked or flat-out negated. If we are perceived as having anything to offer at all, it is, as Peter Singer suggested, in the way that we inspire others, teach them lessons about overcoming obstacles, or engender charitable values. As we saw in the case of Lou and Bill, Green Mountain College's working oxen, disabled animals are viewed as burdens too—impacted by ableist human conceptions of dependency. The work that Lou and Bill were able to perform as able-bodied animals justified their right to live, but when the oxen grew frail the farm was adamant that it was not an animal sanctuary.

Domesticated animals have not only been presented as burdens that need to earn their keep but also as "unnatural," environmentally damaging beings created by humans. In 1948 conservationist and environmentalist Aldo Leopold wrote that a shift in values toward an ethics of ecology could "be achieved by reappraising things unnatural, tame, and confined in terms of things natural, wild, and free."[10] Leopold's celebration of the wild and autonomous in contrast to the unnatural and tame has been influential to traditional framings of environmentalism. Endorsed by various environmentalists, philosophers, and animal welfarists, this viewpoint at its most extreme presents domesticated animals as man-made, dimwitted, or, as we saw in science writer Stephen Budiansky's description, "degenerate" approximations of their "natural" and "wild" counterparts. Even environmentalist John Muir expressed disdain for domesticated animals, celebrating the autonomy of wild goats as "bold, elegant and glowing with life," in contrast to domesticated ones who he described as "only half alive."[11] This has a stunning parallel in commonly held sentiments that disabled people are incomplete or that, in the famous words of Jerry Lewis, to be disabled is to be "half a person."[12]

These views are based on the idea that unlike wild animals, domesticated animals are no longer natural, independent, and autonomous beings. Through domestication they have become extensions of human culture and technology—man-made, without an ecological niche beyond human use, and unfit for the wild or life without human caregivers.

The dependency and unnaturalness of domesticated animals is often referred to in tandem with their supposed "stupidity," as if the fact that they cannot take care of themselves "in the wild" proves their dimwittedness. For example, philosopher and environmentalist J. Baird Callicott celebrates wild animals while arguing that domesticated animals "have been bred to docility, tractability, stupidity, and dependency. It is literally meaningless to suggest that they be liberated. It is, to speak in hyperbole, a logical impossibility."[13] Because these animals are man-made and dependent, they are too stupid to be free—seeking their liberation is pointless.

These are ableist arguments, and, as we've seen, they are also untrue. The intelligence of domesticated farmed animals is all the more striking when one considers that they have been brutally kept in environments completely devoid of mental stimulation for generations; by what criteria does it make sense to judge their cognitive capacities? Even so, the idea that it would be "meaningless" to support a population's liberation because they are "dependent" and "stupid" is chilling. Callicott goes so far as to compare domesticated species with objects, suggesting that there is "something profoundly incoherent . . . in the complaint of some animal liberationists that the 'natural behavior' of chickens and bobby calves is cruelly frustrated on factory farms. It would make almost as much sense to speak of the natural behavior of tables and chairs."[14]

The presumed "unnaturalness" of domesticated animals has led some to conflate the environmental destruction wrought by animal agriculture and other animal industries with domesticated animals themselves, arguing that they are destructive to the environment and at odds with the natural world, including the habitats of wild animals. Although there is no doubt that animal farming and overpopulation has led to massive amounts of environmental destruction—some of the most serious environmental concerns we face—it's important to remember that these problems are created by humans through the forced breeding of animals in environments that are unable to support them. Domesticated animals should not be held responsible—or become the scapegoat—for these human choices. Consider another quote from Callicott: "From the perspective of the land ethic a herd of cattle, sheep, or pigs is as much or more a ruinous blight on the landscape as a fleet of four-wheel drive off-road vehicles."[15]

One wonders what Callicott would say of dependent disabled people going for a stroll or hike in our power wheelchairs. In her work on ableism within environmental movements, Alison Kafer shows how nature narratives are implied to be open only to those who can have an unmediated experience of "the natural." She writes, "A very particular kind of embodied experience [is presented as] a prerequisite to environmental engagement . . . to know the desert requires walking through the desert, and to do so unmediated by technology. In such a construction, there is no way for the mobility-impaired body to engage in environmental practice; all modalities other than walking upright become insufficient, even suspect. Walking is both what makes us human and what makes us at one with nature."[16] Domesticated animals are also suspect; they can never have an unmediated interaction with nature because they are already always polluted by human intervention. Not autonomous and not wild, they are equated with technology that harms nature.

What is left out of these arguments that despise domesticated animals as being dependent, unnatural, and unfree is the unquantifiable violence toward animals domestication has wrought. Domestication has led to the slaughter, commodification, exploitation, and systemic abuse of an unimaginable number of animals. Author Sue Donaldson and philosopher Will Kymlicka write that "for many animal advocates, [domestication] is irredeemably unjust; a world in which humans continue to maintain domesticated animals cannot be a just world."[17]

Because of what many animal advocates see as the inherent violence of domestication, it is common for animal activists to argue that the best thing for animals is to live entirely apart from humans and have nothing to do with us. As domesticated animals are dependent on us for their survival and cannot be separated from human society, however, many argue that they are better off not existing at all.

Animal abolitionists maintain that sentient animals have a right not to be owned, exploited, or killed for human purposes—as philosopher Tom Regan puts it, they demand "empty cages, not larger cages"[18]—and some suggest that domestication has created beings who are so vulnerable to human exploitation that the only ethical solution is to stop breeding them and let them go extinct. The reasoning behind an abolitionist argument for extinction is on one level very simple: if we stop bringing domesticated animals into existence, then humans won't be able to exploit them and make them suffer. This is pretty much the opposite of Temple Grandin's argument. Where Grandin sees animals' ongoing existence as enough of a justification to continue to use and kill them, many animal activists see the suffering and exploitation of domesticated animals as enough of a justification for their extinction. These animal advocates believe that we have a deep responsibility to treat the animals who currently exist with compassion and dignity while they are alive, as well as a responsibility to stop breeding millions of these animals every year—after all, so many animals exist only because humans breed them. Nonetheless, at a certain point a decision will have to be made about whether remaining animals are sterilized or kept from breeding on their own.

I understand why extinction may seem like the most responsible conclusion to the question of domesticated animals—after all we have done, why should we be trusted as caregivers? Even so, I find the extinction argument very troubling, especially when one recognizes the extent to which it is based upon assumptions about dependency, naturalness, and quality of life. Consider this quote by animal advocate and lawyer Gary Francione:

> Domestic animals are neither a real nor full part of our world or of the nonhuman world. They exist forever in a netherworld of vulnerability, dependent on us for everything and at risk of harm from an environment that they do not really understand. We have bred them to be compliant and servile, or to have characteristics that are actually harmful to them but are pleasing to us. We may make them happy in one sense, but the relationship can never be "natural" or "normal." They do not belong stuck in our world irrespective of how well we treat them.[19]

Francione's argument is bizarrely similar to Hugh Fearnley-Whittingstall's statement quoted earlier, even though they are arguing for completely opposed outcomes. Fearnley-Whittingstall argued that domesticated animals' dependency justifies our use of them because we are responsible for them. It seems clear that the dependency and vulnerability of domesticated animals makes people on both sides of the animal debate profoundly uneasy. The ableist assumption that it is inherently bad, even unnatural, to be a dependent human being is here played out across the species divide, showing once again just how much ableism informs our ideas of animal life.

Wild animals are romanticized in these narratives as the autonomous, independent, natural subjects long glorified by Western philosophers. Domesticated animals are seen as pitiable. In a parallel to the "better off dead" narrative of disability, domesticated animals are viewed as "better off extinct." As animal advocates Donaldson and Kymlicka insist, however, "this entire way of understanding domesticated animals is misguided, and indeed morally perverse."[20]

As we've seen with the frequently gross misjudgments of quality-of-life issues people make about disability, it's important to question assumptions about which lives are worth living. In fact it is impossible for me to consider the extinction view without thinking of the history and legacy of eugenics. As historian Charles Patterson shows, early eugenicists were inspired by the way animal breeds could be manipulated to have "better" traits. In the early part of the twentieth century, Charles B. Davenport—a leader in the American eugenics movement and a member of the American Breeders Association, a group devoted to furthering knowledge about genetics, heredity, and breeding—described eugenics as "the science of the improvement of the human race by better breeding." Davenport "stressed the importance of people's genetic history and looked forward to the time when a woman would no more accept a man 'without knowing his biologico-genealogical history' than a stockbreeder would take a sire for his colts or calves who was without pedigree."[21]

The American eugenics movement aimed to perfect the genetic makeup of the population by ridding the genetic pool of "undesirable" traits, which were invariably linked to disability, race, and class. What we have done to farmed animals has already been a form of eugenics—as Donaldson and Kymlicka write, "The overwhelming direction of domestication has been to breed specific traits in animals which increase both their dependency on humans and their utility for humans, with no attention to the animal's own interests."[22] We have selectively bred these animals to make them into better products, better specimens. In human eugenics, perfection meant getting rid of "unwanted" characteristics such as disabilities, while animal breeders have often pursued perfection by enhancing certain characteristics to the point where they easily could be classified as disabilities or deformities.

Now that these domesticated animals are here with us, do we really want to enact another coercive force over their individual lives and species by leading them to extinction based upon assumptions that their lives are less worth living than wild animal lives? I find the idea that the solution to the wrongs of domestication is to erase the very populations we have harmed unsettling. Instead I want to ask how we can dismantle the exploitative systems that have created these injustices in the first place. Part of this involves critiquing the idea that one's life is less valuable, worthy, or even enjoyable if one is vulnerable and dependent. We have made a massive mess in our treatment of domesticated animals, and we must try to figure out solutions that are equally massive in their complexity and nuance.

With regard to disability, I am not arguing that we need to continue to breed and propagate animals who grow so much muscle mass that their bones break under their weight, or animals whose udders produce so much milk that they are prone to broken bones, infection, and lameness. Before we can begin to untangle the ethical issues that we have created through breeding and exploitation, we have to unpack a lot of complex questions about our responsibilities to different breeds of animals, and far more consideration has to go into what disability means for different species and how different animals interact with disability. In short, when it comes to domestication and breeding, there needs to be a more thoughtful conversation about dependency and disability beyond simply using these concepts as a justification for extinction or for exploitation.

Donaldson and Kymlicka write, "Dependency doesn't intrinsically involve a loss of dignity, but the way in which we respond to dependency certainly does," offering the insightful example of a dog pawing at his bowl for dinner. "If we despise dependency as a kind of weakness then when a dog paws his dinner bowl . . . we will see ingratiation or servility. However, if we don't view dependency as intrinsically undignified, we will see the dog as a capable individual who knows what he wants and how to communicate in order to get it—as someone who has the potential for agency, preferences and choice."[23] Does an animal's dependence on human care have to be understood as inevitably negative or exploitative? Is it possible to have a relationship with domesticated animals in which humans recognize the value of these animals with whom we have evolved beyond a simple calculation of mutual advantage?

Caring for animals ethically means listening to what animals are telling us about the care they are receiving and the care they would like to receive. As Lori Gruen suggests, deciphering what animals need and want requires us to not only be actively attuned to our own empathetic responses to animals but also to invest energy in learning about their species' typical behaviors as well as their individual characters. If we tried harder to listen to them, would it challenge the infantilizing image some animal advocates have of animals as "voiceless" beings who simply need our protection? Would our visions for domesticated animals' futures be altered? As Josephine Donovan writes, "It is not so much . . . a matter of caring for animals as mothers (human and nonhuman) care for their infants, but of listening to animals, paying emotional attention, taking seriously—caring about—what they are telling us."[24]

Domesticated animals are dependent on us, which means we cannot simply leave them to their own devices, free from human interaction. But the truth is we cannot really do this for *any* animal (human or non), because we are all affecting one another and our environments all the time—all of us depending on one another—sometimes in terrifyingly intimate ways. Perhaps dependency is so uncomfortable precisely because it demands intimacy. With domesticated animals and with many disabled humans, there has to be involvement and interaction; there can be no illusion of independence. This vulnerability can create frightening opportunities for coercion, but it also holds the potential for new ways of being, supporting, and communicating—new ways of creating meaning across differences in ability and species.

Where are we left if the arguments for both domesticated animal extinction and continued exploitation are inadequate?

Viewing the dependence of domesticated animals through a disability liberation framework reveals new solutions to the problem
of animal exploitation and may also open up a third path in our
relationships with domesticated animals. Instead of continuing to
exploit animals or leading them to extinction, we could realize
our responsibilities to these animals we have co-evolved with,
and whom we also helped create. We could take seriously the
ways domesticated animals contribute to our lives and world, in
ways that don't involve slaughter. We could recognize our mutual
dependence, our mutual vulnerability, and our mutual drive for
life. We could also start listening to what those who need care
are communicating about their own lives, feelings, and the care
they are receiving. As Donaldson and Kymlicka suggest, we could
recognize that we are all citizens of shared communities.

For better or for worse, our co-evolution with domesticated
species has created animals with whom we are deeply entangled,
both ecologically and emotionally. These animals remind us that
we ourselves are a part of nature, but they also remind us that we
are capable of deep coercion and exploitation—that we have too
often dominated those we deem dependent and vulnerable. To do
right by these animals now means respecting their dependence,
their interdependence, and indeed their naturalness as beings who
have just as much of a right to live out their lives on this planet
as we do.

# 18

## The Service Dog

<hr/>

BAILEY WAS ONE DAY AWAY from being "put down" when the rescue organization All Fur Love first found him at a shelter in Bakersfield, California. When people from All Fur Love inquired about Bailey, the shelter staff told them not to bother with him—he was "trouble." They decided to take him anyway.

Bailey is indeed trouble—temperamental, opinionated, stubborn, and the neighborhood ball thief—and he is also a committed friend. During our first year or so together, Bailey went with me everywhere—coffee shops, restaurants, public transit, the grocery store—sporting his very own Service Dog tag and (sometimes) acting every bit the part.

A year or two before I left Georgia for California, I had applied for a service dog. Organizations like the one to which I applied breed, raise, and train mostly Labradors and golden retrievers to provide companionship and physical assistance to disabled people—a necessarily time-consuming process. Only a small percentage of the animals are rescues. By the time I was offered a dog five years later, I had decided that it was important to me to adopt a dog from a shelter, as thousands of animals face euthanasia in pounds and shelters across the country every day. According to the Humane Society of the United States, around 2.7 million purportedly healthy cats and dogs are killed in America annually—about one every eleven seconds (a statistic that says nothing of those who are ill or disabled). Breeding animals adds to this problem by bringing more animals into the world to take up homes that could be given to the countless animals in shelters. With these issues in mind, I declined the trained dog and ended up with Bailey.[1]

Bailey has large sleepy brown eyes, unusually expressive eyebrows, a heavy moustache, and oversized off-white paws. His thick, mostly black coat is clearly meant for snowy weather; it would grow to the ground if we didn't crop it. Weighing in at about 22 pounds, he has the dramatic fur and signature swooping tail of a Lhasa Apso. However, I would bet good money that there's also a dachshund somewhere in his family tree, as he has the very short legs and awkwardly long body of a wiener dog. From this description it may be obvious that Bailey is not your typical service dog. For the physical help I needed—picking things up, turning on and off switches—his body type is totally impractical. In the books I had bought but didn't read for people who want to train their own service dogs, this was probably the number one rule: don't just adopt the first funny-looking animal who gazes into your eyes.

I would be lying if I said that training Bailey came naturally to me. In fact I have learned from Bailey that cross-species communication, even between such compatible beings as canines and humans, is no simple task. Dog trainers are the first to remind people that dog training is actually human training—that most of the work involves learning how to express your needs and desires to your dog while also being able to correctly interpret theirs. This unfortunately did not come naturally to me, and it did not come naturally to Bailey either.

Part of the challenge was that Bailey had many years of unknown traumas to work through—the worst of which manifested as severe separation anxiety. Like most shelter dogs, Bailey's origins are a mystery. It is clear to me, though, that in the two and a half years before he came to us, he went through a lot. You can see it in the photo we have of him from the shelter, crouching in the back of his cage, looking like a terrified swamp creature with leaves, sticks, and other debris knotted and tangled through his disastrously long fur. It was hard enough to teach him to trust that he wasn't going to be abandoned again, let alone train him to pick up my keys off the floor.

Despite my own inability to train myself to train Bailey to help me when I drop things (and his physical inability to reach light switches), Bailey did come to provide an unexpected service for me: he became my mediator to the outside world. Paradoxically, when Bailey and I would move through the world together, I would suddenly feel surprisingly alone. Bailey would attract much of the attention that used to be directed toward me—the stares, the uncomfortable looks, the awkward questions. When that attention was redirected toward him, it turned from discomfort into affection. Although the opposite is certainly true, with service animals regularly being used as a justification to refuse disabled people access into public spaces, I have nonetheless heard similar sentiments from other disabled people: one of the most powerful services animals can provide is a certain kind of social ease, mediating between their human companions and an ableist world.

Over the years, Bailey and I also have learned to understand each other, at least about the things that are most important. He knows how to read his human's emotions, appearing at a moment's notice if David or I are angry or worried, licking our hands and leaning his body up against ours. And we know how to read his emotions as well—the way he holds his tail up stiffly and stands tall when he is unconvincingly trying to be dominant, the way he looks up at me and does his best to curl his whole body to fit on my wheelchair's footrests when he is nervous, or the way he worriedly looks back and braces the sidewalk if one of his humans falls behind when our family goes out for a stroll.

David and I also understand when Bailey is telling us he is in pain. Like many breeds, Lhasa Apsos and dachshunds are predisposed to particular health issues and disabilities related to their breeding. For bulldogs it's heart disease, heart attacks, and difficulty breathing, while Dalmatians are susceptible to hereditary deafness.[2] Dogs like Bailey who have short legs and long backs are prone to patella problems, spinal cord injuries, and slipped disc disease, with which Bailey has been diagnosed.

Many people who haven't seen Bailey when he is in pain ask how I can tell that he is suffering, but it's impossible not to recognize it. His body responds just as mine would if I were in severe pain: his muscles tighten, he stays as still as possible, he cries, he can't get comfortable, and he doesn't want anyone to touch him.

A few years ago, Bailey suddenly began losing control of his back legs. Overnight he went from going on walks and running around our house to being virtually paralyzed. By the time we got him to a surgeon that evening, he was dragging his back legs behind him. My first concern was that he wouldn't survive, but as the fear of him dying thankfully passed, I began to realize that Bailey, my service dog, was now physically disabled himself.

Bailey had emergency surgery the next day. We were extremely fortunate that his rescue organization managed to have a large portion of his medical bills reduced; we never could have afforded it otherwise. When we finally brought him home, Bailey was still unable to use his back legs and he had lost control of his bowel and bladder. When he needed to go out, David would either carry him or walk him, outfitted with a sort of sling-like contraption made out of one of my scarves under his back legs. For the most part, Bailey seemed to be surprisingly nonchalant about it all, still managing to maneuver to his favorite pee spots (which, in the sling, made him look like an old-fashioned lawn mower) or to anyone nearby for a scratch or two. But when we tried to leave him alone or when a large dog approached him, his anxieties would reappear, heightened due to an evident awareness of his increased vulnerability.

Bailey's days going out with me on long public excursions were cut short by the surgery. Long walks seem to inflame his back pain, and my arms are not strong enough to pick him up if he gets tired. Most importantly, though, Bailey is still with us. He is doing well, but he'll always walk with a gimpy swagger, he'll always be slower than other dogs, and when he attempts to run he'll always seem to have a separate driver in his rear end. He also will always be at risk of another disc slipping in his spine. Since his surgery he has had numerous mild episodes, which thankfully we have been able to manage with medications and care. After generations of human intervention, his back is simply too long for the rest of his body.

As I write this, five years to the day since Bailey first came to live with me and David, we are still together. He lies beside me on the bed he has made out of his blanket under my desk, snoring louder than any human being I know. Although he rarely travels around town with me anymore, he has given me priceless company during the endless hours I have spent writing this book. I am extremely grateful that Bailey found his way into our lives, but the irony of our relationship is not lost on me: I originally wanted to get a dog in part to make my life easier, and instead I ended up with a disabled dog. David and I are undoubtedly Bailey's service humans.

Bailey is still my service dog, attentive to my emotions, needs, and whereabouts, his very presence helping to mediate between me and the ableism I encounter when we go on our daily walks together. And I gladly embrace being his service human as much as I can. I coat his medications in peanut butter, I make sure he doesn't go up and down stairs (he's the only elevator companion I have ever known to enjoy the smelly ones the best), and I try to help him through his anxiety and episodes of pain. But I fear that one day another disc will slip, causing him huge amounts of discomfort and pushing my own limitations as his caregiver. I often say that I wish I could just remove a few of his vertebrae or put him in a magic back-smushing machine—and then it dawns on me that I am wishing I could cure him.

Mostly though, there is a sense of something appropriate —beautiful actually—about being a gimped-up, dependent, inefficient, incapable human supporting and being supported by my inefficient, dependent, and gimped-up dog. Two vulnerable, interdependent beings of different species learning to understand what the other one needs. Awkwardly and imperfectly, we care for each other.

# Acknowledgments

WHEN I BEGAN *BEASTS OF BURDEN* in 2010 I had no idea where to begin or how to make it happen. To a visual artist just out of graduate school, writing a nonfiction book seemed like an utterly mysterious process. What I did have, though, was an amazing community of friends, family, and mentors who all believed in me and my project. Without this incredible support, this book would not have been written.

I am extremely grateful for the generous support of The New Press, and I am indebted to everyone there who has had a hand in the book's creation. I am especially lucky to have received the guidance and wisdom of Sarah Fan. Sarah's belief in and commitment to *Beasts of Burden*, and her deep understanding of what I was trying to achieve with it, proved invaluable. Jed Bickman also offered solid advice and much-needed support in the book's final stages. My profound gratitude to all the editors and production staff at The New Press who have helped me realize this project.

Tremendous thanks are due as well to Amy Scholder, who was unwavering in her encouragement from the earliest days of *Beasts of Burden*. Amy's initial edits and suggestions have stayed with me over the many years I've worked on this book, and I am a far better writer because of them. Thanks as well to Jeanann Pannasch and Sam Huber.

The ideas for this book were born during my time in the Department of Art Practice at the University of California,

Berkeley. Words cannot express how grateful I am for the community of friends and mentors that emerged from my time there. I am particularly appreciative of Katherine Sherwood and Susan Schweik, whose steadfast support and loving mentorship have meant the world to me.

I am immensely fortunate to have found another community of mentors and friends in the Department of Social and Cultural Analysis and the broader NYU community. The department has supported me not only as a PhD student, but as an author, an activist, and a new mom. I am grateful to have ended up in such a caring and genuinely politically engaged program. Thank you to everyone I have learned from at NYU.

I am forever indebted to those who braved sections of *Beasts of Burden* at a variety of readable and unreadable stages: Jean Stewart, Margaret Price, Bethany Stevens, Lori Gruen, and Robert Jones, who all offered immensely thoughtful analysis and necessary critiques. To those who courageously read the whole project, all I can say is: thank God you did! Greg Youmans, Alison Kafer, my sister Astra, and my parents, Maria and Will: your suggestions, critiques, encouragement, and belief in *Beasts of Burden* are what made it possible. I am grateful beyond words. Immense thanks are also due to Carol Adams and Rebecca Solnit for the countless encouraging words about my project over the years, and for reading the manuscript and offering such generous words of support for it.

I am indebted to all the people who agreed to share their thoughts and stories for *Beasts of Burden*. Sincere gratitude to Michael Bérubé, Susan Schweik, Dawn Prince-Hughes, Jenny Brown, Harold Braswell, and Daniel Salomon. I am especially grateful to Peter Singer for graciously agreeing to be interviewed. Dozens of friends and strangers filled out questionnaires or sat down for conversations with me to discuss disability and animal rights in *Beasts of Burden*'s early days. Although they did not all end up in the final version of the book, each and every one of them shaped the project and my thinking in profound ways. Thanks as well to Yve Laris Cohen for driving me around upstate New York to conduct interviews. I am also very grateful to Dennis Walton, Mike Ervin, and Ethan Persoff for their last-minute work to make sure we could reproduce various images, and to Marisa Hernández for her help with references.

Thank you to the Culture and Animals Foundation for the early support of *Beasts of Burden*—the grant I received from the foundation gave momentum to the book early on. I am also so grateful for the many opportunities I have had over the years to share this work at conferences and in classrooms. The impact of the feedback I received at these events is evident throughout these pages.

I am honored to have had versions of some of the chapters in *Beasts of Burden* included elsewhere. Thank you to Claire Jean Kim and Carla Freccero for including chapter 13 in their 2013 special edition of *American Quarterly, Species/Race/Sex*. Thanks also to Carol Adams and Lori Gruen for including portions of chapter 17 in their 2014 edited collection *Ecofeminism: Feminist Intersections with Other Animals and the Earth*. I am also grateful to Judy K.C. Bentley, Kim Socha, and JL Schatz for including portions of chapter 3 in their special issue of *JCAS, Eco-Ability the Intersection of Earth Animal and Disability*. Thanks as well to *Qui Parle* and Katrina Dodson for including my work in the 2011 issue, *At the Intersections of Ecocriticism*. Some portions of chapters 9 and 17 were included in the piece and are reprinted here with permission.

*Beasts of Burden* is only here because of my remarkable families, including the beautiful crip community I call home. The ideas in this book have been indelibly shaped by these glorious people. Bethany Stevens and Alison Kafer should largely be blamed for the radical crip I have become. I surely would be an abysmally less fun and smart person without them, and my book would be even worse off. Leroy Moore started a disabled writers group that even from far away gave me a sense of solidarity in the too often solitary practice of writing. Jean Stewart was always there for me when writing got tough, with her porch, wine, pita bread, and fierce sense of justice. Margaret Price knew writing can be tedious and humbling, and so along with encouraging words, she sent me a popcorn maker so that I would at least not go hungry as I wrestled through the text. The late and sorely missed Paul Longmore gave me writing advice, telling me that if I wrote every day, at some point I'd realize I had written a book. It would take me many more pages to name you all—I know, I tried—but every one of you who I have danced with, been arrested with, protested with, made art with, learned with, struggled with, laughed with: thank you. I am also deeply indebted to the disability organizations and activist groups I have learned from over the past twelve years: ADAPT, CUIDO, Sins Invalid, and in particular the Society for Disability Studies.

The Wallace family has shown me so much love and friendship, never failing to ask me how the book is coming along and always offering to help. To Julia, Laura and Evan, Rachel and Chris, Jeremy, and Francie: thank you. I am so grateful to be a part of your adventures.

To the Taylors, I like to think that this is a book that would have made those funny hippie kids who prank called fur companies, and sang songs about not eating at McDonald's, proud. Perhaps one of us would have even reviewed it in *K.A.R.E.!* To my beloved Alex, Nye, and Astra, thanks for the years of debating animal issues and everything else under the moon. I am always still learning from you all. To my parents, Maria and Will, my gratitude is boundless. This book is most definitely a product of our family! Not only because it's weird, and because it has a passionate animal liberation message, but because it is a project that came from my heart, and from a sense of justice—from the things you two taught me a project should be based in.

Two of the most important contributors to *Beasts of Burden* have not read it. My dog Bailey has been there from the beginning and his significance to my life and my thinking about animals is evident throughout these pages. I thank him for giving so much to us, and loving us so fiercely.

During the book's last rounds of edits, Leonora Fenix was born. Although she has yet to read it, Leonora contributed substantially to the last edits. Whether it was lack of sleep, new mom hormones, or all the joy she brought me daily, somehow many things about my book became clearer—sections that had always troubled me were cut, others were added, and unfinished parts that had puzzled me seemed less puzzling. I am overjoyed that she is part of our lives and grateful beyond words that I get to be her mama. I am also so thankful to my mom, Maria, and to Francie, for coming to stay with us multiple times to help with child care so I could finish editing.

Finally, no one read *Beasts of Burden* as thoroughly and thoughtfully—and as many times—as David Wallace. David surely deserves an award for reading the book repeatedly, sometimes even out loud to me. The fact that I kept asking him to do so is a testament to how essential he was to the writing of the book. His genuine enthusiasm for the ideas and his steadfast belief that I would finish it were unwavering and gave me the stamina and confidence to continue working on it over the years. Without his thoughts and his heart this book would not be here. Thank you, David, for giving so much to this project.

# Notes

**Prologue: Chicken Truck**

1. United Poultry Concerns, "Chickens," accessed October 26, 2013, http://www.upc-online.org/chickens/chickensbro.html.

2. United Poultry Concerns, "Chickens."

**1. Strange but True**

1. Fiona Campbell, *Contours of Ableism* (New York: Palgrave Macmillan, 2009), 17.

**2. What Is Disability?**

1. World Health Organization, "Summary: World Report on Disability," 2011, http://whqlibdoc.who.int/hq/2011/WHO_NMH_VIP_11 .01_eng.pdf.

2. United Nations, "Some Facts About Persons with Disabilities," fact sheet, 2006, 2013, http://www.un.org/disabilities/convention/facts.shtml.

3. Fiona Campbell, *Contours of Ableism* (New York: Palgrave Macmillan, 2009), 22.

4. See Ellen Samuels, *Fantasies of Identification: Disability, Gender, Race* (New York: New York University Press, 2014).

5. Samuels, *Fantasies of Identification*, 2.

6. See Kim Nielsen, *A Disability History of the United States* (Boston: Beacon Press, 2012).

7. "Differently Abled—Disability Language on My Mind," *Cripwheels* (blog), accessed October 19, 2013, http://cripwheels.blogspot.com/2011/01 /differently-abled-disability-language.html.

8. Michael Bérubé, foreword to *Claiming Disability: Knowledge and Identity*, by Simi Linton (New York: New York University Press, 1998), viii.

9. Alison Kafer, "Compulsory Bodies: Reflections on Heterosexuality and Able-bodiedness," *Journal of Women's History* 15, no. 3 (2003): 78.

10. For more information on ADAPT, visit their website, accessed September 10, 2013, http://www.adapt.org.

11. Centers for Medicare Services, *CMS 2012 Nursing Home Action Plan* (Baltimore, MD: Centers for Medicare Services, 2012), ii, accessed October 26, 2013, http://www.cms.gov/Medicare/Provider -EnrollmentandCertification/CertificationandComplianc/downloads /nursinghomedatacompendium_508.pdf; and North Carolina Department of Health and Human Services, ICF/MR Branch Newsletter, October 2002, http://www.ncdhhs.gov/dhsr/mhlcs/pdf/icfnewsletter/icfmroctnewsltr.pdf.

12. Toshio Meronek, "Disability Advocates, Nursing Home Industry Battle for Health Care Dollars for Aging, Disabled," *Truthout*, April 28, 2013, http://www.truth-out.org/news/item/15985-disability-advocates-nursing -home-industry-battle-for-health-care-dollars-for-aging-disabled.

13. Centers for Disease Control and Prevention, "Nursing Home Care," http://www.cdc.gov/nchs/fastats/nursingh.htm; Centers for Medicare Services, *Nursing Home Compendium 2012 Edition* (Centers for Medicare Services, 2012), 153, http://www.cms.gov/Medicare/Provider -Enrollment-andCertification/CertificationandComplianc/downloads /nursinghomedatacompendium_508.pdf.

14. Genworth, "Genworth 2013 Cost of Care Survey," 5, https:// www.genworth.com/dam/Americas/US/PDFs/Consumer/corporate /130568_032213_Cost%20of%20Care_Final_nonsecure.pdf.

15. National Center on Elder Abuse, "Abuse of Residents of Long Term Care Facilities," fact sheet, 2010, http://www.ncea.aoa.gov/Resources /Publication/docs/NCEA_LTCF_ResearchBrief_2013.pdf.

16. SCAN Foundation, "Fact Sheet: Summary of the California 2011–2012 Enacted Budget: Impact on Older Adults and People with Disabilities," July 2011, http://www.udwa.org/pdf_docs/2011 /Scan_Foundation_Budget_TSF-FactSheet-21.pdf.

17. Rosemarie Garland-Thomson, "From Wonder to Error—A Genealogy of Freak Discourse in Modernity," introduction to *Freakery: Cultural Spectacles of the Extraordinary Body*, ed. Rosemarie Garland Thomson (New York: New York University Press, 1996), 4.

18. See Michael Oliver, *The Politics of Disablement: A Sociological Approach* (New York: St. Martin's Press, 1990).

19. Margaret Price, *Mad at School* (Ann Arbor: University of Michigan Press, 2014), 134.

20. Mia Mingus, "Changing the Framework: Disability Justice: How Our Communities Can Move Beyond Access to Wholeness," *Resist*, December 2010, http://www.resistinc.org/newsletters/articles/changing-framework -disability-justice.

21. World Health Organization, "Disabilities and Rehabilitation," accessed September 10, 2013, http://www.who.int/disabilities/media/events /idpdinfo031209/en.

22. United Nations Enable, "Convention on the Rights of Persons with Disabilities," accessed September 10, 2013, http://www.un.org/disabilities /convention/facts.shtml.

23. Shaun Heasley, "More Than 1 in 4 With Disabilities Living in Poverty," *Disability Scoop*, September 14, 2011, accessed September 10, 2013, http: //www.disabilityscoop.com/2011/09/14/more-1-in-4-poverty/13952.

24. World Bank, "Poverty and Disability," accessed October 19, 2013, http://web.worldbank.org/WBSITE/EXTERNAL/TOPICS/EXT SOCIALPROTECTION/EXTDISABILITY/0,,contentMDK:20 193783~menuPK:419389~pagePK:148956~piPK:216618~theSite PK:282699,00.html.

25. United Nations Enable, "Disability and Employment Fact Sheet 1: Employment of Persons with Disabilities: Fact Sheet 1," accessed September 10, 2013, http://www.un.org/disabilities/default.asp?id=255.

26. U.S. Department of Labor, Bureau of Labor Statistics, "Persons with a Disability: Labor Force Characteristics—2009," U.S. Department of Labor, August 25, 2010, http://www.bls.gov/news.release/archives /disabl_08252010.pdf.

27. Tom Harkin, "Disability Employment: Are We at the Tipping Point?," *Huffington Post*, July 16, 2012, http://www.huffingtonpost.com/sen-tom -harkin/disability-employment-are_b_1677380.html.

28. Marta Russell and Jean Stewart, "Disablement, Prison, and Historical Segregation," *Monthly Review* 53, no. 3 (2009), http://monthlyreview.org /2001/07/01/disablement-prison-and-historical-segregation.

29. Mark Sherry, *Disability Hate Crimes: Does Anyone Really Hate Disabled People?* (Surrey, UK: Ashgate Publishing Limited, 2010), 15.

30. Paul K. Longmore and Lauri Umansky, introduction to *The New Disability History: American Perspectives* (New York: New York University Press, 2001), 7.

31. Douglas C. Baynton, "Disability and the Justification of Inequality in American History," in Longmore and Umansky, *New Disability History*, 52.

32. Deborah Stone, *The Disabled State: Health, Society Policy* (Philadelphia: Temple University Press, 1984). See also Ravi Malhotra and Marta Russell, "Capitalism and Disability," *Socialist Registrare* 38 (2002): 211–28; and

Nirmala Erevelles, *Disability and Difference in Global Contexts: Enabling a Transformative Body Politic* (New York: Palgrave Macmillan, 2011).

33. See Susan M. Schweik, *The Ugly Laws: Disability in Public* (New York: New York University Press, 2009).

34. See Samuels, *Fantasies of Identification*.

35. Erevelles, *Disability and Difference in Global Contexts*, 68–71.

36. Samuels, *Fantasies of Identification*, 178.

37. Steven A. Gelb "Darwin's Use of Intellectual Disability in *The Descent of Man*," *Disability Studies Quarterly* 28, no. 2 (December 5, 2008), http://dsq-sds.org/article/view/96.

38. See Londa L. Schiebinger, *Nature's Body: Gender in the Making of Modern Science.* (New Brunswick, NJ: Rutgers University Press, 1993).

39. Michelle Jarman, "Coming Up from Underground: Uneasy Dialogues at the Intersections of Race, Mental Illness, and Disability Studies," in *Blackness and Disability: Critical Examinations and Cultural Interventions*, ed. Christopher M. Bell, (East Lansing: Michigan State University Press, 2011), 10.

40. Mingus, "Changing the Framework."

## 3. Animal Crips

1. Scott McBurney, "Congenital Limb Deformity in a Red Fox," Canadian Cooperative Wildlife Health Centre 6, no. 1 (1999), 9–10.

2. "My Bionic Pet: Nature (VIDEO)," *Nature*, April 9, 2014, http://www.pbs.org/wnet/nature/my-bionic-pet-my-bionic-pet/8696.

3. Franz DeWaal, *Good Natured: On the Origins of Right and Wrong in Humans and Other Animals* (Cambridge, MA: Harvard University Press, 1996), 44.

4. "Chris P. Bacon, Disabled Pig, Charms with Tiny Wheelchair After Escaping Death (VIDEO)," *Huffington Post*, February 5, 2013, http://www.huffingtonpost.com/2013/02/05/chris-p-bacon-disabled-pig-wheelchair_n_2626078.html.

5. "Mozu the Snow Monkey: Nature," directed by Nigel Cole (1989; Toronto, ON: E1 Entertainment, 1989), DVD.

6. Jeffrey Moussaieff Masson, *The Pig Who Sang to the Moon: The Emotional World of Farm Animals* (New York: Ballantine Books, 2003), 82.

7. Marc Bekoff, *The Emotional Lives of Animals: A Leading Scientist Explores Animal Joy, Sorrow, and Empathy and Why They Matter* (Novato, CA: New World Library, 2008), 3.

8. "Cute Alert: Goose Looks After Blind Dog," *Metro*, April 21, 2011, http://metro.co.uk/2011/04/21/buttons-the-goose-looks-after-baks-the-blind-dog-652701.

9. De Waal, *Good Natured*, 48.

10. Ibid.

11. Ibid., 52.

12. Ibid., 48.

13. Ibid.

14. PETA, "Factory Farming: Cruelty to Animals," accessed October 19, 2013, http://www.peta.org/issues/animals-used-for-food/factory-farming.aspx.

15. United Poultry Concerns, "Debeaking," fact sheet, accessed October 19, 2013, http://www.upc-online.org/merchandise/debeak_factsheet.html.

16. Masson, *Pig Who Sang to the Moon*, 67.

17. Karen Davis, "The Battery Hen: Her Life Is Not for the Birds," United Poultry Concerns, accessed July 17, 2013, http://www.upc-online.org/batthen.html.

18. Masson, *Pig Who Sang to the Moon*, 67–68. "Scientists, like the veterinary Professor John Webster of the University of Bristol School of Veterinary Medicine, who exposed this situation, have been accused of being speculative, or worse, anthropomorphic." More recent studies have supported these scientists' findings by showing that if offered a choice between regular feed and a feed that includes an anti-inflammatory and pain-reducing drug, that "lame" hens will choose the enhanced feed, leading researchers to conclude that "the lame broiler chickens are in pain and that this pain causes them distress from which they seek relief." C.A. Weeks, et al. "The Behaviour of Broiler Chickens and Its Modification by Lameness," *Applied Animal Behaviour Science* 67 (2000): 111–125.

19. Masson, *Pig Who Sang to the Moon*, 151.

20. Humane Society of the United States, *An HSUS Report: The Welfare of Cows in the Dairy Industry* (Washington, D.C.: Humane Society of the United States, 2009), http://www.humanesociety.org/assets/pdfs/farm/hsus-the-welfare-of-cows-in-the-dairy-industry.pdf.

21. Vegetarian Society, "Cattle: Fact Sheet," accessed October 24, 2013, https://www.vegsoc.org/sslpage.aspx?pid=561.

22. Armelle Casau, "When Pigs Stress Out," *New York Times*, October 7, 2003, http://www.nytimes.com/2003/10/07/science/when-pigs-stress-out.html.

23. Gail Eisnitz, *Slaughterhouse: The Shocking Story of Greed, Neglect, and Inhumane Treatment Inside the U.S. Meat Industry* (Amherst, NY: Prometheus Books, 2006), 82.

24. Eisnitz, *Slaughterhouse*, 100.

25. Laura Entis, "Will the Worst Bird Flu Outbreak in US History Finally Make Us Reconsider Factory Farming Chicken?," July 14, 2015, accessed November 12, 2015, http://www.theguardian.com/vital-signs/2015/jul/14

/bird-flu-devastation-highlights-unsustainability-of-commercial-chicken
-farming.

26. Robert Uhlig, "10 Million Animals Were Slaughtered in Foot and
Mouth Cull," *The Telegraph*, January 23, 2002, http://www.telegraph.co.uk
/news/uknews/1382356/10-million-animals-were-slaughtered-in-foot-and
-mouth-cull.html.

27. Matthew Scully, *Dominion: The Power of Man, the Suffering of Animals,
and the Call to Mercy* (New York: St. Martin's Press, 2003), ix–x.

28. Entis, "Worst Bird Flu Outbreak."

29. Jim Wappes, "Report Finds $1.2 Billion in Iowa Avian Flu Dam-
age," *Center for Infectious Disease Research and Policy*, August 18, 2015, accessed
November 12, 2015, http://www.cidrap.umn.edu/news-perspective/2015
/08/report-finds-12-billion-iowa-avian-flu-damage.

30. Swift & Company, *Easy Does It*, reprinted by Ethan Persoff, "Com-
ics with Problems #24—D-Doh-D-Don't Bruise That Pig!," accessed January 14, 2013, http://www.ep.tc/problems/24.

31. Ibid.

32. Humane Society of the United States, "Rampant Animal Cruelty at
California Slaughter Plant," January 30, 2008, http://www.humanesociety
.org/news/news/2008/01/undercover_investigation_013008.html.

33. Mercy for Animals, "Auction Atrocities: California Livestock Market
Abuse Exposed," accessed July 17, 2013, http://www.mercyforanimals.org
/auction/video.aspx.

34. Vegan Outreach, "How Does Drinking Milk Hurt Cows?," accessed
January 14, 2013, http://www.veganoutreach.org/dairy.

35. "Downer Cow Ban Initially Rejected by USDA Finally Passed,"
*Examiner.com*, March 15, 2009, http://www.examiner.com/article/downer
-cow-ban-intially-rejected-by-usda-finally-passed.

36. Animal Welfare Institute, "Legal Protections for Nonambulatory (or
'Downed') Animals," accessed January 14, 2013, http://awionline.org/sites
/default/files/uploads/documents/fa-lawsrelatedtononambulatoryanimals
-020612.pdf.

37. Animal Welfare Institute, "Legal Protections for Nonambulatory (or
'Downed') Animals."

38. Anna Bassett, "Technical Advice Fact Sheet No. 1: Welfare and
Belgian Blue Cattle," Animal Welfare Approved, 2009, http://www
.animalwelfareapproved.org/wp-content/uploads/2009/08/TAFS
-1-Welfare-and-Belgian-Blue-Cattle-9-22-09.pdf.

39. Kim Severson, "An Unlikely Way to Save a Species: Serve it for Dinner," *New York Times*, April 30, 2008, http://www.nytimes.com/2008/04
/30/dining/30come.html.

40. Humane Society of the United States, "Warning: Anti-Fur Brochure," 2000, https://web.archive.org/web/20081203133831/http://files.hsus.org /web-files/PDF/AntiFurWarningBro_2000.pdf.

41. PETA, "Ailing Elephants Forced to Perform," September 22, 2010, http://www.peta.org/b/thepetafiles/archive/2010/09/22/ailing-elephants -forced-to-perform.aspx. In March 2015 Ringling Bros. and Barnum & Bailey made the unexpected announcement that it will be eliminating its elephant acts by the year 2018, citing animal welfare concerns. The announcement comes on the heels of a lawsuit against Feld Entertainment (Ringling Bros.' parent company) brought by the U.S. Department of Agriculture for alleged violations of the Animal Welfare Act. In 2011 a settlement was reached (allowing the company to avoid admitting any wrongdoing) for $270,000, the largest settlement in the Animal Welfare Act's four-decade history. A yearlong investigation in *Mother Jones* found that elephants performing with Ringling Bros. were "whipped with bullhooks, trapped in train cars filled with their own feces, and chained in place for a good part of their lives." Thanks to the persistent work of animal advocates, public opinion has shifted so much that numerous cities have now placed bans on bullhooks. However, there are no signs that acts involving tigers, lions, bears, and other circus animals will be eliminated any time soon. See James Gerkin, "Ringling Bros. Circus To Phase Out Elephant Acts" *The Huffington Post*, March 5, 2015, http://www.huffingtonpost.com/2015/03/05/ringling -bros-elephants_n_6807340.html, and Deborah Nelson, "The Cruelest Show on Earth," *Mother Jones*, November/December 2011 issue, http://www .motherjones.com/environment/2011/10/ringling-bros-elephant-abuse.

42. Dawn Prince-Hughes, *Songs of the Gorilla Nation* (New York: Three Rivers Press, 2005), 37.

43. Laura Smith, "Zoos Drive Animals Crazy," *Slate*, June 2014, accessed November 2015, http://www.slate.com/blogs/wild_things/2014/06/20/ani mal_madness_zoochosis_stereotypic_behavior_and_problems_with_zoos .html.

44. Laurel Braitman. *Animal Madness: How Anxious Dogs, Compulsive Parrots, and Elephants in Recovery Help Us Understand Ourselves* (New York: Simon and Schuster, 2014), 199.

45. Smith, "Zoos Drive Animals Crazy."

46. Jenny Brown, e-mail communication with the author, December 1, 2012.

47. Fernanda Santos, "A Rescued Goat Gets a Chance for a Normal Life," *New York Times*, May 1, 2008, http://www.nytimes.com/2008/05/01 /nyregion/01goat.html.

## 4. The Chimp Who Spoke

1. Roger Fouts, *Next of Kin: What Chimpanzees Have Taught Me About Who We Are* (New York, New York: William Morrow and Company, 1997), 145.

2. Fouts, *Next of Kin*, 133.

3. Ibid.

4. Ibid., 134–35, 142.

5. Ibid., 355.

6. Ibid., 133, 134.

7. Ibid., 248.

8. Ibid., 283, 284.

9. *Project Nim Chimpsky*, directed by. James Marsh (2011; Los Angeles, CA: Roadside Attractions, 2011), DVD.

10. Fouts, *Next of Kin*, 285–86.

11. Ibid., 284.

12. Ibid., 354.

13. Margret A. Winzer, *The History of Special Education: From Isolation to Integration*. (Washington, D.C.: Gallaudet University Press, 1993), 18.

14. Gallaudet University, "The Abbe Charles Michel de l'Epee," accessed November, 2015, http://giving.gallaudet.edu/HOF/pastinductees/the-abbe-charles-michel-de-lepee.

15. Douglas C. Baynton, "'Savages and Deaf-Mutes': Evolutionary Theory and the Campaign Against Sign Language in the Nineteenth Century," in *Deaf History Unveiled: Interpretations from the New Scholarship*, ed. John Vickrey Van Cleve (Washington, D.C.: Gallaudet University Press, 1993).

16. Baynton, "'Savages and Deaf-Mutes,'" 93.

17. *American Annals of the Deaf*, ed. Edward Allen Fay (Washington, D.C.: Conference of Superintendents and Principals of American Schools for the Deaf, 1910), 179; Carol Padden, *Deaf in America: Voices from a Culture* (Cambridge, MA: Harvard University Press), 52.

18. Baynton, "'Savages and Deaf-Mutes,'" 52.

19. Ibid., 53: "and an oralist educator concluded in 1897 that 'these signs can no more be called a language than the different movements of a dog's tail and ears which indicate his feelings.'"

20. Diane L. Beers, *For the Prevention of Cruelty: The History and Legacy of Animal Rights Activism* (Athens: Ohio University Press, 2006), 29.

21. Henry Childs Merwin, *Dogs and Men* (New York: Houghton Mifflin, 1910), 42.

22. Baynton, "'Savages and Deaf-Mutes.'"

23. Margalit Fox, *Talking Hands: What Sign Language Reveals About the Mind* (New York: Simon & Schuster, 2007), 36.

24. Nicholas Mirzoeff, "The Silent Mind: Learning from Deafness," *History Today*, July 1992, 24.

25. Hess, Elizabeth, *Nim Chimpsky: The Chimp Who Would Be Human* (New York: Bantam Books, 2008), 18.

26. *The Cove*, directed by Louie Psihoyos (Santa Monica, CA: Lions Gate Entertainment, 2009), DVD.

27. George Johnson, "Chimp Talk Debate: Is It Really Language?," *New York Times*, June 6, 1995, accessed October 12, 2013, http://www.nytimes .com/1995/06/06/science/chimp-talk-debate-is-it-really-language.html.

28. Mel Y. Chen, *Animacies: Biopolitics, Racial Mattering, and Queer Affect* (Durham, NC: Duke University Press, 2012); Chen, *Animacies*, 91.

29. Chen, *Animacies*, 91.

## 5. Ableism and Animals

1. Daniel Salomon, "From Marginal Cases Linked Oppressions: Reframing the Conflict Between the Autistic Pride and Animal Rights Movements," *Journal for Critical Animal Studies* 8, no. 1 (2010): 48.

2. Harold Braswell, in discussion with the author, May 5, 2011.

3. Marc Bekoff, *The Animal Manifesto: Six Reasons for Expanding Our Compassion Footprint* (Novato, CA: New World Library, 2010), 27.

4. PETA, "Got Autism? Learn About the Link Between Dairy Products and the Disorder," accessed November 12, 2014, http://www.peta.org /features/got-autism-learn-link-dairy-products-disease.

5. Rory Freedman and Kim Barnouin, *Skinny Bitch* (Philadelphia: Running Press, 2005).

6. Breeze Harper, "Situating Racialization, Racisms, and Anti-Racisms: Critical Race Feminist and Socio-spatial Spatial Epistemological Analysis of Vegan Consciousness in the USA" (PhD diss. in progress, University of California, Davis), 23.

7. Ella Wheeler Wilcox, "The Voice of the Voiceless," quoted in *For the Prevention of Cruelty: The History and Legacy of Animal Rights Activism* by Diane L. Beers (Athens: Ohio University Press, 2006), 59.

8. The 2004 Sydney Peace Prize lecture delivered by Arundhati Roy at the Seymour Theatre Centre, University of Sydney, November 4, 2004.

9. Stephen Drake, "Connecting Disability Rights and Animal Rights: A Really Bad Idea," *Not Dead Yet*, October 11, 2010, http://www.notdeadyet .org/2010/10/connecting-disability-rights-and-animal.html.

10. Michael Pollan, *The Omnivore's Dilemma: A Natural History of Four Meals* (New York: Penguin Group, 2009), 315.

11. Alexandra Topping, "Yvonne the Cow Is Caught After Three Months on the Run," *The Guardian*, September 2, 2011, http://www.theguardian.com/world/2011/sep/02/yvonne-cow-caught-three-months.

12. Jeffrey St. Clair, "Let Us Now Praise Infamous Animals," foreword to *Fear of the Animal Planet: the Hidden History of Animal Resistance* by Jason Hribal (Oakland, CA: AK Press, 2010), 16.

13. Mel Y. Chen, *Animacies: Biopolitics, Racial Mattering, and Queer Affect* (Durham, N.C.: Duke University Press, 2012), 115–121.

14. Eugene Linden, "Can Animals Think?" *Time Magazine*, August 29, 1999, http://content.time.com/time/magazine/article/0,9171,30198,00.html.

15. Hribal, *Fear of the Animal Planet*, 116.

16. Ibid., 93.

17. Ibid., 25.

18. St. Clair, "Let Us Now Praise Infamous Animals," 16.

19. "I Am Scared and Don't Want to Die," YouTube, uploaded May 29, 2009, https://www.youtube.com/watch?v=LUkHkyy4uqw.

20. Daniel Salomon, "From Marginal Cases Linked Oppressions: Reframing the Conflict Between the Autistic Pride and Animal Rights Movements," *Journal for Critical Animal Studies* 8, no. 1 (2010): 2.

21. See Lori Gruen, *Ethics and Animals an Introduction* (New York: Cambridge University Press, 2011), 57.

22. Peter Singer, *Animal Liberation: A New Ethics for Our Treatment of Animals*, 2nd ed. (1975; New York: New York Review of Books, 2009), 237.

23. Salomon, "From Marginal Cases Linked Oppressions," 52.

24. Licia Carlson and Eva Feder Kittay, *Cognitive Disability and Its Challenge to Moral Philosophy* (West Sussex, UK: John Wiley & Sons, 2010), 318.

25. Pollan, *Omnivore's Dilemma*, 312.

26. Cathryn Bailey, "On the Backs of Animals: The Valorization of Reason in Contemporary Animal Ethics," in *The Feminist Care Tradition in Animal Ethics: A Reader*, ed. Josephine Donovan and Carol J. Adams (New York: Columbia University Press, 2007), 346.

27. Margaret Price, *Mad at School: Rhetorics of Mental Disability and Academic Life* (Ann Arbor: University of Michigan Press, 2011), 9.

28. Price, *Mad at School*, 26.

29. Bailey, "On the Backs of Animals," 345.

30. Peter Singer, *Rethinking Life and Death: The Collapse of Our Traditional Values* (New York: St. Martin's Griffin, 1994), 213.

31. Michael Bérubé, "Equality, Freedom, and/or Justice for All: A Response to Martha Nussbaum," in *Cognitive Disability and Its Challenge to*

*Moral Philosophy*, ed. Eva Feder Kittay (Hoboken, NJ: John Wiley & Sons, 2010), 106.

32. Rachel Adams, "Didn't You Get Tested?," *Salon*, April 28, 2013, http://www.salon.com/2013/04/28/all_the_ways_you_judge_my_son.

33. G.L. Krahn, L. Hammond, and A. Turner, "A Cascade of Disparities: Health and Health Care Access for People with Intellectual Disabilities," *Mental Retardation and Developmental Disabilities Research Reviews* 12, no. 1 (2006): 70–82, http://www.ncbi.nlm.nih.gov/pubmed/16435327.

34. Susan Donaldson James, "Mom Says Mentally Impaired Tot Heartlessly Denied Transplant," ABC News, January 17, 2012, http://gma.yahoo.com/mom-says-tot-mental-delays-heartlessly-denied-transplant-160808540--abc-news.html.

35. Charles Camosy, "Amelia Rivera and Medical Morality," *Washington Post*, January 18, 2012, http://www.washingtonpost.com/blogs/guest-voices/post/amelia-rivera-and-medical-morality/2012/01/18/gIQA1ZxE8P_blog.html.

36. Jenna Glatzer, "A Genetic Death Sentence," *Salon*, December 8, 2000, accessed October 13, 2013, http://www.salon.com/2000/12/08/heart_transplant.

37. Hugh Raffles, "Jews, Lice, and History," *Public Culture* 19, no. 3 (October 1, 2007): 525.

38. Ellie Turner, "Steakin' Claim for Freedom," *NT News*, September 4, 2011, http://www.ntnews.com.au/article/2011/09/04/257941_ntnews.html.

39. Louis Leakey, telegram to Jane Goodall, 1960.

40. Ker Than, "First Pictures: Wild Fish Uses Tools," *National Geographic*, July, 2011, http://news.nationalgeographic.com/news/2011/07/pictures/110713-tool-using-fish-science-tuskfish-australia-use-tools.

41. David Derbyshire, "Magpies Grieve for Their Dead," *Daily Mail*, October 25, 2009, http://www.dailymail.co.uk/sciencetech/article-1221754/Magpies-grieve-dead-turn-funerals.html.

42. "Prairie Dogs' Language Decoded by Scientists," CBC News, June 21, 2013, http://www.cbc.ca/news/technology/story/2013/06/21/science-prairie-dog-language-decoded.html.

43. Bijal P. Trivedi, "Sheep Are Highly Adept at Recognizing Faces, Study Shows," *National Geographic*, November 7, 2001, http://news.nationalgeographic.com/news/2001/11/1107_TVsheep.html.

44. F. Range et al., "Visual Categorization of Natural Stimuli by Domestic Dogs," *Animal Cognition* 11, no. 2 (2008).

45. Marc Bekoff and Jessica Pierce, *Wild Justice: the Moral Lives of Animals* (Chicago: University of Chicago Press, 2009).

46. Bekoff and Pierce, *Wild Justice*, x.

47. Barry Sanders, *Sudden Glory: Laughter as Subversive History* (Boston: Beacon Press, 1995), 3; Mary Bates, "Tickling Rats for Science," *Wired*, September 9, 2013, http://www.wired.com/wiredscience/2013/09/tickling-rats-for-science.

48. Peter Singer and Jim Mason, *The Ethics of What We Eat: Why Our Food Choices Matter* (Melbourne, Victoria: Text Publishing Company, 2006), 131.

49. Michael Hopkin, "Fish 'Personalities' Shaped by Life Experience," *Nature*, November 22, 2006, http://www.nature.com/news/2006/061120/full/news061120-5.html.

50. Fishcount, Humane Slaughter, accessed November, 2015, http://fishcount.org.uk/fish-welfare-in-commercial-fishing/humane-slaughter.

51. Jonathan Safran Foer, *Eating Animals* (New York: Little, Brown, 2009), 193.

52. Radhika Sanghani, "Chickens 'Cleverer Than Toddlers,'" *Telegraph*, June 19, 2013, http://www.telegraph.co.uk/science/science-news/10129124/Chickens-cleverer-than-toddlers.html; "The Hidden Lives of Chickens," PETA, accessed October 24, 2013, http://www.peta.org/issues/animals-used-for-food/hidden-lives-of-chickens.aspx.

53. PETA, "Hidden Lives of Chickens."

54. Fiona Macrae, "Can Chickens REALLY Be Cleverer Than a Toddler?," *Daily Mail Online*, June 18, 2013, accessed October 13, 2013, http://www.dailymail.co.uk/sciencetech/article-2344198/Chickens-smarter-human-toddlers-Studies-suggest-animals-master-numeracy-basic-engineering.html.

55. Maggie Koerth-Baker, "Kids (and Animals) Who Fail Classic Mirror Tests May Still Have a Sense of Self," *Scientific American*, November 29, 2010, http://www.scientificamerican.com/article.cfm?id=kids-and-animals-who-fail-classic-mirror.

56. Koerth-Baker, "Kids and Animals."

57. Michael Bérubé, in discussion with the author, September 1, 2011.

58. Lori Gruen, "Entangled Empathy: An Alternate Approach to Animal Ethics," in *The Politics of Species*, ed. Raymond Corbey (New York: Cambridge University Press, 2013), 224.

59. Christopher Cox, "Consider the Oyster: Why Even Strict Vegans Should Feel Comfortable Eating Oysters by the Boatload," *Slate*, April 7, 2010, http://www.slate.com/articles/life/food/2010/04/consider_the_oyster.html.

60. Marc Bekoff, "Vegans Shouldn't Eat Oysters, and If You Do You're Not Vegan, So . . ." *Huffington Post,* 2010, http://www.huffingtonpost.com/marc-bekoff/vegans-shouldnt-eat-oyste_b_605786.html.

61. Michael Pollan, "The Intelligent Plant: Scientists Debate a New Way

of Understanding Flora," *New Yorker,* December 23, 2013, http://www
.newyorker.com/magazine/2013/12/23/the-intelligent-plant. In the end,
even if we come to a point where we learn that plants feel pain and experience their lives in ways that would make using and eating them morally ques-
tionable, this would still not be an argument for killing and eating animals.
The vast majority of human beings can live thriving, healthful lives without
eating animal products, whereas none of us could survive without eating
any plants. Even if our goal was to harm fewer plants, eating farmed animals
would still not be the solution, because to be turned into meat these animals
must eat huge amount of plant matter every day—plant matter that could be
used to feed far more people than an animal's flesh and excretions can.

## 6. What Is an Animal?

1. Franz Kafka, "A Report to an Academy," Kafka Project, accessed
October 13, 2013, http://www.kafka.org/index.php?aid=161.

2. Harriet Ritvo, "On the Animal Turn," *Daedalus* 136 (Fall 2007), 119.

3. Edward Tyson, *Orang-Outang, sive Homo-Sylvestris; or, The Anatomy of
a Pygmie, Compared with That of a Monkey, an Ape, and a Man* (London: n.p.,
1699), fig 1.

4. Londa L. Schiebinger, *Nature's Body: Gender in the Making of Modern
Science* (New Brunswick, NJ: Rutgers University Press, 1993), 5.

5. Schiebinger, *Nature's Body,* 84.

6. Susan Crane, *Animal Encounters: Contacts and Concepts in Medieval Britain* (Philadelphia: University of Pennsylvania Press, 2012), 49.

7. Edward Long, *History of Jamaica, volume II: Reflections on Its Situation,
Settlements, Inhabitants, Climate, Products, Commerce, Laws and Government*
(Montreal: McGill-Queen's University Press, 2003), 278, 279.

8. Jennifer Morgan, *Laboring Women: Reproduction and Gender in New
World Slavery* (Philadelphia: University of Pennsylvania Press, 2011), 168.

9. Steven A Gelb, "Darwin's Use of Intellectual Disability in *The Descent
of Man,*" *Disability Studies Quarterly* 28, no. 2, December 5, 2008, http://dsq
-sds.org/article/view/96.

10. See Matt Cartmill and David Pilbeam. "One Hundred Years of Paleo-
anthropology." *American Scientist* 74 (1986): 410–20.

11. Jacques Derrida and David Wills. "The Animal That Therefore I Am
(More to Follow)," *Critical Inquiry* 28, no. 2 (2002): 392.

12. Schiebinger, *Nature's Body,* 45.

13. Chen, *Animacies,* 4.

14. Schienbinger, *Nature's Body,* 81.

15. Schiebinger, *Nature's Body,* 78.

16. See, for example, Jennifer Morgan, "'Some Could Suckle over Their Shoulder': Male Travelers, Female Bodies, and the Gendering of Racial Ideology, 1500–1770," *William and Mary Quarterly:* 54, no. 1 (January 1997): 167–92.

17. Schiebinger, *Nature's Body*, 55.

18. Meg Mcsherry Breslin, "Anna Stonum, 40, Activist for Disabled," *Chicago Tribune*, February, 1999, http://articles.chicagotribune.com/1999-02-13/news/9902130089_1_disability-rights-accessible-public-transit-accessible-public-transportation.

19. Liat Ben-Moshe, and Justin J.W. Powell, "Sign of Our Times? Revis(it)ing the International Symbol of Access," *Disability & Society* 22, no. 5 (August 2007): 492.

20. Ben-Moshe and Powell, "Sign of Our Times?," 501.

## 7. The Chimp Who Remembered

1. Roger Fouts, *Next of Kin: What Chimpanzees Have Taught Me About Who We Are* (New York: William Morrow, 1997), 355.

2. Fouts, *Next of Kin*, 202.

## 9. Animal Insults

1. Rosemarie Garland-Thomson, *Extraordinary Bodies: Figuring Physical Disability in American Culture and Literature* (New York: Columbia University Press, 1997), 72–74, 77.

2. Garland-Thomson, *Extraordinary Bodies*, 77.

3. "World's 'Ugliest Woman' Julia Pastrana Buried 153 Years On," BBC News, February 13, 2013, http://www.bbc.co.uk/news/world-latin-america-21440400.

4. Licia Carlson, "Philosophers of Intellectual Disability," in *Cognitive Disability and Its Challenge to Moral Philosophy*, ed. Licia Carlson and Eva Feder Kittay (Chichester, West Sussex: John Wiley & Sons, 2010), 323.

5. National Council on Disability, "Forty Years After the Willowbrook Consent Decree, NCD Celebrates How Far We've Come," accessed November 15, 2015, https://www.ncd.gov/newsroom/05042015.

6. Dan Barry, "The 'Boys' in the Bunkhouse," *New York Times*, March 8, 2014, http://www.nytimes.com/interactive/2014/03/09/us/the-boys-in-the-bunkhouse.html.

7. D.L. Adams and Kimberly Socha, "Shocking into Submission: Suppressive Practices and Use of Behavior Modification on Nonhuman Animals, People with Disabilities, and the Environment," in *Earth, Animal, and Dis-*

*ability Liberation: Eco-Ability and Inclusive Education*, ed. Anthony J. Nocella II, Judy K.C. Bentley, and Janet M. Duncan (New York, NY: Peter Lang Publishing, 2012), 1.

8. Susan M. Schweik, *The Ugly Laws: Disability in Public* (New York: New York University Press, 2009), 97, 99, 100.

9. Mel Y. Chen, *Animacies: Biopolitics, Racial Mattering, and Queer Affect* (Durham, NC: Duke University Press, 2012), 95.

10. Cary Wolfe, *Animal Rites: American Culture, the Discourse of Species, and Posthumanist Theory* (Chicago: University of Chicago Press, 2003), 8.

11. Schweik, *The Ugly Laws*, 314.

12. Diane L. Beers, *For the Prevention of Cruelty: The History and Legacy of Animal Rights Activism* (Athens: Ohio University Press, 2006), 80.

13. Eric Baratay, and Elisabeth Hardouin-Fugier, *Zoo: A History of Zoological Gardens in the West* (London: Reaktion Books, 2003), 110.

14. Baratay, *Zoo*, 117–118.

15. Licia Carlson, *The Faces of Intellectual Disability: Philosophical Reflections* (Bloomington, IN: Indiana University Press, 2010), 161.

## 10. Claiming Animal

1. J. Tithonus Pednaud, "Percilla—The Monkey Girl," *Human Marvels*, accessed April 13, 2015, http://www.thehumanmarvels.com/percilla-the-monkey-girl.

2. *Sideshow—Alive on the Inside*, dir Lynn Dougherty (1999; 2005), DVD.

3. Robert Bogdan, *Freak Show: Presenting Human Oddities for Amusement and Profit* (Chicago: University of Chicago Press, 1988), 1, 279–81.

4. Bogdan, *Freak Show*, 280.

5. Robert Bogdan, in discussion with the author, June 5, 2013.

6. Petra Kuppers, *Disability and Contemporary Performance: Bodies on the Edge* (London: Routledge, 2004), 20.

7. Rachel Adams, *Sideshow U.S.A.: Freaks and the American Cultural Imagination* (Chicago: University of Chicago Press, 2001), 42.

8. Lehrer's most recent rendering of her dog Zora was *Zora: How I Understand* (36" x 50"), a mixed-media drawing on paper and Mylar the artist created in 2010—a year after Zora died. This image is a self-portrait of Lehrer with Zora, who was elderly and dying at the time. The woman's fingers are entangled in the dog's fur. Her head is a red cascade of hair as she burrows her face into the dog's back. The dog's body is in profile and the woman is on her knees behind the dog, her arms reaching under the creature's belly, crisscrossing as she tightly—though clearly tenderly—embraces the animal. The

dog stares out at us, one eye cloudy from blindness, her mouth open, tongue and teeth visible, in an expression of dog contentment, even happiness, which so many of us humans are familiar with. Although her tail is down, it seems at any moment that it will begin to wag—like the image was caught in that second right as the dog realized something pleasant was going to happen, but before her tail would begin to betray her anticipation. The dog's joy is contrasted with the human's devastation.

9. Laura Swanson, *Homemade Bull*, 2011. The bull's body towers over the gallery visitors, two huge white tusks protruding forward. The bull's shoulders are broad and curve into a large arch. Like a drooping tulip, the tail is stiffly erect, pointing upward until it suddenly folds unto itself and dangles down. The muscular bull has a hide made of large gray moving blankets that are pinned and sewn together. Parts of the blankets are frayed giving the impression of hair or fur. The bull has a large forehead that seems to roll forward and onto where the eyes would be. The two huge round nostrils that sit side by side on the bull's face give the sense of a steady and direct gaze instead.

Gallery visitors approach the bull and put their faces up close to the nostrils and gaze in. From afar it looks as if they are intimately kissing the creature, their faces deeply nuzzled in the bull's nose. The visitors are actually looking into a room covered with green floral wall paper. Inside are a few piles of books, a bed and pillow with an embroidered peacock, posters on the wall, potted plants, a radio, and a large mirror. There is even the head of a goat, made of papier-mâché, mounted to the wall. The bull's nostrils create a sort of bay window. The books include Frantz Fanon's *The Wretched of the Earth* and Irving Goffman's *Stigma*. The bull is lumbering, clumsy, and as the title describes, homemade. The bull is also a demanding presence, one that people seem to feel compelled to be near.

Although Swanson is not necessarily taking on the identity of the bull, the bull is a place of refuge. No one is allowed in the bull besides Swanson. The bull is a place "to read critical theory," according to the artist. From the book titles we have a sense of what sort of theory Swanson is reading; she is unpacking identity and oppression.

10. See Cary Wolfe, *What Is Posthumanism?*. (Minneapolis: University of Minnesota Press, 2010).

## 11. Freak of Nature

1. Wes Ishmael, "Dealing with Curly Calf," *BEEF*, December 1, 2008, accessed October 13, 2013. http://beefmagazine.com/genetics/1201-curly -calf-issue.

## 12. All Animals Are Equal (But Some Are More Equal Than Others)

1. Peter Singer, *Animal Liberation: A New Ethics for Our Treatment of Animals*, 2nd ed. (1975; New York: New York Review of Books, 2009).

2. Stephen Drake, "Connecting Disability Rights and Animal Rights: A Really Bad Idea," Not Dead Yet, October 11, 2010, accessed October 13, 2013, http://www.notdeadyet.org/2010/10/connecting-disability-rights-and-animal.html.

3. Eunjung Kim, "Why Do Dolls Die? The Power of Passivity and the Embodied Interplay Between Disability and Sex Dolls," *Review of Education, Pedagogy, and Cultural Studies* 34 (2012): 94.

4. Singer, *Animal Liberation*, 191–92. It's important to note that Singer thinks *all* human infants are not full persons, because they do not yet have the continuation of self that children and adults do. He makes it clear that infants nonetheless still have interests (such as avoiding pain) because they are sentient, but he doesn't think they have the same interest in staying alive that children and adults do.

Singer does ask a valuable question that is rarely quoted: "If society decides that severely impaired infants must live, is society prepared to take on the task of giving them adequate care?" In *Should the Baby Live? The Problem of Handicapped Infants* (New York: Oxford University Press, 1985), co-written with Helga Kuhse, Singer and his co-author Kuhse write about the inadequacies of institutions, which are often overpopulated and understaffed, and about the lack of government funding for alternative care. It's an important point: if we agree that disabled infants should survive, how are we to make a better place for them within our society? Singer does support improvements to services for disabled people, but instead of trying to find examples of how such necessary care might be done better, ultimately he points to infanticide as a solution.

5. Julia Driver, "The History of Utilitarianism," in *The Stanford Encyclopedia of Philosophy*, edited by Edward N. Zalta, winter 2014, Accessed November 13, 2015, http://plato.stanford.edu/archives/win2014/entries/utilitarianism-history.

6. Singer, *Animal Liberation*, 2.

7. Singer, *Animal Liberation*, 4–5.

8. Peter Singer, *Writings on an Ethical Life* (New York: Harper Collins, 2001), 192.

9. Singer, *Animal Liberation*, 9.

10. Steven Best, "Philosophy Under Fire: The Peter Singer Controversy," Dr. Steven Best's website, accessed October 13, 2013, http://www.drstevebest.org/PhilosophyUnderFire.htm.

11. Personhood is a controversial subject among philosophers. Generally

speaking, the term is used differently in philosophy than its everyday confla-tion with the term "human being." Philosopher Lori Gruen writes that in the philosophical tradition "the notion of 'personhood' is used to identify the value or worth of someone, and it has also been used to identify who has 'rights' and who is the subject of ethical duties and obligations." Lori Gruen, "Entangled Empathy: An Alternate Approach to Animal Ethics," in *The Politics of Species*, ed. Raymond Corbey (New York: Cambridge University Press, 2013), 57.

12. Because Singer is a utilitarian, he takes many factors into consideration to try to find the outcome that will minimize suffering: the feelings of the birth parents, the likelihood that other parents might want to adopt the child, how the resources and time spent prolonging a life might otherwise be spent, whether a "replacement" baby could bring the parents more happiness if they chose to conceive again, and of course the quality of life the infant will have as he or she grows older. Peter Singer, *Practical Ethics* (New York: Cambridge University Press, 2011), 186.

13. Michael Pollan, *The Omnivore's Dilemma: A Natural History of Four Meals* (New York: Penguin, 2009), 327.

14. Singer, *Practical Ethics*, 102.

15. Licia Carlson, *The Faces of Intellectual Disability: Philosophical Reflections* (Bloomington: Indiana University Press, 2009), 10–11.

16. Harriet McBryde Johnson, "Unspeakable Conversations," *New York Times Magazine*, February 16, 2003, accessed October 13, 2013, http://www.nytimes.com/2003/02/16/magazine/unspeakable-conversations.html.

17. Kim, "Why Do Dolls Die?," 95.

18. Gary Francione, *Introduction to Animal Rights: Your Child or the Dog?* (Philadelphia: Temple University Press, 2000), 138.

19. Anne McDonald, "Crip Time," Anne McDonald Centre, accessed October 14, 2013, http://www.annemcdonaldcentre.org.au/crip-time.

20. Johnson, "Unspeakable Conversations."

21. Peter Singer, in discussion with the author, April 17, 2012.

22. Alison Kafer, *Feminist, Queer, Crip* (Bloomington, IN: Indiana University Press, 2013), 43.

23. Neil Marcus, *Storm Reading*, play in collaboration with Rod Lathim, Roger Marcus, and Access Theater, 1996. The play is discussed in "Occupying Disability: An Introduction," in *Occupying Disability: Critical Approaches to Community, Justice, and Decolonizing Disability*, ed. Pamela Block, Devva Kasnitz, Akemi Nishida, and Nick Pollard (New York: Springer, 2015).

24. Robert McRuer, *Crip Theory: Cultural Signs of Queerness and Disability* (New York: NYU Press, 2006), 207.

25. Biklen, Sari Knopp, and Charles R. Moseley. "'Are You Retarded?'

'No, I'm Catholic' Qualitative Methods in the Study of People with Severe Handicaps," *Journal of the Association for Persons with Severe Handicaps (JASH)* 13, no. 3 (September 1, 1988): 160. For information on David Goode see, "David Goode: World Without Words," Temple Press, accessed July 20, 2016, http://www.temple.edu/tempress/titles/1022_reg.html. Thank you to Susan Schweik for directing me to this story.

26. Kafer, *Feminist, Queer, Crip*, 2.

27. Johnson, "Unspeakable Conversations."

28. Peter Singer, *Writings on an Ethical Life* (New York: HarperCollins, 2001), xvii.

29. Johnson, "Unspeakable Conversations."

30. Best, "Philosophy Under Fire."

31. Ibid.

32. Fiona Campbell, *Contours of Ableism* (New York: Palgrave Macmillan, 2009), 166.

33. Kafer, *Feminist, Queer, Crip*, 27.

34. Ibid., 3.

35. Eli Claire, *Exile and Pride* (Cambridge, MA: South End Press, 1999), 7.

36. Susan Schweik, in discussion with the author, June 26, 2012.

37. Paul Longmore, "The Second Phase: From Disability Rights to Disability Culture," in *Disability: The Social, Political and Ethical Debate*, ed. Robert M. Baird, Stuart E. Rosenbaum, and S. Kay Toombs (Amherst, NY: Prometheus Books, 2009), 147.

38. Gary L. Francione, *Introduction to Animal Rights: Your Child or the Dog?* (Philadelphia: Temple University Press, 2010), 142.

39. Lori Gruen, "Samuel Dubose, Cecil the Lion and the Ethics of Avowal: Protesting Against One Injustice Doesn't Mean You Privilege It over Another," *Aljazeera America*, July 31, 2015, http://america.aljazeera.com/opinions /2015/7/samuel-dubose-cecil-the-lion-and-the-ethics-of-avowal.html.

40. According to a 2015 Gallup poll 62 percent of American say animals deserve some protection but can still be used for the benefit of humans. Surprisingly, an additional 32 percent of Americans believe animals should be given the same rights as people (this is up from 25 percent in 2008). Rebecca Riffkin, "In U.S., More Say Animals Should Have Same Rights as People," Gallup, May 18, 2015, accessed August 5, 2015, http://www.gallup.com/poll /183275/say-animals-rights-people.aspx.

41. Johnson, "Unspeakable Conversations."

### 13. Toward a New Table Fellowship

1. The Feral Share art event, Headlands Center for the Arts, Sausalito, CA, September 19, 2010.

2. Michael Pollan, *The Omnivore's Dilemma: A Natural History of Four Meals* (New York: Penguin, 2009), 313.

3. Jonathan Safran Foer, *Eating Animals* (New York: Little, Brown, 2009), 32.

4. Alicia Harvie and Timothy A. Wise, "Sweetening the Pot: Implicit Subsidies to Corn Sweeteners and the U.S. Obesity Epidemic," Global Development and Environment Institute Policy Brief No. 9, February 1, 2009, Tufts University, http://grist.files.wordpress.com/2009/02/pb09 -01sweeteningpotfeb09.pdf.

5. Bob Torres and Jenna Torres, *Vegan Freak: Being Vegan in a Non-Vegan World* (Colton, NY: Tofu Hound Press, 2005).

6. Diane Beers, *For the Prevention of Cruelty: The History and Legacy of Animal Rights Activism in the United States* (Athens, OH: Swallow Press, 2006), 16.

7. Lori Gruen, Breeze Harper, and Carol J. Adams, "What's Wrong with Only White Men Judging a Contest Defending Meat-Eating?," Carol J. Adams's website, March 24, 2012, http://caroljadams.blogspot.com/2012/03 /whats-wrong-with-only-white-men-judging.html.

8. Pollan, *Omnivore's Dilemma*, 314.

9. Safran Foer, *Eating Animals*, 55.

10. Eva Feder Kittay and Licia Carlson, eds., *Cognitive Disability and Its Challenge to Moral Philosophy* (Hoboken, NJ: John Wiley & Sons, 2010), 318.

### 14. Romancing the Meat

1. Temple Grandin and Catherine Johnson, *Animals Make Us Human: Creating the Best Life for Animals* (Boston: Houghton Mifflin Harcourt, 2009), 297.

2. Slow Food USA, "Ark of Taste in the USA," accessed October 14, 2013, http://www.slowfoodusa.org/ark-of-taste-in-the-usa.

3. Allison Aubrey, "Heritage Turkeys: To Save Them, We Must Eat Them," *The Salt* (blog), NPR, November 23, 2011, http://www.npr.org /blogs/thesalt/2011/11/23/142703528/heritage-turkeys-to-save-them-we -must-eat-them.

4. Slow Food USA, "Ark of Taste in the USA."

5. Jonathan Safran Foer, *Eating Animals* (New York: Little, Brown, 2009), 203.

6. Michael Pollan, *Omnivore's Dilemma: A Natural History of Four Meals* (New York: Penguin, 2009), 322.

7. Hugh Fearnley-Whittingstall, *The River Cottage Meat Book* (Berkeley, CA: Ten Speed Press, 2007), 18.

8. Madeline Ostrander, "Joel Salatin: How to Eat Animals and Respect Them, Too," *Yes!*, March 27, 2011, http://www.yesmagazine.org/issues/can -animals-save-us/joel-salatin-how-to-eat-meat-and-respect-it-too.

9. Pollan, *Omnivore's Dilemma*, 320.

10. Alison Kafer, *Feminist, Queer, Crip* (Bloomington, IN: Indiana University Press, 2013), 131.

11. Pollan, *Omnivore's Dilemma*, 310.

12. John Stuart Mill, *Three Essays on Religion* (New York: Holt, 1878), 31.

13. Marc Bekoff and Jessica Pierce, *Wild Justice: the Moral Lives of Animals* (Chicago: University of Chicago Press, 2009), vii.

14. Jenny Brown, *The Lucky Ones: My Passionate Fight for Farm Animals* (New York: Penguin, 2012), 208–9.

15. Jess Bidgood, "Oxen's Fate Is Embattled as the Abattoir Awaits," *New York Times,* October 28, 2012, http://www.nytimes.com/2012/10/29/us oxens-possible-slaughter-prompts-fight-in-vermont.html.

16. Jess Bidgood, "A Casualty amid Battle to Save College Oxen," *New York Times,* November 12, 2012, http://www.nytimes.com/2012/11/13/us /vermont-college-euthanizes-one-ox-spares-another.html.

17. Marti Kheel, *Nature Ethics: An Ecofeminist Perspective* (Lanham, MD: Rowman & Littlefield, 2008), 141.

18. Martha Nussbaum, *Frontiers of Justice: Disability, Nationality, Species Membership* (Cambridge, MA: Harvard University Press, 2006), 3.

19. Martha Nussbaum, "Justice," in *Examined Life: Excursions with Contemporary Thinkers*, ed. Astra Taylor (New York: New Press, 2009), 118.

20. See Stephen Budiansky, *The Covenant of the Wild: Why Animals Chose Domestication* (New Haven, CT: Yale University Press, 1999).

21. Pollan, *Omnivore's Dilemma*, 120.

22. Fearnley-Whittingstall, *River Cottage Meat Book*, 25.

23. These authors suggest that we couldn't grow enough sustainable food without farmed animals; manure is necessary to maintain soil fertility, so we depend on animal agriculture to grow our vegetable crops. This argument misses an obvious point: animals do not need to be killed to poop. In fact, all of the positive impact that domesticated animals have on crops and soil happens while the animals are alive. Even the common practice of using blood, bone, feathers, and other discarded animal parts as compost depends not on slaughter so much as on the simple inevitability that animals die—and they could die naturally rather than be killed for profit. Slaughter is simply not a necessary component of plant-based agriculture. Although profit from

animal products is largely what keeps farmers invested in raising animals, killing animals does not have to be essential to our farming methods or, more important, our relationship with domesticated species.

Vegan organic (or "veganic") farming may also be an option. The United Kingdom has a certification process for "stock-free" farming, which is a system of cultivation that excludes artificial chemicals, livestock manures, and animal remains. Many farmers in the United States already practice such farming by rotating their crops and using "green manure" (essentially an uprooted cover crop, which is one grown specifically to be returned back to the soil to enrich it). Whether or not this form of farming is practical on a large scale, why has so little research been done to explore it, especially considering the vast and still growing interest in sustainable farming?

Too many people lack imagination about the possibility of sustainable vegan agriculture. People have managed to grow food under constrained circumstances in a myriad ways. The fact that it has never been a human priority to develop farming methods that don't rely on animal products (such as blood and manure) and that minimize harm to field animals (who often die during farming processes) says more about the paradigm of human domination over animals than it does about the viability of sustainable, vegan agriculture.

24. Fearnley-Whittingstall, *River Cottage Meat Book*, 16.

25. Budiansky, *The Covenant of the Wild*, 122–123.

26. Kafer, *Feminist, Queer, Crip*, 130.

27. James McWilliams, "Patriarchal Plots of Power," James McWilliams's website, October 29, 2012, http://james-mcwilliams.com/?p=2549.

28. Emily Matchar, "Is Michael Pollan a Sexist Pig?," *Salon*, April 27, 2013, http://www.salon.com/2013/04/28/is_michael_pollan_a_sexist_pig.

29. Kim Q. Hall, "Talk: Toward a Queer Crip Feminist Politics of Food," April 22, 2012, Interdisciplinary Humanities Center, University of California, Santa Barbara, CA.

30. Michael Pollan, *Food Rules: An Eater's Manual* (New York: Penguin, 2009), 20.

31. Nikki Henderson, "Food, Justice and Sustainability," panel discussion, Oakland, CA, January 26, 2012.

32. Food Empowerment Project is a nonprofit founded by Lauren Ornelas in 2006; see "About F.E.P.," http://www.foodispower.org/about-f-e-p.

33. Pollan, *Omnivore's Dilemma*, 331.

34. TempleGrandin.com, "About Temple Grandin," accessed November 15, 2015, http://www.templegrandin.com.

35. Temple Grandin, *Thinking in Pictures: My Life with Autism* (New York: Vintage Books, 2006), 24.

36. Jim Sinclair, "If You Love Something, You Don't Kill It," response to

Temple Grandin, AR-News Google group, February 7, 2010, https://groups
.google.com/forum/#!msg/ar-news/EawJhTvbGck/-acJC81KPSAJ.

37. Nicolette Hahn Niman, *Righteous Porkchop: Finding a Life and Good
Food Beyond Factory Farms* (New York: Collins Living: 2009), 168–69.

## 15. Meat: A Natural Disaster

1. Henning Steinfeld et al., *Livestock's Long Shadow: Environmental Issues
and Options* (Rome: Food and Agriculture Organization of the United
Nations, 2006), accessed October 14, 2013, http://www.fao.org/docrep/010
/a0701e/a0701e00.HTM.

2. Robert Goodland and Jeff Anhang, "Livestock and Climate
Change," World Watch Institute report, November–December 2009, 11,
http://www.worldwatch.org/files/pdf/Livestock%20and%20Climate%20
Change.pdf.

3. Drew T. Shindell, Greg Faluvegi, Dorothy M. Koch, Gavin A.
Schmidt, Nadine Unger, and Susanne E. Bauer, "Improved Attribution of
Climate Forcing to Emissions," *Science* 326, no. 5953 (October 30, 2009):
716–18, doi:10.1126/science.1174760.

4. Goodland and Anhang, "Livestock and Climate Change," 13.

5. Christopher L. Weber and H. Scott Matthews, "Food-Miles and the
Relative Climate Impacts of Food Choices in the United States," *Environmental Science and Technology* 42 (2008): 3512–13.

6. U.S. Department of Agriculture, *2002 Census of Agriculture,* June 2004.

7. In Vitro Meat Consortium, "In Vitro Meat Consortium Preliminary Economics Study Project 2907," March 2008, http://invitromeat.org
/images/Papers/invitro%20meat%20economics%20study%20v5%20%20
march%2008.pdf.

8. Steinfeld et al., *Livestock's Long Shadow,* xx.

9. Vaclav Smil, "Harvesting the Biosphere: The Human Impact," *Population and Development Review* 37(4): 613–36. The proportions are of mass
measures in dry weight.

10. Jonathan Safran Foer, *Eating Animals* (New York: Little, Brown, 2009),
32.

11. Sergio Margulis, "Causes of Deforestation of the Brazilian Amazon,"
Washington, D.C.: World Bank, 2004, https://openknowledge.worldbank
.org/handle/10986/15060.

12. Mario Herrero, Petr Havlík, Hugo Valin, An Notenbaert, Mariana C.
Rufino, Philip K. Thornton, Michael Blümmel, Franz Weiss, Delia Grace,
and Michael Obersteiner, "Biomass Use, Production, Feed Efficiencies, and
Greenhouse Gas Emissions from Global Livestock Systems *PNAS* 110 no.52
(2013): 20888–93, doi:10.1073/pnas.1308149110.

13. Goodland and Ahang, "Livestock and Climate Change," 12.

14. Boris Worm et al., "Impacts of Biodiversity Loss on the Ocean Ecosystem Services," *Science* 314 (2006): 790.

15. R. Sansoucy, "Livestock—A Driving Force for Food Security and Sustainable Development," *World Animal Review* 88, no. 1 (1997), http://www.fao.org/docrep/v8180t/v8180t07.htm; Anup Shah, "Beef," *Global Issues*, accessed November 2015, http://www.globalissues.org/article/240/beef.

16. Nirmala Erevelles, "The Color of Violence: Reflecting on Gender, Race, and Disability in Wartime," in *Feminist Disability Studies*, ed. Kim Q. Hall (Bloomington, IN: Indiana University Press, 2011), 119–120.

17. David Wallinga, "Concentrated Animal Feeding Operations: Health Risks from Air Pollution," Institute for Agriculture and Trade Policy, November 2, 2004, http://www.iatp.org/files/421_2_37388.pdf, quoted in Food Empowerment Project, "Environmental Justice," http://www.foodispower.org/environmental-racism.

18. Food Empowerment Project, "Environmental Justice," *Food Empowerment Project*, accessed October 15, 2013, http://www.foodispower.org/environmental-racism.

19. Safran Foer, *Eating Animals*, 4.

20. Stacy Finz, "Niman Ranch Founder Challenges New Owners," *San Francisco Chronicle*, February 22, 2009, accessed October 15, 2013, http://www.sfgate.com/news/article/Niman-Ranch-founder-challenges-new-owners-3249982.php.

21. Lindsey Wilkes-Edrington, "Farm Worker Conditions Likened to Modern Slavery," *Huffington Post* video, February 1, 2013, accessed October 20, 2013, http://www.huffingtonpost.com/2013/02/01/farm-worker-conditions-modern-slavery-video_n_2593772.html.

22. Centers for Disease Control and Preventions, "Agriculture," accessed October 20, 2013, http://www.cdc.gov/niosh/topics/agriculture; Centers for Disease Control and Prevention, "Pesticide Illness & Injury Surveillance," accessed October 15, 2013, http://www.cdc.gov/niosh/topics/pesticides.

23. See "About F.E.P.," http://www.foodispower.org/about-f-e-p; Food Empowerment Project, "Produce Workers," accessed October 15, 2013, http://www.foodispower.org/produce-workers.

24. Michele Ver Ploeg, "Access to Affordable and Nutritious Food: Measuring and Understanding Food Deserts and Their Consequences," U.S. Department of Agriculture report to Congress, 2009, 35.

25. Kimberly Morland et al., "Neighborhood Characteristics Associated with the Location of Food Stores and Food Service Places," *American Journal of Preventative Medicine* 22, no. 1 (2002): 23, 26. Establishing what exactly is considered healthy and for whom is another food justice challenge. For

decades the USDA has promoted milk and dairy products by declaring that everyone should be getting two to three servings of dairy a day. Yet the Food Empowerment Project (FEP) reports, "While 95% of Asians, 60–80% of African Americans and Ashkenazi Jews, 80–100% of American Indians, and 50–80% of Latinos are lactose intolerant, only a very small proportion of individuals of northern European descent experience any pain as a result of consuming lactose-filled milk products." (U.S. Department of Health and Human Services, "Lactose Intolerance: Information for Health Care Providers," NIH no. 05-5305B, accessed October 15, 2013, http://www.nichd.nih .gov/publications/pubs/Documents/NICHD_MM_Lactose_FS_rev.pdf.) As scholars such as A. Breeze Harper and John Robbins have shown, this bias in favor of dairy is a form of institutionalized nutritional racism, which leads many to become sick with symptoms such as nausea, abdominal pain, cramping, diarrhea, bloating, and flatulence, especially in communities that are least likely to have access to dairy-free alternatives. A study by the FEP reports that "dairy alternatives were only available in approximately 3% of market locations in lower-income areas, which have proportionally much larger populations of ethnic minorities. In comparison, dairy alternatives were available at 23% of locations in higher-income neighborhoods." Food Empowerment Project, "Food Deserts," accessed October 15, 2013, http:// www.foodispower.org/food-deserts.

26. Food Empowerment Project, "Dietary Diseases," accessed October 26, 2013, http://www.foodispower.org/dietary-diseases.

27. World Health Organization, "Q&A on the Carcinogenicity of the Consumption of Red Neat and Processed Meat," October 2015, http://www .who.int/features/qa/cancer-red-meat/en.

28. U.S. Government Accountability Office (hereafter GAO), *Workplace Safety and Health: Safety in the Meat and Poultry Industry, while Improving, Could Be Further Strengthened* (Washington, D.C.: U.S. GAO 2005), 3, 9, http://www.gao.gov/new.items/d0596.pdf, cited in Food Empowerment Project, "Slaughterhouse Workers," accessed October 15, 2013, http://www .foodispower.org/slaughterhouse-workers.

29. Ryan J. Foley, "Jury Awards $240 Million to 32 Mentally Disabled Iowa Turkey Plant Workers for Years of Abuse," *Huffington Post*, May 1, 2013, http://www.huffingtonpost.ca/2013/05/01/jury-awards-240-million -_n_3194042.html.

30. Dan Barry, "The 'Boys' in the Bunkhouse: Toil, Abuse and Endurance in the Heartland," *New York Times*, March 2014, http://www.nytimes.com/ interactive/2014/03/09/us/the-boys-in-the-bunkhouse.html.

31. Eric Schlosser, "The Chain Never Stops: Thousands of Meatpacking Workers Suffer Crippling Injuries Each Year. A Special Report from Inside the Nation's Slaughterhouses," *Mother Jones*, July 2001 http://www.motherjones .com/politics/2001/07/dangerous-meatpacking-jobs-eric-schlosser.

32. GAO, *Workplace Safety and Health*, 7.

33. Schlosser, "Chain Never Stops."

34. Gail Eisnitz, *Slaughterhouse: The Shocking Story of Greed, Neglect, and Inhumane Treatment Inside the U.S. Meat Industry* (Amherst, NY: Prometheus Books, 2006), 271–72.

35. Eisnitz, *Slaughterhouse*, 273.

36. Schlosser, "The Chain Never Stops."

37. Lance Compa, *Blood, Sweat, and Fear: Workers' Rights in U.S. Meat and Poultry Plants* (New York: Human Rights Watch, 2005), 6, http://www .hrw.org/node/11869/section/5, quoted in Food Empowerment Project, "Slaughterhouse Workers."

38. Compa, *Blood, Sweat, and Fear*, 6; Eisnitz, *Slaughterhouse*, 274.

39. Toxics Steering Group, "Concentrated Animal Feedlot Operations (CAFOs) Chemicals Associated with Air Emissions," Michigan Department of Environmental Quality, May 10, 2006, http://www.michigan.gov /documents/CAFOs-Chemicals_Associated_with_Air_Emissions_5-10 -06_158862_7.pdf , cited in Food Empowerment Project, "Factory Farm Workers," accessed October 15, 2013, http://www.foodispower.org/factory -farm-workers.

40. "Livestock Confinement Dusts and Gases," Iowa State University report, 1992, 4, http://nasdonline.org/static_content/documents/1627 /d001501.pdf, cited in Food Empowerment Project, "Factory Farm Workers."

41. "Whistleblower on the Kill Floor: Interview with Virgil Butler and Laura Alexander," *SATYA*, February 2006, http://www.satyamag.com /feb06/butler.html.

42. Jennifer Dillard, "A Slaughterhouse Nightmare: Psychological Harm Suffered by Slaughterhouse Employees and the Possibility of Redress Through Legal Reform," *Georgetown Journal on Poverty Law & Policy*, September 24, 2007, accessed October 15, 2013, http://papers.ssrn.com/sol3/papers .cfm?abstract_id=1016401, cited in Food Empowerment Project, "Slaughterhouse Workers."

43. "Whistleblower on the Kill Floor."

44. Compa, *Blood, Sweat, and Fear*, 6.

45. "No Relief: Denial of Bathroom Breaks in the Poultry Industry," accessed May 25, 2016, https://www.oxfamamerica.org/static/media/files /No_Relief_Embargo.pdf.

46. Schlosser, "Chain Never Stops."

47. Eisnitz, *Slaughterhouse*, 274–75.

48. Peter Singer, *Writings on an Ethical Life* (New York: HarperCollins, 2001), 192.

49. Erevelles, *Disability and Difference*, 29.

50. Eli Clare, *Brilliant Imperfection: Grappling with Cure*, unpublished manuscript, Duke University Press, 2017.

## 16. A Conflict of Needs

1. Dennis Walton, personal communication with author, October 16, 2013; *Courage in Life and Politics: The Dona Spring Story*, directed by Lindsay Vurick and Valerie Trost, YouTube, uploaded January 17, 2009, https://www.youtube.com/watch?v=XwNthNhXDtA.

2. *Courage in Life and Politics*.

3. John Selawsky, "The Party Loses One of Its Finest Members, Dona Spring, 1953–2008," *Green Pages* 12, no. 2 (Fall 2008): 2, http://gp.org/greenpages-blog/pdf/GreenPages-Fall-08.pdf.

4. Joan Clair, "Dona Spring: An Act of Kindness," accessed October 15, 2013, http://www.donaspring.com/JoanClairArticleDonaS.htm.

5. "AMA Animal Research Action Plan," June 1989, 5, http://issuu.com/conflictgypsy/docs/amaactionplan?e=3660395/3662139.

6. Richard Kurti, *The Monkey Wars* (Oxford: Oxford University Press, 1994), 145.

7. "AMA Animal Research Action Plan," 2.

8. F. Barbara Orlans, *In the Name of Science: Issues in Responsible Animal Experimentation* (New York: Oxford University Press, 1993), 47.

9. Ibid.

10. Ibid., 47–48.

11. Ibid., 49.

12. "AMA Animal Research Action Plan," 6.

13. Orlans, *In the Name of Science*, 48.

14. Ibid. See also PETA, "Pound Seizure: The Shame of Shelters," accessed April 7, 2015, http://www.peta.org/issues/Companion-Animals/pound-seizure-the-shame-of-shelters.aspx.

15. "Jerry's Orphans Protest the MDA Telethon," Kids Are All Right website, accessed April 7, 2015, http://www.thekidsareallright.org/story.html.

16. See Joseph Shapiro, *No Pity: People with Disabilities Forging a New Civil Rights Movement* (New York: Three Rivers Press, 1994).

17. U.S. Department of Agriculture, Animal and Plant Health Inspection Service, "Annual Report Animal Usage by Fiscal Year," November 28, 2014, http://swemgovdocs.blogs.wm.edu/2011/11/09/annual-report-animal-usage-by-fiscal-year.

18. Gary Francione, *Introduction to Animal Rights: Your Child or the Dog?* (Philadelphia: Temple University Press, 2000), 34.

19. Ibid., 56–58. See also "Questions and Answers About Biomedical Research"; and National Agriculture Library, "Animal Welfare Act," U.S. Department of Agriculture, accessed October 25, 2013, http://awic.nal.usda .gov/government-and-professional-resources/federal-laws/animal-welfare -act.

20. Francione, *Introduction to Animal Rights*, 36–49.

21. Daniel G. Hackam, and Donald A. Redelmeier, "Translation of Research Evidence from Animals to Human," *Journal of the American Medical Association* 296 (2006): 1731–32.

22. Jarrod Bailey, "An Assessment of the Role of Chimpanzees in AIDS Vaccine Research," *Alternatives to Laboratory Animals* 36 (2008): 381–428. See also C. Ray Greek, *Sacred Cows and Golden Geese : The Human Cost of Experiments on Animals* (New York: Continuum, 2000).

23. Junhee Seok et al., "Genomic Responses in Mouse Models Poorly Mimic Human Inflammatory Diseases," *Proceedings of the National Academy of Sciences* 110 (2013): 3507–12. See also Johns Hopkins Center for Alternatives to Animal Testing, "About Us: Center for Alternatives to Animal Testing," accessed October 25, 2013, http://caat.jhsph.edu/about/inde x.html.

24. Vurick, *Courage in Life and Politics*

25. Clair, "Dona Spring."

26. Carol J. Adams, *The Sexual Politics of Meat: A Feminist-Vegetarian Critical Theory* (New York: Bloomsbury Publishing USA, 2015), 21–24.

27. Food and Agricultural Organization of the United Nations and World Health Organization, "Chapter 2. Food-Based Approaches to Meeting Vitamin and Mineral Needs," in *Human Vitamin and Mineral Requirements* (Rome: FAO Food and Nutrition Division, 2001), http://www.fao.org/docrep/004 /Y2809E/y2809e08.htm#bm08; "Position of the American Dietetic Association: Vegetarian Diets," *Journal of the American Dietetic Association* 109, no. 7 (2009): 1266; Physicians Committee for Responsible Medicine, "Vegetarian Foods: Powerful for Health," http://www.pcrm.org/health/diets/vegdiets /vegetarian-foods-powerful-for-health; British Medical Association, "Diet, Nutrition & Health," report, 1986, 49; Paul N. Appleby et al., "The Oxford Vegetarian Study: An Overview," supplement, *American Journal of Clinical Nutrition* 70 (1999): 525S–31S, http://ajcn.nutrition.org/content/70/3/525s .full.pdf; T. Colin Campbell, *The China Study: The Most Comprehensive Study of Nutrition Ever Conducted and the Startling Implications for Diet, Weight Loss and Long-Term Health* (Dallas, TX: BenBella Books, 2006).

28. Winston J. Craig, Ann Reed Mangels, and American Dietetic Asso-

ciation, "Position of the American Dietetic Association: Vegetarian Diets," *Journal of the American Dietetic Association* 109, no. 7 (July 2009): 1266–82.

29. Vurick, *Courage in Life and Politics*.

## 17. Caring Across Species and Ability

1. Christine Kelly, "Building Bridges with Accessible Care: Disability Studies, Feminist Care, Scholarship, and Beyond," *Hypatia* 28, no. 4 (2012): 3, doi:10.1111/j.1527-2001.2012.01310.x.

2. Carol Adams and Josephine Donovan, *The Feminist Care Tradition in Animal Ethics* (New York: Columbia University Press, 2007), 3.

3. Ibid., 3.

4. Ibid., 6.

5. Ibid., 4.

6. Lori Gruen, "Entangled Empathy: An Alternate Approach to Animal Ethics," in *The Politics of Species*, ed. Raymond Corbey (New York: Cambridge University Press, 2013), 224.

7. Eva Feder Kittay, "The Personal Is Philosophical Is Political," in *Cognitive Disability and Its Challenge to Moral Philosophy*, ed. Eva Feder Kittay (Hoboken, NJ: John Wiley & Sons, 2010), 405–407.

8. Michael Oliver, *The Politics of Disablement: A Sociological Approach* (New York: St. Martin's Press, 1990), 91.

9. Michael Bérubé, "Equality, Freedom, and/or Justice for All: A Response to Martha Nussbaum," in *Cognitive Disability and Its Challenge to Moral Philosophy*, ed. Eva Feder Kittay (Hoboken, NJ: John Wiley & Sons, 2010), 102.

10. Aldo Leopold, *A Sand County Almanac* (New York: Oxford University Press, 1949), ix.

11. Marti Kheel, *Nature Ethics: An Ecofeminist Perspective* (Lanham, MD: Rowman & Littlefield, 2008), 5; John Muir, "The Wild Sheep of California," *Overland Monthly* 12 (1874): 359.

12. Jerry Lewis, "What if I Had Muscular Dystrophy?" *Parade*, September 2, 1990.

13. J. Baird Callicott, *In Defense of the Land Ethic: Essays in Environmental Philosophy* (Albany: State University of New York Press, 1989), 30.

14. Callicott, *In Defense of the Land Ethic*, 30.

15. Ibid.

16. Alison Kafer, *Feminist, Queer, Crip* (Bloomington: Indiana University Press, 2013), 132.

17. Sue Donaldson and Will Kymlicka, *Zoopolis: A Political Theory of Animal Rights* (New York: Oxford University Press, 2011), 83.

18. Tom Regan, *Empty Cages: Facing the Challenge of Animal Rights* (Lanham, MD: Rowman & Littlefield Publishers, 2004), 10.

19. Gary L. Francione, "'Pets': The Inherent Problems of Domestication," *Animal Rights: The Abolitionist Approach* (blog), 2012, accessed October 18, 2013, http://www.abolitionistapproach.com/pets-the-inherent-problems-of -domestication.

20. Donaldson and Kymlicka, *Zoopolis*, 83.

21. Charles Patterson, *Eternal Treblinka: Our Treatment of Animals and the Holocaust* (New York: Lantern Books, 2002), 83.

22. Donaldson and Kymlicka, *Zoopolis*, 75.

23. Ibid., 84.

24. Josephine Donovan, "Feminism and the Treatment of Animals: From Care to Dialogue," *Signs* 31, no. 2 (2006): 305.

## 18. The Service Dog

1. Humane Society of the United States, "Pet Overpopulation," accessed October 26, 2013, http://www.humanesociety.org/ issues/pet_overpopulation/http://www.humanesociety.org/issues/ pet_overpopulation.

2. "Genetic Welfare Problems of Companion Animals—Deafness," Universities Federation for Animal Welfare, accessed October 26, 2013, http:// www.ufaw.org.uk/DEAFNESSDALMATION.php.

# About the Author

**Sunaura Taylor** is an artist and writer based in New York City. She has written for *AlterNet, American Quarterly, BOMB,* the *Monthly Review, Qui Parle,* and *Yes!* magazine and has contributed to the books *Ecofeminism, Defiant Daughters, Occupy!, Stay Solid,* and *Infinite City.* Taylor and Judith Butler's conversation is featured in the film *Examined Life* and the book of the same name, published by The New Press.

# Celebrating 25 Years of Independent Publishing

# Other Titles of Interest from The New Press

*Ethics: Subjectivity and Truth*
by Michel Foucault, edited by Paul Rabinow

*Foodopoly: The Battle Over the Future of Food and Farming in America* by Wenonah Hauter

*Gristle: From Factory Farms to Food Safety (Thinking Twice About the Meat We Eat)*, edited by Moby and Miyun Park

*In Praise of Love* by Alain Badiou with Nicolas Truong

*The Self Beyond Itself: An Alternative History of Ethics, the New Brain Sciences, and the Myth of Free Will* by Heidi M. Ravven